STEPHEN KING
AND PHILOSOPHY

Great Authors in Philosophy

General Editor: Jacob M. Held,
editor of *Dr. Seuss and Philosophy*

The Great Authors and Philosophy series is for anyone who ever wondered about the deeper ideas in their favorite authors' books. Comprising entertaining, concise, and accessible takes on the philosophical ideas that classic and contemporary authors and their work convey, the books in this series bring together philosophical perspectives enhanced and illuminated by beloved stories from our culture.

Current and Forthcoming Titles in the Series

Stephen King and Philosophy, edited by Jacob M. Held
Jane Austen and Philosophy, edited by Mimi Marinucci
Mark Twain and Philosophy, edited by Alan Goldman

STEPHEN KING
AND PHILOSOPHY

Edited by Jacob M. Held

ROWMAN & LITTLEFIELD
Lanham • Boulder • New York • London

Published by Rowman & Littlefield
A wholly owned subsidiary of
The Rowman & Littlefield Publishing Group, Inc.
4501 Forbes Boulevard, Suite 200, Lanham, Maryland 20706
https://rowman.com

Unit A, Whitacre Mews, 26-34 Stannary Street, London SE11 4AB, United
Kingdom

Distributed by NATIONAL BOOK NETWORK

British Library Cataloguing in Publication Information Available

Library of Congress Cataloging-in-Publication Data
Names: Held, Jacob M., 1977– editor.
Title: Stephen King and philosophy / edited by Jacob M. Held.
Description: Lanham : Rowman & Littlefield, 2016. | Series: Great authors and
    philosophy | Includes bibliographical references and index.
Identifiers: LCCN 2016016519 (print) | LCCN 2016020596 (ebook) | ISBN
    9781442253841 (pbk. : alk. paper) | ISBN 9781442269767 (electronic)
Subjects: LCSH: King, Stephen, 1947—Criticism and interpretation. | Philoso-
    phy in literature.
Classification: LCC PS3561.I483 Z8784 2016 (print) | LCC PS3561.I483
    (ebook) DDC 813/.54—dc23
LC record available at http://lccn.loc.gov/9781442253841

∞ ™ The paper used in this publication meets the minimum requirements of
American National Standard for Information Sciences Permanence of Paper
for Printed Library Materials, ANSI/NISO Z39.48-1992.

Printed in the United States of America

For Wallace,
One of my reminders of what matters.

CONTENTS

The Shining's Overlook Hotel as Heterotopia   147
   Elizabeth Hornbeck

10 Broadcast Dystopia: Power and Violence in *The Running*
   Man and *The Long Walk*   161
   Joseph J. Foy and Timothy M. Dale

11 Stephen King and the Art of Horror   173
   Greg Littmann

12 "You Weren't Hired to Philosophize, Torrance": The Death
   of the Author in *The Shining*   195
   Charles Bane

13 What Happens to the Present When It Becomes the Past:
   Time Travel and the Nature of Time in *The Langoliers*   207
   Paul R. Daniels

14 Notes on Foreknowledge, Truthmaking, and
   Counterfactuals from *The Dead Zone*   219
   Tuomas W. Manninen

15 Time Belongs to the Tower   231
   Randall Auxier

16 Ur 88,416   253
   Randall Auxier

17 From Desperation to Haven: Horror, Compassion, and
   Arthur Schopenhauer   277
   Jacob M. Held

Index   299

Ka-tet: Author Biographies   309

INTRODUCTION

On Writing Popular Philosophy

Jacob M. Held

I've been working in the philosophy and popular culture genre for years, since the very beginning of my career, in fact. My career is intimately tied to, and in fact inseparable from, work on popular culture. But it has come at a cost. I've had to combat naysayers who diminish my work as lacking in some aspect they deem essential to legitimate philosophy or academic scholarship—perhaps it's too readable, too relatable. Real philosophy is dense, impenetrable, so esoteric as to be unknown, and so obscure as to be irrelevant. But I've also had to combat my own expectations, the suspicion that even if I don't recognize the naysayers, their intuitions may be correct. Maybe what I do is trivial, the philosophical equivalent of a Big Mac and fries.

I have reconciled myself with myself on this matter; and the answer lies between nihilism and eudaimonism. Anything I do, in the cosmic view of things, will be trivial. Everything will be forgotten. And even if it's remembered, why does that matter? If I seek to emulate Aristotle or Kant, and should I succeed, what do I gain? They gain nothing from their notoriety; they are long dead. And were they never to have appeared would the world have missed them, lamented the absence of unknown geniuses? Surely not. Someone would've filled their vacant seats, someone else who now would also be long dead. And so here nihilism creeps in. Nothing matters in the long run because, as the economist John Maynard Keynes (1883–1946) so eloquently put it, in the long run we're all dead. But it can't end there. Rejecting the desire for reputation or recognition frees one up for something else, namely, magnanimity, or eudaimonia. So I reject the criticisms, both proffered by my discipline and academic peers, and leveled against me by my own worst critic, myself, and accept who I in fact am, a philosopher who can't but engage with popular culture, who has to do philosophy that is relevant, relatable, and yes . . . fun. It's all I can do, so I'll do it well. But then there's always someone ready with a jibe, ready to force me to relive, yet again, this inner drama.

So I'd like to begin with an anecdote. This series, the Great Authors and Philosophy series, was years in the making. There were some false starts, but finally I got the call, or rather the e-mail, and then the contract. I was offered two books to start the series: one on Stephen King and another on Jane Austen.[1] I jumped at the chance to edit the Stephen King book. It'd be an excuse to read a ton of Stephen King, plus it's truly ripe material for this style book. I began sending out a call for abstracts and soliciting essays from friends and colleagues. Then I got a response from one of my colleagues, a friend, who actually contributed to this book, a response that irritated me.

I had sent out an e-mail indicating that the inaugural volume of the "Great Authors" series would be a book I was editing on Stephen King, and I received the response: "When did Stephen King become a great author?" My first thought: "When did you become a critic, you ass?" But I stepped back and realized that in this singular sentence were all the criticisms waged against me, my work, and my field for the past decade. And a response came to me. Why had I not seen this before? I don't have to justify what I do. The burden of proof is on the critic. And this type of dismissal of popular art, culture, or philosophy is more often indicative of an unjustified snobbery than a legitimate assessment of rigor or worth.

The type of criticism indicated above, whether it is aimed at philosophy and popular culture generally or Stephen King specifically evinces a repugnant snobbery. Now, I'm not a relativist. All things are not equally valuable. I am not against standards or judgment. Standards are good, and standards need to be maintained, but standards relevant to and tied to the essence of a thing or practice. Snobbery is something else; it speaks to the snob, not to the quality of that which they criticize. Consider the snob.

The idea that King isn't a great author, but instead pulp or garbage fiction, is not uncommon. He even adopts a self-deprecating demeanor when he equates his work to the literary equivalent of McDonald's—not the finest cuisine available, but good enough and enjoyed by millions. So someone disparages you and your choice of reading material, say, *'Salem's Lot*, while that individual chooses a "classic," *A Farewell to Arms*. Your popular fiction is about vampires, the other person's is about war. Yours is only forty years old, his or hers almost ninety. Or perhaps someone criticizes your taste in films or television programs as juvenile. For instance, a snob may claim that men dressing in drag and engaging in slapstick humor is beneath them, juvenile, base. Monty Python and the Kids in the Hall is lowbrow humor. But the same phenomena, namely, cross-dressing tomfoolery, is acceptable and high art if it's done by "The Bard." These types of examples point out the foolishness behind the snob's critique and lay bare its motivation, not the maintenance of high standards for comedy or literature, but the maintenance of one's position as a snob or critic. One who lauds Shakespeare while disparaging Monty Python both fails to appreciate Monty Python, and often merely demonstrates that they have tied their self-worth to the stature of Shakespeare. If Shakespeare is great, then surely some of that greatness rubs off on the critic who lauds Shakespeare and sets him above all others. They are the elite and occupy a privileged position because they can appreciate truly great works like those of their chosen author, Shakespeare. Their sense of worth is tied to their tastes, their consumptive habits, and in order to maintain their status as "better than," they must first disparage "the common," or "the banal." Snobbery is nothing short of the adult version of playground politics, raising one's own position by lowering another, and just as on the playground it says nothing about the victim of the insult and everything about the instigator. Snobbery of this sort cannot go unchecked. It is not legitimate criticism. So although I've made peace with this line of criticism, for the most part, I'd be remiss if I didn't respond, even preemptively, in a book on Stephen King and philosophy.

POPULAR FICTION, POPULAR PHILOSOPHY

The academic assault on popular art is well documented and can be summed up as the idea that mass art in being accessible to a large group of people must somehow lack depth or content. The idea seems to be that if a great many people "get it" there must be nothing to get, or it appeals to the lowest common denominator. But this line of criticism fails to appreciate that esoteric is not equivalent to valuable. Some things are esoteric for a reason. Sometimes nobody has heard about some work of art, or nobody appreciates an artist because there is nothing there. Some authors and artists deserve to remain unknown. Likewise, popular doesn't have to mean valueless or worthless. Shakespeare, to go back to the example above, was popular art. Pay your half penny, grab a seat at the Globe, and listen to some fart jokes, watch guys dress in drag, and maybe even see a murder or two. But arguments against mass art abound including the well-worn idea that it's "formulaic, not unique; that it is a commodity, and, therefore, neither is it disconnected from society and practical concerns, nor is it disinterested . . . that the responses it does elicit are 'canned.'"[2] But as Noël Carroll points out, things can be popular and valuable. "Like most human practices, mass art involves worthy and unworthy examples (morally, politically, and aesthetically), and it is at the level of particular cases that praise or blame seems appropriate."[3] So let's consider Stephen King on his own merits.

Let's begin with a definition of literature.

> What is literature but the expression of moods by the vehicle of symbol and incident? And are there not moods which need heaven, hell, purgatory, and fairyland for their expression. . . . Nay, are there not moods which shall find no expression unless there be men who dare to mix heaven, hell, purgatory, and fairyland together, or even to set the heads of beasts to the bodies of men.[4]

Literature is a vehicle for expressing moods as well as truths about the human condition, and so whatever means are necessary to express these moods are grist for the literary mill; and sometimes what needs to be expressed can only be done through the monstrous, for sometimes the human condition is monstrous, defined by the breach of the boundaries between the sacred and the profane, the normal and the abnormal, good and evil, right and wrong. Sometimes only a monster will do, so we need a monster story. Sometimes what is human is horrific, so we need a horror story. Stanley Fish notes, "It is not that the presence of poetic qualities compels a certain kind of attention but that the paying of a certain kind of attention results in the emergence of poetic qualities."[5] Fish's point, when read in conjunction with Yeats's quote above, suggests that the value of literature is to be found in whether or not the work communicates with the reader in a way to which the reader can relate. If this is the mark of literature, then great literature is literature that speaks to deep, fundamental human truths and experiences in a way that is relatable to the reader and that may provoke engagement or facilitate insight into these truths and experiences. If these truths and experiences are about breaches of the normal, then surely horror has a place in literature, and in fact may proffer deep engagement with the most profound aspects of our existence. Sometimes only horror can say what needs to be said. Note the opening words of "The Call of Cthulhu," by another northeastern master of horror, H. P. Lovecraft (1890–1937):

> The most merciful thing in the world, I think, is the inability of the human mind to correlate all its contents. We live on a placid island of ignorance in the midst of black seas of infinity, and it was not meant that we should voyage far. The sciences, each straining in its own direction, have hitherto harmed us little; but someday the piecing together of dissociated knowledge will open up such terrifying vistas of reality, and of our frightful position therein, that we shall either go mad from the revelation or flee from the deadly light into the peace and safety of a new dark age.[6]

The idea expressed in the above quote, namely, that the awareness of the inconsequential nature of our existence will lead us to despair, or perhaps into nihilism, is driven home only through engagement with the Cthulhu mythos, through the affective experience of encountering the Deep Ones, the Old Ones, or cruel or mad Elder Gods. These tales leave us existentially shaken and so reinforce the importance of locating and shoring up values that orient us as human beings toward each other and our world. Alice Crary notes, "A novel, in virtue of its tendency . . . to invite a distinctive pattern of affective reactions, may lead us to the rational conviction that a new way of looking at the regions of human life with which it is concerned is correct."[7] Martha Nussbaum reiterates the point that only fiction can adequately or well describe some things.[8] Horror shakes us up, shows us what truly matters.

In philosophy, so often theory loses touch with reality and becomes abstract thinking divorced from the lives of actual humans. Yet the truths revealed in academic philosophy are often relevant to our lives if only they could be brought back to earth, brought back to us humans and shown to connect to our deepest commitments. It's the role of narrative to do this, to bridge the gap between philosophy as abstract theory, ideas in the ether, and life as lived on the ground. Looking back at Lovecraft's opening words from "The Call of Cthulhu," we can see the message of the work: it's about confronting our finitude, about our place in the universe, our apparent purposelessness or meaninglessness. It's about nihilism. Whether it be in "Dagon," "The Call of Cthulhu," *The Whisperer in Darkness*, or *At the Mountains of Madness*, confrontation with an ancient, malevolent enormity when well expressed forces the reader to engage with finitude in a way simple exegesis or philosophical dialogue does not. Horror literature is capable of expressing elements of the human condition in ways philosophical discourse often cannot. Horror thereby becomes a component of philosophical discourse. This is one sense in which I would argue that Stephen King is a great author; he is a master of drawing out our deepest commitments and forcing us to reaffirm our most cherished values.

EXISTENTIAL HORROR

Noël Carroll notes that "the attraction of supernatural horror is that it provokes a sense of awe which confirms a deep-seated human conviction about the world, viz., that it contains vast unknown forces."[9] Although in this case he is referencing Lovecraft, no doubt with the quote from "The Call of Cthulhu" noted above in mind, he is speaking to the genre itself. Carroll calls this attraction a paradox of the heart insofar as we are attracted to that which horrifies us. We are attracted to wonder, the sublime, the awesome, something before which we tremble in the recognition that we may be destroyed by or lost in it. It is terrifying in that it inspires terror, as do the deepest and most profound mysteries of the universe, for they rightfully put us in our place as insignificant, cosmically speaking. But supernatural horror, or horror in general, doesn't just speak to this awe and wonder. It also provokes a response. Horror, done well, speaks to meaning and order in a frightful universe. Horror is reassuring even as it unsettles us.

Where Carroll uses the term "supernatural horror," King refers to "existential horror."[10] In existential horror one wonders, "Why is this happening?" and is offered the response, "Because it is." Such horror puts humanity in the same helpless position Lovecraft places it, but not necessarily because of the looming threat of the Old Ones or the Deep Ones. Sometimes the horror, sometimes the threat, is just part of being human. It is this sense of vulnerability that horror speaks to. But horror's response is often reassuring. Horror throws us into uncertainty, unmasks our vulnerability, but then steers us toward a resolution, a reaffirmation of those values that we hold dear and that ultimately define us. It is in this sense that horror is existential, as well as conservative. Horror often seeks to conserve those values that matter most to who we are.

Carroll notes that the conservatism of horror may often mask a political ideology rooted in racism, or other less than admirable values. He notes Lovecraft's own racist undertones.[11] Surely he is right. *The Shadow over Innsmouth* does speak to miscegenation fears, the concern that mingling pure blood with a tainted strain will produce a monstrous mongrel stock, one that threatens our way of life and humanity's very existence. It also speaks to a "genetics = destiny" narrative that has fostered and reinforced racist narratives throughout history. But not all conservatism seeks to conserve that which is sinister. Although historically conservatism may have sought to conserve white supremacy, one can also speak to conserving moral value, decency, meaning, and order, and not all orders are racist, sexist, or xenophobic. This is the conservatism King speaks to in using the self-described "pompous" metaphor of the horror tale evoking the outbreak of Dionysian madness in an Apollonian existence. He claims that the horror tale evinces a disturbing crack between our normal world and chaos, but that in the end the nightmare is over and a "steady state [is] restored. . . . Equilibrium never felt so good."[12] This steady state, this equilibrium, is about the normal, and order that allows us to function as humans, that facilitates our well-being, as opposed to chaos and disorder. Read *Desperation* and/or *The Regulators*. We'd rather live in a world without Tak, and if seeking order in the face of Tak's chaos is conservative, if seeking a world where good/right/love triumphs over evil/wrong/hatred is conservative, then so be it. Horror is rooted in transgression, the breaking of the bounds of normalcy, pushing the limits of the acceptable. But it does so to elucidate the limits of human existence, the limits of the human condition, and once the breach is too great it aims at resolution, a way home again to order and meaning in the face of a chaotic world.

The themes in the horror genre lend themselves naturally to interrogating the limits of the human condition, and the emotional response generated by horror motivates our engagement with these themes. King refers to horror as a "dance of dreams."[13] Horror, he claims, awakens the child in us and, he notes, children are bent. Children think around corners. Horror invigorates our imagination, requiring us to think around the corners of life. In this way horror helps us to reenvision what matters most. King notes, "If the horror story is our rehearsal for death, then its strict moralities make it also a reaffirmation of life and good will and simple imagination."[14] Horror is conservative, and some things matter enough that they ought to be conserved. Horror challenges our norms, pushes them to the limits, and often times breaks them to smithereens, only to have them come back restructured, reconfigured, and reinforced. "So the norm emerges stronger than before; it has been, so to say, tested; its superiority to the abnormal vindicated."[15] In this sense, horror may actually be able to do more than philosophy. It may be able to express what the dry and flat language of academia fails to capture: the necessity of cultivating a praiseworthy and truly human existence in the face of suffering and doubt. Horror literature can be transformative, or a protreptic in favor of living a praiseworthy, examined life rooted in community and built on foundational commitments to well-being. Human beings are motivated by more than simply logic and evidence. We need more than mere arguments to motivate us to pursue what is most important, and here literature may prove to be a needed complement to the project of academic philosophy.

THE PHILOSOPHICAL EQUIVALENT OF
A BIG MAC AND FRIES?

So let's return to the academic concern, the idea that somehow popular philosophy, or philosophy that engages with popular culture, isn't valuable as philosophy. But what is philosophy? What is its purpose? Philosophy itself seems to be nothing other than a critical, methodological approach to all facets of the human condition in an attempt to find and ground meaning and thus craft a praiseworthy existence. So a legitimate question to ask is whether literature, in this case horror, is helpful in this endeavor. We might also ask whether horror literature is an invitation to do philosophy or philosophy proper. That is, does horror simply raise philosophical issues or is it doing philosophy itself? This is similar to the question Edward Harcourt poses when he wonders if literature is an example of moral philosophy or an invitation to do moral philosophy.[16] And although I think this is a valuable question, I'll not address it in depth here. We know fiction can instigate and motivate philosophical thinking and it seems prima facie true that often in works of literature theories, doctrines, and policies are proffered, interrogated, or refuted in ways akin to strict academic philosophy. What I find most pressing for this current book is recognition of the fact that fiction provides a bridge between academic philosophy and the common, lived, and relatable experiences of the majority of humankind. Thus, by means of engaging with literature academic philosophers are able to overcome the "curse of knowledge" of their discipline, the fact that they often cannot speak to nonacademics about their field since their vocabulary is too technical or obtuse, and so their wisdom, their hard-won truths go unacknowledged. And if you are rarely read, and never understood, what good is there in your work, other than a self-satisfied pat on the back? At least you know that you know about something nobody else knows about. But intellectual masturbation seems a shallow end for the task of academic philosophy. Wisdom is for all of us; the examined life is not for academics alone. All this leads to the conclusion that philosophy, if it is to be relatable and so relevant, needs to operate in the idioms of those people to whom it is trying to relate, to whom it is relevant. Plato used myth, Saint Augustine used confessionals, and we'll use Stephen King. Horror can act as an opportunity to raise important questions, interrogate ideas and themes, reaffirm our deepest commitments, motivate us toward a reflective life, and do so in a way relatable to people as they actually exist in a way relevant to their actual lives.

Philosophers are prone to use thought experiments. It's just unfortunate that so many of them are poorly constructed, or simply fall flat. But in fiction we have entire worlds severed from our own, yet remarkably similar and relevantly analogous so that we are free to explore and play with any concept imaginable all the while being left with an avenue back to our world where the lessons learned in Haven, Castle Rock, or Mid-World can be brought to bear on our lives. Fiction offers philosophy much-needed assistance. As noted by Nussbaum, fiction offers the opportunity to present "a fine rendering of [a particular] life." She notes that often in fiction, only "language this dense . . . can adequately tell the reader what [the author] believes to be true."[17] Additionally, Harcourt states, "Form is inseparable from content: some contents require a non-argumentative form to be conveyable at all."[18] This point is similar to one raised by Colin McGinn regarding moral philosophy. McGinn claims that in and through novels we live life's many challenges, we live them in ways that force sympathy and empathy, that drive us to be connected to other humans that equally suffer and thus reconnect us to our commitment to others, and ultimately to those values, hopes, dreams, and ideals that define us. He states, "The fictional work can make us *see* and *feel* good and evil in a way no philosophical tract can—unless it takes on board what literary works achieve so well."[19] Through fiction our ethical knowledge is "aesthetically mediated," and this mediation forms a bridge between the truths of academic philosophy and the narratives of our everyday lives. This harkens back to what King says about children being "bent" and "thinking around corners." It relates back to horror being a "dance of dreams" where our imagination is rekindled. Horror can play a crucial role in providing the narrative through which we can access the full range of experiences that define human existence, play out scenario after scenario, and bring back this experiential knowledge to our lives, and it does so beginning with an emotional response, by triggering our prerational commitment to those foundational values that define who we are. Horror reminds us why we care about those things about which we do care. King is a great author because he is a master of generating this experience. I only wish academic philosophy was as adept at communicating these truths about the human condition. We can try. It is in this spirit that I offer you *Stephen*

King and Philosophy, the first in the Great Authors and Philosophy series.

NOTES

1. Being edited by Mimi Marinucci and sure to be amazing. We also now have a third volume, *Mark Twain and Philosophy*, in the works with Alan Goldman on board as editor.

2. Noël Carroll, *A Philosophy of Mass Art* (Oxford: Clarendon, 1998), 89.

3. Carroll, *Philosophy of Mass Art*, 184.

4. William Butler Yeats, "A Teller of Tales," in *The Celtic Twilight* (London: Forgotten Books, 2007), 5.

5. Cited in Paisley Livingston, "Literature," in *The Oxford Handbook of Aesthetics*, ed. Jerrold Levinson (Oxford: Oxford University Press, 2005), 543.

6. H. P. Lovecraft, "The Call of Cthulhu," in *The New Annotated H. P. Lovecraft*, ed. with a forward and notes by Leslie S. Klinger, introduction by Alan Moore (New York: Liveright, 2014), 124.

7. Alice Crary from "Does the Study of Literature Belong within Moral Philosophy?" *Philosophical Investigations* 23, no. 4 (2000), cited in Edward Harcourt, "Literature, Moral Thinking, and Moral Philosophy," in *Intuition, Theory and Anti-Theory in Ethics*, ed. Sophie Grace Chappell (Oxford: Oxford University Press, 2015), 213.

8. See Martha Nussbaum, *Love's Knowledge* (New York: Oxford University Press, 1990).

9. Noël Carroll, *The Philosophy of Horror; or, Paradoxes of the Heart* (New York: Routledge, Chapman and Hall, 1990), 162.

10. See Stephen King, "What's Scary": a forenote to the 2010 edition of *Danse Macabre* (New York: Gallery Books, 2010).

11. Carroll, *Philosophy of Horror*, 196.

12. King, *Danse Macabre*, 422.

13. King, *Danse Macabre*, 436.

14. King, *Danse Macabre*, 436.

15. Carroll, *Philosophy of Horror*, 201.

16. See Harcourt, "Literature, Moral Thinking, and Moral Philosophy."

17. Martha Nussbaum, quoted in Harcourt, "Literature, Moral Thinking, and Moral Philosophy," 8.

18. Harcourt, "Literature, Moral Thinking, and Moral Philosophy," 8.

19. Colin McGinn, *Ethics, Evil, and Fiction* (Oxford: Clarendon, 1997), 176.

I

THERE IS NO GOD IN DESPERATION

Tak and the Problem of Evil

C. Taylor Sutton and Jacob M. Held

There is something about the worlds Stephen King creates—Haven, Castle Rock, Mid-World—that speak to a fundamental aspect of human existence: life is full of suffering. We are immersed in a world of loss and define ourselves by how we respond. The horrors King paints, although often supernatural, are more often mirrors of the mundane world of banal human existence. Sure, vampires are scary, but 'salem's Lot wasn't pleasant before they arrived. And although Tak decimates Desperation, David Carver had known loss before he ever entered that small Nevada town. In fact, for most of King's stories the supernatural merely augments the amount of suffering his characters experience, but not the fact that they suffer fundamentally. We are always already awash in evil, in pain and suffering. This is the human condition, and it is a problem we have collectively been seeking to rectify since we had the intelligence to recognize it. We wonder: "Why do we suffer?" And the religiously minded among us ponder: "Why would God allow so much suffering?"

In *Desperation*, David Carver speaks to God. He has a one-on-one relationship with Him. God offers David advice and at times instructs him. There are also indications that God intervenes to save David (e.g., by allowing him to squeeze through jail bars far too narrow for his head). But even so, even with God as his copilot, David has doubts. David saw his sister, Pie, killed by Collie Entragian and left at the bottom of the stairs like a discarded rag doll. Later he sees her dangling from a clothes hook: "Pie who walked around ants on the sidewalk because she didn't want to hurt them."[1] He sees his mother possessed by Tak, used up, and thrown away. His father dies before his very eyes. David knows God, David speaks to God, and yet he also knows suffering. So where is God, and what good is He?

Desperation, aside from being a fantastic Stephen King horror novel, is an exploration into the problem of evil as classically presented by philosophers and theologians. If God exists, and if God is all-powerful and good, then why does evil exist? With respect to this problem, David Hume (1711–1776) notes in his *Dialogues concerning Natural Religion* that "Epicurus's old questions are yet unanswered. Is [God] willing to prevent evil, but not able? Then is he impotent. Is he able, but not willing? Then is he malevolent. Is he both able and willing? Whence then is evil?"[2] This is the problem of evil.

THE WORLD IS SUNK IN EVIL

The existence of God is supposed to be a comforting thought for the believer, all hellfire and damnation aside. That an omniscient, omnipotent, and perfectly benevolent (omnicompetent for short) being exists, created, and oversees this world should provide us some sense of assurance. But believing in a God seems cold comfort when you're watching an ancient evil tear through town wearing your mother's skin. Ask David Carver. So the problem of evil poses a challenge to the theistic belief in an omnicompetent and personal God. If He is all-powerful and perfectly good, why is there so much evil in the world; why does He cause, or simply allow, it to happen? Can He prevent it? Then why doesn't He? Is there a reason for it? If God can eliminate Tak, then why doesn't He? What reason could there be for allowing Tak to rampage the earth?

Evil can't just be ignored. One can't explain it away as a nonproblem claiming we're just too sensitive or it's not really all that bad. There are evils in the world. Brian's mom is all too aware of this fact. Her son is hit by a drunk driver, thrown into a neighbor's home, and lies listless in a coma. To add insult to injury, the drunk doesn't even remember hitting her son, so he is spared the memories of his transgression. How merciful! But what kind of God allows such a thing? What kind of God allows a boy to be run down by a drunk, and the drunk to not even have to suffer the inner torment of remembering his deed? Brian's mom knows what kind of God— "*A God who loves drunks and hates little boys!*"[3] That is, no God at all. God is either cruel, or He simply doesn't exist. So in responding to the problem of evil one must be able to explain or make consistent the very real nature of these evils with a classic depiction of God as omnicompetent creator and ruler of the cosmos. Many find the two propositions, namely, the existence of evil in this world and the existence of an all-powerful and morally perfect God, to be mutually exclusive. The existence of evil is meant to disprove God.

Most often, arguments against theism that focus on the problem of evil are evidentiary arguments. That is, the person attempting to refute theism, or the idea of an omnicompetent God, does so by claiming that the amount of evil present in the world is evidence against the claim that such a God exists. Basically, the amount of evil in the world is testimony against the existence of a traditionally conceived, monotheistic God. As Hume illustrates in his *Dialogues*, by means of his character Demea: "All the goods of life united would not make a very happy man: But all the ills united would make a wretch indeed; and any one of them almost (and who can be free from every one), nay often the absence of one good (and who can possess them all) is sufficient to render life ineligible."[4] Beginning from this position, the ills of this life weigh heavily against existence, and thus they weigh heavily against the claim that a perfect and good God is present.

There are ample examples of this line of doubting. Recall the story of Job from the Old Testament. Job, a pious and good man, is afflicted with the most horrendous of ills, from the death of his family and destruction of his farm to his being rendered an invalid due to his physical afflictions, all at the hand of God as a test of faith. But from Job's perspective it is all undeserved suffering of the gravest kind. He laments, "I am blameless; I regard not myself; I loathe my life. It is all one; therefore I say, he destroys both the blameless and the wicked. When disaster brings sudden death, he mocks at the calamity of the innocent."[5] David Carver clearly suffers as did Job. He also loses everything, for no apparent reason, and with no relief in sight.

In a more modern accounting, Albert Camus (1913–1960), in his story *The Plague*, approaches the issue from the perspective of a Catholic priest administering to a plague-stricken city. A boy is afflicted with the disease and in a detailed account the reader is subjected to the last moments of this child's tortured existence. After the young child dies one of the men assisting the priest, in response to the priest's claim that God is beyond comprehension and deserves our love even in the face of this evil, retorts: "Until my dying day I shall refuse to love a scheme of things in which children are put to torture."[6] These types of accounts all use the existence of seemingly inexplicable or unnecessary suffering as evidence against theism, against the existence of a perfect and good God. The fact of evil is data against the explanatory hypothesis that the world is the construct of a benevolent, all-powerful creator God. God as a quasi-scientific hypothesis isn't supported by our observations.

THERE IS NO GOD IN DESPERATION

In contemporary philosophy there are several approaches to this problem. We'll begin with William Rowe (1931–2015). Rowe's argument is perhaps the most influential in the philosophical literature. Rowe's case boils down to the basic idea that the existence of unnecessary or superfluous suffering is evidence against God, thus making atheism a more rational belief. Let's begin by considering the amount of suffering in the world. It's immense. Rowe focuses specifically on evils that seem to have no purpose whatsoever. He presents an example of a fawn dying in a forest fire.[7] The fawn dies slowly and unobserved so its death can't incite compassion. In this case, the fawn's slow death and the concomitant pain and suffering appear to serve no greater purpose. For what good could the unobserved slow, agonizing death of a fawn serve? Rowe admits we might just lack imagination enough to envision a plan where it makes sense. We simply can't see from a God's-eye point of view. But he also notes that these types of incidences occur quite often. There are many cases of suffering on this planet that seem to follow this pattern; there is a great deal of apparently superfluous suffering in the world. We don't need Tak nailing cats to road signs to cause such pain. There are ample examples of both human wickedness and naturally occurring pain for us to begin to wonder whether it is necessary or creates some greater good we just don't see. People don't have to be possessed by Tak to murder children, or stranded in Desperation to be attacked and killed by snakes, wolves, or spiders. Our world is one where children die of snakebite, where infants are abused by parents, where death comes randomly, violently, and often too slowly. Where is God?

Rowe concludes, given the evidence, that God is nowhere. The existence of these kinds of evils, this amount of seemingly unnecessary suffering is enough evidence to warrant disbelief, to justify the claim that God, at least a God traditionally conceived as omnicompetent, doesn't exist. But for Rowe, this isn't a conclusive case. There is rational support for atheism given our observations, but he is what he terms a friendly atheist, and so acknowledges that there might still be reasons for theists to believe, even if the evidentiary case is quite strong against the existence of God. Even though it seems apparent there is no God in Desperation, David Carver does still pray. Others aren't so charitable.

Paul Draper isn't so sure that theism is a rational belief. Beginning from a position very similar to Rowe, and pursuing an evidentiary case from evil against theism, Draper offers his "hypothesis of indifference." Draper simply asks whether or not there is an alternative hypothesis to theism that explains the fact of evil better. Seeing theism as a quasi-scientific hypothesis meant to explain the phenomenon of human existence, he considers an alternative: "HI [Hypothesis of indifference]: neither the nature nor the condition of sentient beings on earth is the result of benevolent or malevolent actions performed by non-human persons."[8] Draper aims to rule out supernatural explanations to account for the facts of human existence. Although more complex than will be presented here, his argument boils down to the inability to explain the presence of pain as a positive good for human beings. Pain, he argues, serves no evident evolutionary good. In addition, assuming (and it's a big assumption) that all pain is intrinsically bad, and all pleasure intrinsically good, the presence of so much pain seems to fly in the face of the ostensible goal a creator God would have for humans, namely, their good, which Draper defines as pleasure.

Now clearly there are several problems with this line of thinking. First, pain can at times be good, as when it is instructive. One scholar, Nelson Pike, makes this point using the illustration of a parent forcing "a child to take a spoonful of bitter medicine." Likewise we might consider parents allowing children to suffer to develop and grow therefrom. Often pain is educative.[9] Secondly, God isn't necessarily a hedonist, one who aims for pleasure as the highest good, and may seek an end for us other than simply pleasure, such as flourishing, or redemption. Recall David's response to Johnny Marinville when he despairs of their condition: "But life is more than just steering a course around pain. That's something you used to know, Mr. Marinville."[10] Life may be about more than avoiding pain and pursuing pleasure. Finally, Draper's argument, even more so than Rowe's above, rests on the ability of humanity to comprehend the existence of evil in the grand scheme of the cosmos, an endeavor difficult for limited human reason. However, this is not to discount Draper's point. If theism is to be a rational belief for humans, then it ought to be based on evidence available to human beings. Here, we have to ask what is more plausible, what is more rational to believe, either that there is a mysterious, omnicompetent being that creates a world of immense suffering for a reason only He comprehends, or that given all evidence available to us it seems more likely that our existence is not the result of supernatural forces but rather the happenstance of evolutionary processes. Draper is making an inference to the best explanation, and the evidence at hand seems to fit better with an account that does not include supernatural entities, than one that does. Therefore, atheism is the best possible explanation given the evidence available to us.

Let's recap. Evil exists, and in not insignificant amounts. The amount and type of suffering and pain, of evil, that exists poses a problem for theists insofar as they have to explain how their vision of a God as omnipotent and morally perfect fits with a world of horrendous pain and suffering, pain and suffering that on the face of it a good God would seek to eliminate as far as possible. But evil persists, so God is either incompetent, or not good. Either way theism falters in the face of evil. Yet it's not so cut and dried. The evidentiary arguments above all rely on the same presumption, that we, as humans, are able to draw a decisive or at least warranted conclusion about the nature of God and the cosmos from our admittedly limited perspective. Herein may lay the fundamental problem.

If we claim that we see no reason for evil, is that a claim about God or about us? Is our lack of imagination proof against God? Is our claim to be able to engineer a better world not simply an example of arrogance, a profound epistemic hubris? As one scholar notes, when it comes to someone claiming to know how evil plays a role in the world, "we must ask him why he thinks he is in a position to know things of this sort. We might remind him of the counsel of epistemic humility that was spoken to Job out of the whirlwind. . . . 'Knowest thou the ordinances of heaven? Canst thou set the dominion thereof in the earth?'"[11] The claim that we have enough evidence from our observations to determine there is no possible, or even probable, account in which evil might exist alongside a perfect God speaks to our hubris. So perhaps the problem of evil is a human problem, one of an egotistical mind-set, an anthropocentric bent in our thinking and perspective. We phrase the problem of evil as one of our suffering, frustration of our ends, our wants and desires, and then condemn God for failing to provide us with a world we deem worthy of us, one in which we are contented. In addition, one might respond to these arguments not with demands for humility but with appeals to faith. Perhaps, "If we have realized the magnitude of the theistic proposal, cognizance of suffering thus should not in the least reduce our confidence that it is true. When cognizance of suffering does have this effect, it is perhaps because we had not understood the sort of being theism proposes for belief in the first place."[12] At the end of *Desperation*, David comes to this sort of realization. Throughout the book he iterates time and again, and concedes that God is cruel. Yet he responds to Johnny's note and the reference to 1 John 4:8 that "God is love" with the statement "Oh, yes . . . I guess he's sort of . . . everything."[13] God is cruel, and God is love. God is everything, including inscrutable. The theistic proposal asserts a God that is everything, that means a personal, loving God, as well as one that is cruel in our eyes, and often too demanding. Perhaps this is the kind of problem that simply can't be solved. Perhaps it's just beyond us. How might we offer an account?

GOD IS LOVE, CRUEL . . . EVERYTHING: DEFENSES AND THEODICIES

To put it more plainly: We've set up a powerful challenge to theism, perhaps even the most powerful challenge to belief that there is. We've looked at the world, and said, "Here! Here is evidence, *strong* evidence, which makes it unlikely that there is a God." What sort of answer should, or could, the theist give in return?

What sort of answer *could* the theist give? After all, you might think that there's no way the theist could reasonably respond to all the evil in the world, and that the right answer for the theist is to just give up the ghost. This is not totally unheard of. Rowe himself started a theist, and even attended seminary, but became an atheist over time at least in part due to the argument from evil. So one possible option for theists is to simply cease being theists, and accept the argument from evil as convincing. This seems to be the route Marinville himself might have taken, growing more and more resistant to the idea of God in the face of everything that has happened in his life. If it weren't for David's presence, it may even have happened for the rest of the survivors of Desperation (if they survived without him at all).

Yet, David never accepts the atheistic argument from evil. While he's not exactly sitting in a philosophy seminar, weighing his theoretical options, he is at least aware of the problem of evil. His friend's suffering, the loss of his family; all these things make him pause, and threaten to break him. But still he remains a theist. Granted, he does have the benefit of getting to talk to God. Regardless, many philosophically aware theists in the world, both historically and today, are familiar with the problem of evil but don't find it convincing. So it seems that there are at least some ways that the theist might respond.

We can classify and organize these responses by the *kind* of answer they try to give to the problem of evil. At its heart, the problem of evil is about a tension between the existence of God and the existence of evil and suffering in the world. The theist, like a smart chess player or strategist, can approach this tension in a few different ways, with each falling into one of two general types: she might attempt to dissolve the initial tension, weakening the atheistic argument and stopping it from ever getting off the ground, or she can attempt to resolve the tension that exists, giving additional reasons why these two ideas can coexist. Not every philosopher organizes responses this way, but for our purposes let's stick to two of the most common types of response: *defenses* and *theodicies*.

Defenses are the attempts to defuse the problem itself. A good defense can show that there is no tension between God and evil, and thus there is no good reason to advance the argument from evil in the first place. These can come in two flavors: broad defenses and specific defenses. A broad defense is not unlike a movie shotgun, affecting every aspect of the problem and simply blowing it away. Perhaps the simplest broad defense available to the theist is simply to deny the existence of any true evil or suffering—no evil, no problem. Evil is simply a problem of perception. What we call or see as evil really is not, we're just looking through an anthropocentric or human-tinted lens. This is generally unconvincing for a variety of reasons, not the least of which is that we generally consider evil and suffering to actually exist in some fashion. Try telling Brian's mother, for example, that despite her child's being hit by a car there is no true suffering or evil in the world, that she's just being selfish, or spoiled. She would find it no more convincing than anyone else. That is not to say that the strategy is totally without merit. Some early church fathers such as Saint Augustine (354–430 CE) considered evil a "privation" or corruption of good, so evil is no more a real thing than darkness (an absence of light) or cold (the absence of heat). Thus, in a technical sense, there is no real *thing* whose existence causes problems for the claim that God exists. In addition, Augustine goes on to remind us that we can't see the whole, but only our limited view of the world so there may be good we fail to see in what we perceive to be evil. Finally, he would remind us that God owes us nothing, we are His creation and as created are mutable, are subject to suffering, but He does not owe us an account of His creation and its goodness.[14] But for one interrogating the world and finding true misery, these seemingly flippant responses won't be convincing.

Another simple, but often unappealing, defense would be for the theist to argue that God lacks one of the characteristics necessary for there to be tension. All the characteristics of omnicompetence (power, knowledge, goodness, etc.) are necessary for most versions of the problem of evil to have any traction, and removing any one characteristic by making claims that this version of God is more likely to exist would weaken the atheistic argument significantly. If God were not all-powerful, say, we would not expect God to prevent all evils. The same is true if God were not perfectly good, or did not know about some evils, or was not a person in any way and thus could not be responsible. God couldn't be held to account for what happens in Desperation if He can't stop Tak, doesn't know what he's doing, or simply doesn't care. The theist can thus say that the atheistic argument proves that the classical God does not exist in the face of evil, but some other version still can. But then who would worship a God, and would He be worthy of worship, if He couldn't or wouldn't stop Tak? So this response is very unappealing to any theist who affirms the classical picture of God, the one with which we are currently working.

One can also argue that we're simply not in a position to weigh the evidence about God's existence and evil, similar to what Augustine was suggesting above. Michael Bergmann argues that "we have no good reason" to think that the goods we are aware of, or the evils we are aware of, are representative of all the goods and evils out there, nor do we have good reason to think the connections between these goods and evils are representative of all the possible entailments between possible goods and the permissibility of evils.[15] In other words, we're "in the dark" about what sorts of goods there might be in the world, and we're similarly blind to whether these goods might justify the existence of evil. It's not that we know nothing about good and evil in the world—we just don't know enough to give the mere existence of evil any real evidentiary weight in our decision to affirm the existence of God. We have *no real reason* to think that our evidence is anything resembling the total evidence out there, which takes the metaphorical wind out of the problem of evil's sails and defuses any tension it claims exists.

If these sorts of broad defenses are a philosophical shotgun, defusing the tension in some sweeping fashion, then specific defenses are scalpels. They play a similar role as other defenses, defusing tension and weakening the initial argument, but do so by targeting specific claims rather than the atheistic argument as a whole, and without showing specific reasons God would allow the existence of evil. One specific defense is to follow Richard Swinburne and claim that some evils simply don't pose a problem for theism, given that the theist can explain away other evils. Swinburne argues, quite straightforwardly, that if the theist can give an explanation for why God might allow a large swath of evils or suffering, there is good reason to think that an omnipotent, omniscient, eternal being like God might also have reason to allow the ones that human theists cannot discern. This is not unlike citing the success of science in the past at explaining mysteries as reason to think that we will be able to someday explain other mysteries via science. It's happened so many other times before that it is at least reasonable to think that it will happen again. That is not to say it's guaranteed, but it at least provides warrant for belief. Consider David Carver. While contemplating his fate and that of his friend, Brian, David seems to come to the conclusion that his fate in Desperation is related to his praying when Brian was looking like he wouldn't recover. He prayed, "God, make him better. If you do, I'll do something for you. I promise." Marinville notes, "And now it's payback time."[16] In this instance, David is seeking a rationale for his suffering, that it's payback for God's favor, and if it works in this case, there's no reason a similar logic or form of reasoning couldn't apply in other cases as well. For instance, perhaps the suffering they all experience in Desperation is for a greater good, or payback for past wrongs.

All of the above are ways for the theist to defuse the tension between the existence of God and the existence of evil in the world, ways to say, "There's no problem here," when presented with evidence of evil. But what about the theist who does see tension between these two claims? It seems she has but two options: one, to concede the nonexistence of God, if she has been convinced of such, or two, find some philosophical reason that resolves the apparent tension between evil and God. If she takes the second option, then we can say that she is offering a *theodicy*, an argument that justifies the existence of God and the existence of evil in the world. Rather than defusing the atheistic argument itself and preventing it from getting off the ground, a theodicy argues *in spite of* the atheistic argument and gives reasons why theism should still be taken as correct.

Many of the reasons given in theodicies follow a general pattern or theme: allowing evil in the world *seems* like a horrible thing, but in reality it allows, and is justified because of, some greater, higher-order good that can only be attained by allowing the existence of evil. Consider pain and exercise: Pain is something that (in general) we consider bad, what J. L. Mackie would call a "first-order evil." It has no real parts, it's just plain bad. So if this were all we had to evaluate things, we might judge exercise to be a bad thing as well—after all, it causes pain to those who do it. But most of us know that exercise is more complicated than that. Exercise has more to it than just pain; it has great benefits as another important part, and most of us would agree that those benefits outweigh the downside of some discomfort. Exercise is thus what Mackie calls a "second-order good," something good that has a first-order evil as an unavoidable part. Theodicies often try to paint a picture of something analogous to exercise: they acknowledge that there are first-order evils in the world, and on their own this would be a problem for claims about God's existence. But in reality, the theodicy might claim, that first-order evil is part of a second- (or higher-) order good! It's thus OK for this evil to exist, since there is something beneficial that makes it worth it for God to allow it.

One such picture of a second-order good is painted by King himself through the words of Reverend Martin—God is cruel, but God's cruelty is refining. This sort of idea, known in academic circles as the "soul-making theodicy" advanced by John Hick (1922–2012), holds that all the bad things in the world are actually a kind of great good. In particular, the evils of the world give us mortals the chance to overcome challenges and temptations, and grow fit for communion with God. As David's spiritual guide Reverend Martin points out, maybe God's cruelty, that is, evil, is refining. "We're the mine, and God is the miner,"[17] as Marinville puts it. This situation, Hick argues, is a greater good than if we were simply made in a state of perfect virtue or innocence, and so justifies the presence of evil over its potential absence. Admittedly, this does little to justify animal suffering like Rowe's fawn in the forest fire, but not every philosopher or theologian counts such "natural evil" against the existence of God, instead focusing on so-called moral evils such as murder and other human actions. Depending on what sorts of evils one cites in the atheistic argument, this theodicy can be considered either more or less convincing.

Among those that focus on moral evils, a common line of argument is the "free-will" theodicy, which comes in a few different flavors. We see an example of one of these in the idea of the "free-will covenant" that David and Reverend Martin refer to in passing. Despite all that God wants to happen in Desperation, He cannot make David or Johnny or anyone else do something they don't want to, because that would take away their free will, and this is apparently worth the risk of folks not following the plan. What "free-will" theodicies have in common, however, is the notion that human freedom to act, and to act without being caused by some outside force to act, is valuable enough that God permits the great evils born of our freedom. Even if we misuse free will, the argument goes, the world is a better place than if we were forced to do the right thing by God or some other cause. Swinburne in particular argues that our freedom is only as valuable as the range of actions that we're able to perform; if we were not free to commit great evils and could only choose to perform some small range of acts, then what sort of freedom do we really have? What value would it have? It would be like playing a board game where each player can only move forward and being praised for not going back.

While intuitive, the free-will theodicy has more than a few challenges. The first, and by no means the least, is that it assumes that human beings have free will, which is itself a major philosophical question. Second, while freedom in general may certainly be valuable, it is not clear that the ability to perform any sort of evil is. If I build some kind of autonomous cleaning robot, few would say that I could improve it by giving it the capability to murder, even if it is not programmed to use that capability. Furthermore, it (like many other theodicies) ignores all the natural evils in the world, like diseases, natural disasters, and accidents.

Some other theodicies do focus on natural evils, however. These arguments claim that it is important, and beneficial, for the universe to be governed by natural laws, like the laws of physics. These laws allow regular, intentional action to take place, but at the unavoidable consequence of allowing individuals to be harmed by them. The laws of thermodynamics make it possible for humans to be killed by forest fires, but the benefits of having consistent laws governing heat and energy outweigh the costs of any related harms. Perhaps evil, as Saint Thomas Aquinas (1225–1274) notes, is needed to preserve the whole. The goodness exists in the whole of created being, as a work of art, and evil thus serves its part as a necessary element therein.[18] In terms of convincingness, this is not the strongest theodicy. It gives no account of moral evils, and so is incomplete in an important sense, much like some of the above "moral" theodicies with regard to natural evils. It is also subject to a number of serious objections, such as the ease with which God could presumably still save lives from natural disasters while otherwise preserving the laws; for example, God could prevent a massive earthquake that would kill millions and no one would be the wiser, while still allowing geological events to be governed in general by natural laws.

In the end, many types of responses can be offered, from defenses to theodicies. The limit to our ability to respond to this problem is simply the limit of our imagination. So there can be as many responses and theodicies as there are authors who can imagine them. And that may, in fact, be the crux of the problem. What really are the limits of the discussion when the topic is something ineffable like God? We might even despair of ever making progress on this topic. Perhaps it's all hot air. Perhaps there's no point to discuss this.

... ONLY *CAN DE LACH*. EVIL ISN'T A GOD PROBLEM— HELD'S CONCLUSION

The problem of evil won't readily be resolved by simple philosophical argument. It is more often than not a personal matter, one affected by experiences and one's perspective as much as by reason and evidence. I want to begin with perspective.

The problem of evil is fundamentally a human problem. We devise it. We recognize ills in the world, things that affront us, upset us, often rightly, and frustrate our ends. We call these evil. But this belies an anthropocentric worldview, as if the world were created for us, and not simply for us, but for us to have a pain-free, obstacle-free, easy, and contented life. Paul Draper's hypothesis of indifference begins from the idea that he has to explain away, better than the theistic hypothesis, pain, namely, our lamentable condition. But as an evidentiary argument against theism it begins from a problematic stance, that somehow the human condition could, or rather, ought to be otherwise. But can a finite existence, an embodied existence be other than one of limitation, and insofar as limited, frustrated and so rife with suffering? We are finite, we are temporal, and we are embodied. "The idea of a world without evil, is the idea of a world without differentiation and finiteness. It is, in short, a self-contradiction and an absurdity, and to create an absurdity is not the mark of omniscience, nor is it a limitation of power to be unable to produce a self-contradiction."[19] We experience limitation and embodiment as pain or evil. But it is the necessary condition of life as limited, as finite, even if we sometimes see the pain as too great or the suffering as unnecessary. So is this an evidentiary claim against theism, or a claim that humans, by design, are fundamentally flawed and not worthy of existence? Is the claim simply that the existence of humans and God is mutually exclusive, such that humans are proof against God because we are such failed experiments only an incompetent could have, or would have, created us? There is no inconsistency in our inability to grasp the rationale that permits what we perceive as grave evils and the perfection of God. There does appear to be a great amount of evidence against a morally perfect and all-powerful God, but that's only because of how we perceive evil and conceive of God. My point is simply that perhaps this debate focuses on an irresolvable problem. Can we ever have enough or the right kind of evidence to discredit the belief in an omnicompetent God?

In evidentiary arguments from the problem of evil we are entertaining the idea that the existence of certain types or amounts of evil is sufficient evidence to militate against a belief in God, classically conceived. The question is about whether the amount and kind of evil presented is evidence against a rational person believing in an omnicompetent God. We're asking about epistemic warrant, and if our belief is reasonable. Here, Peter van Inwagen offers help. To paraphrase van Inwagen: if we are in no position to assign a probability to the concurrence of suffering and theism, or rather, if we are in no epistemically justified position to assess whether the suffering that exists is more or less likely than not given God's existence, then we have no epistemic warrant to make an evidentiary claim from suffering and evil against a belief in God.[20] Simply put, like Job, we are in no position, we lack the requisite knowledge, to make a reasoned judgment about whether or not the suffering we experience and perceive is consistent with God, a, by definition, ineffable and inscrutable being. The introduction of God into any discussion necessarily adds an element of mystery, of epistemic opacity. Often this means believers will rely on faith and nonbelievers will remain unmoved by theistic appeals. So in the end we will come to an impasse, while the problem of suffering remains.

The problem of evil is the problem of suffering. It isn't a God problem, it's a human problem. The problem of evil

> is often treated as the problem of why God allows evil. The enquiry then takes the form of a law-court, in which Man, appearing both as judge and accuser, arraigns God and convicts him of mismanaging his responsibilities. We then get a strange drama, in which two robed and wigged figures apparently sit opposite each other exchanging accusations. But this idea, seems . . . unhelpful. If God is not there, the drama cannot arise. If he is there, he is surely something bigger and more mysterious than a corrupt or stupid official. Either way, we still need to worry about a different and more pressing matter.[21]

That "more pressing matter" is human suffering. No defense or theodicy will cause one who raised the issue to relent. If we raise the problem of evil in earnest, then simply being told a comforting story about God and how all the suffering we and others endure is "justified" according to this account won't assuage our concerns, it won't make the suffering any less real, it won't help us cope with the harshness of human existence in the here and now. No Bible story is going to satisfy Brian's mom or comfort the denizens of Desperation. Johnny, David, and the others aren't going to be appeased with a pat on the head and a religious platitude about God working in mysterious ways. Especially when those mysterious ways involve a psychopathic ancient demon rampaging through town. What they need is a strategy to cope with the suffering they experience, which isn't an argument to be refuted, but a condition to be tolerated, and perhaps redeemed. Likewise, proving God is absent or nonexistent would be a hollow victory. You'd have demonstrated that no God exists, only by thoroughly providing an account of how miserable this life truly is. And again, you're still stuck with the misery. As one scholar notes, although interesting, this debate often misses the point. The real question is "Am I glad that I am alive? Or is my existence, on the whole, something which I regret?"[22] In the work of Stephen King, pain is always front and center; suffering infuses his work. And so the reader sees most clearly that the problem of evil is not a God problem, it is a human problem.

So if God can't save us, if we can't define away the problem of evil, what is an appropriate response? I think compassion holds the key, but that discussion can wait for a later chapter.[23] Read on, for now. There are other conclusions than these.

"THE SPIRITUAL STATE OF UNBELIEF IS DESPERATION": MARINVILLE, DESPAIR, AND FAITH WITHOUT BELIEF

We need not conclude, pace Held, that the problem of evil is unsolvable. The problem is difficult, as is attempting to change the opinions of either side of the debate. It might even be so difficult that it has never happened, and is unlikely to happen in the future. But this doesn't mean that the problem is *unsolvable*, any more than difficulty surrounding any problem in philosophy proves that that problem is unsolvable.[24]

Even if philosophers never agree whether we have free will or not, even if no one can convince anyone else to adopt one's views on the matter, it's plain that there *is* still an answer to the question. It is either true that we are free in our actions and responsible for what we do, or it is not.[25] In other words, there is an answer out there somewhere.

The same is true for the problem of evil. Only a fool would deny that there is evil out there in the world—even if there are no forces like Tak hiding under the earth, there are other, all too normal, sources of suffering and tragedy out there. It is also true that either an omnicompetent God exists or not, in the same way that a line is either straight or not. One of those two options is correct, and so an answer exists. And to paraphrase many theologians and philosophers, the answer *matters*—if God exists, the implications for our lives are immense. Ignoring God's existence would be like Johnny's threat to leave the job in Desperation unfinished and just drive off. You'd be living a lie, ignoring a fundamental fact of the world, and sooner or later the implications would catch up to you. God's existence would mean changes for our views about the universe, ethics, ourselves, the way we ought to live, the purpose of humanity, and so forth. It matters.

So what should we do about this? In the face of such a fundamental question, and lacking an answer or any certain way to reach one, it seems that we risk despair—we risk *desperation*. It's all too easy for us to give up on deep questions and try to lose ourselves in . . . anything. The idea of burying ourselves in work, Netflix, booze, or something else is all too familiar for most of us. And this isn't always a bad thing. Sometimes, for the sake of recuperating or resting, we *need* to get away. The problem arises when we try and stay away. We grow afraid of going back to the difficult, the demanding, the uncomfortable. We start inventing new ways to amuse and distract ourselves, doing anything we can to avoid ourselves and our responsibilities. Danish philosopher Søren Kierkegaard (1813–1855) aptly called this state "despair," and it is the exact state Johnny Marinville has spent the latter part of his life in.[26] Ignoring his spirit in favor of his *sarx*, Johnny did everything he could to cope with Vietnam and forget it. He considers going right back to that life instead of finishing Tak and closing the China Shaft.

But this isn't the right course of action, nor the best one for him. "Its mark is on you," David says. "It will let you go, but you'll wish you'd stayed when you start smelling Tak on your skin."[27] Running away leaves Tak in the world. Ignoring a question still leaves it demanding an answer. It won't go away. Even if you do something that would be otherwise good, it will stink of Tak—of desperation. That's no way to live. King knows this, Johnny knows this, and we know it.

Thankfully, King also draws a road map out of desperation for us. If we look to the conversation that young Johnny has with David in the spirit world, we get a glimpse of how we might avoid desperation. It may not be the only answer, but it is the answer that King seems to give to us:

> "Never mind *can tah* and *can tak*, at least for now. We have bigger fish to fry, so pay attention. What is faith?"
>
> That one was easy. "The substance of things hoped for, the evidence of things not seen."
>
> "Yeah. And what is the spiritual state of the faithful?"
>
> "Um . . . love and acceptance. I think."
>
> "And what is the opposite of faith?"
>
> That was tougher—a real hairball, in fact. . . . "Disbelief?" he ventured.
>
> "No. Not disbelief but *un*belief. The first is natural, the second willful. And when one is in unbelief, David, what is one's spiritual state?"
>
> He thought about it, then shook his head. "I don't know."
>
> "Yes you do."
>
> He thought about it and realized he did. "The spiritual state of unbelief is desperation."[28]

Looking at this conversation, we can actually "work backward" to see what we should do. Desperation is the spiritual state of unbelief, the opposite of faith. That may sound weird to those who lean atheistic, but bear with me. Here, King is drawing a distinction between merely not believing and willfully turning away from belief. In the novel, where divine acts and miracles are (relatively) common, willfully refusing to believe is willfully refusing to engage the truth, intentionally avoiding the matter. In our world, where the truth is somewhat less clear, the matching act would be intentionally and willfully refusing to engage the question—refusing to even *look* for the truth. This is the kind of running away that characterizes desperation and despair, and whose opposite is faith.

Rather than mere semantics, this makes an important point. The opposite of desperation is faith, but that doesn't mean that we should automatically believe in God simply because we lack an answer. That's just not rational. Instead, King/Johnny's point is that we should respond with the opposite of desperation, the opposite of wildly and intentionally ignoring the question, and whatever this is, he calls faith.

But isn't that wrong? Doesn't faith require belief? Surprisingly, not always. And some philosophers would argue that belief isn't even fundamental to faith. Jonathan Kvanvig, among others, has explored what the academic world calls "non-cognitive" faith.[29] This sort of faith is "non-cognitive" because it's not based on what sort of propositions you believe or what ideas you have. That kind of faith is usually captured in statements like, "I have faith that . . ." Cognitive faith is a common kind of faith, but it's not the only sort, nor is it the most basic one. That honor, Kvanvig says, belongs to a kind of commitment to an ideal, something similar to trust, but different. It's the kind of faith that is captured by "faith in" statements, as in "I have faith in Kevin," or "I have faith in democracy." Kvanvig calls this faith *affective* faith, because it affects you in some way. It is the sort of faith that changes behavior and drives you to act, and belief has very little to do with it.

Take a Little League ballplayer, about David's age. After striking out every time he was at bat, the boy makes a promise to himself that this will never happen again, and really commits to the idea of getting better. In Kvanvig's words:

> Such a reaction can generate an orientation or disposition toward various efforts at becoming better, in hopes of doing so (or at least some aversion to the idea that any efforts of any sort are hopeless), and display a kind of self-trust or self-reliance and perhaps some trust of others who may be recruited to help in the project. Our youngster makes a commitment to a certain kind of future. It might be an intense commitment or more casual in its firmness, but when he carries through on this commitment, he will be properly characterized as being faithful to it, or pursuing his goal faithfully.[30]

This kid doesn't necessarily believe anything at all. He may think quite often that this will in fact happen again, and believe himself to be a terrible baseball player. But so long as he remains committed to himself and that possible future, he has faith in that future and himself.

I think it is this sort of faith that we should have in light of the problem of evil, the sort of faith that is the opposite of desperation. Desperation drives us to run away from problems with the stink of Tak on our skin, to bury ourselves in booze and sex and endless distractions. But having faith in something, be it ourselves, the truth, reason, or even God, will drive us to take up the problem of evil in a constructive, creative way. Thus we have what Saint Anselm (1033–1109) calls "faith seeking understanding." Anselm states, "I do not understand so that I may believe; but I believe so that I may understand."[31] His belief, his faith, drives him to understanding. Even without an answer we can continue to try and discover the truth. This sort of faith is not just assuming an answer to the problem of evil and committing oneself to confirming it, but is rather like Kvanvig's affective faith: a commitment to and care for the subject matter of philosophy and the problem of evil. It is caring about the question and its answers, caring enough for the truth that one continues to investigate despite the difficulty. It is this kind of faith that drove Anselm to try and demonstrate God's existence, despite already being a priest. It is this kind of commitment that brings Johnny back in the final chapters. It is this kind of commitment that can allow us to face one of the most difficult problems in philosophy with determination and courage. It is a kind of faith required by both atheists and theists, demanded by our integrity as reflective beings, and necessary lest we persist in desperation.

NOTES

1. Stephen King, *Desperation* (New York: Viking, 1996), 499.

2. David Hume, *Dialogues concerning Natural Religion*, in *Principal Writings on Religion including* Dialogues concerning Natural Religion *and* The Natural History of Religion, ed. J. C. A. Gaskin (Oxford: Oxford University Press, 1993), 100.

3. King, *Desperation*, 167.

4. Hume, *Dialogues concerning Natural Religion*, 98.

5. From the book of Job 9:21–23, in *The Problem of Evil: Selected Readings*, ed. Michael L. Peterson (Notre Dame, Ind.: University of Notre Dame Press, 1992), 25–26.

6. Albert Camus, from *The Plague*, anthologized as *Physical Suffering and the Justice of God*, in *The Problem of Evil*, ed. Michael L. Peterson (Notre Dame, Ind.: University of Notre Dame Press, 1992), 78.

7. See William Rowe, "The Problem of Evil and Some Varieties of Atheism," in *The Problem of Evil*, ed. Marilyn McCord Adams and Robert Merrihew Adams (Oxford: Oxford University Press, 1990), 126–37.

8. Paul Draper, "Pain and Pleasure: An Evidential Problem for Theists," in *God and the Problem of Evil*, ed. William L. Rowe (Malden, Mass.: Blackwell, 2001), 181.

9. See Nelson Pike, "Hume on Evil," in *The Problem of Evil*, ed. Marilyn McCord Adams and Robert Merrihew Adams (Oxford: Oxford University Press, 1990), 40.

10. King, *Desperation*, 533.

11. Peter van Inwagen, "The Problem of Evil, the Problem of Air, and the Problem of Silence," in *God and the Problem of Evil*, ed. William L. Rowe (Malden, Mass.: Blackwell, 2001), 218.

12. See Stephen J. Wykstra, "The Humean Obstacle to Evidential Arguments from Suffering: On Avoiding the Evils of 'Appearance,'" in *The Problem of Evil*, ed. Marilyn McCord Adams and Robert Merrihew Adams (Oxford: Oxford University Press, 1990), 160.

13. King, *Desperation*, 690.

14. For a good summation of this line of Augustine's thinking, see William E. Mann, "Augustine on Evil and Original Sin," in *The Cambridge Companion to Augustine*, ed. Eleonore Stump and Norman Kretzmann (Cambridge: Cambridge University Press, 2001).

15. Michael Bergmann, "Skeptical Theism and Rowe's New Evidential Argument from Evil," *Nous* 35 (2001): 278–96.

16. King, *Desperation*, 619.

17. King, *Desperation*, 499.

18. For a clear discussion of this point, see Jacques Maritain, "St. Thomas and the Problem of Evil: The Aquinas Lecture, 1942" (Milwaukee, Wis.: Marquette University Press, 1942).

19. Errol E. Harris, "The Problem of Evil: The Aquinas Lecture, 1977" (Milwaukee, Wis.: Marquette University Publications, 1977), 42.

20. For the full argument, see van Inwagen, "Problem of Evil."

21. Mary Midgley, *Wickedness: A Philosophical Essay* (London: Routledge & Kegan Paul, 1984), 1.

22. William Hasker, "On Regretting the Evils of This World," in *The Problem of Evil: Selected Readings*, ed. Michael L. Peterson (Notre Dame, Ind.: University of Notre Dame Press, 1992), 154.

23. See chapter 17 in this volume.

24. See David Chalmers, "Why Isn't There More Progress in Philosophy?" *Philosophy* 90 (2015).

25. There are, of course, many more options than these two.

26. Soren Kierkegaard, *The Sickness unto Death: A Christian Psychological Exposition for Upbuilding and Awakening* (Princeton, N.J.: Princeton University Press, 1983).

27. King, *Desperation*, 567.

28. King, *Desperation*, 499–500.

29. Jonathan Kvanvig, "The Idea of Faith as Trust: Lessons in Non-Cognitive Approaches to Faith," in *Reason and Faith*, ed. Michael Bergmann and Jeffrey Brower (Oxford: Oxford University Press, 2016).

30. Kvanvig, "Idea of Faith as Trust," 11.

31. Anselm of Canterbury, *Proslogion*, in *The Major Works including Monologion, Proslogion, and* Why God Became Man, ed. Brian Davies and G. R. Evans (Oxford: Oxford University Press, 2008), 87.

2

FEMALE SUBJECTIVITY IN *CARRIE*

Kellye Byal

In response to the enormous popularity of *Carrie*, Stephen King writes, "One reason for the success of the story in both print and film, I think, lies in this: Carrie's revenge is something that any student who has ever had his gym shorts pulled down in Phys Ed or his glasses thumb-rubbed in study hall could approve of."[1] Indeed, *Carrie* is a novel to which any student can relate. What makes it interesting is that "any student" is personified by a teenage girl. Coming-of-age novels frequently use female protagonists, from Charlotte Brontë's *Jane Eyre* to Judy Blume's *Are You There God? It's Me, Margaret*. What sets Carrie apart from the others are her supernatural abilities—as well as her body—as a source of transformation.

Carrie White's telekinetic power acts for her when she cannot: made powerless by her mother's abuse in the form of religious fervor and tormented by her peers, she finds new agency in her mental capabilities. King clearly suggests that the transition from girl to woman as well as helpless teen to powerful supernatural entity is intentional, which raises all sorts of questions concerning Carrie's identity. Particularly, how does Carrie White grapple with femininity throughout the novel? And how does femininity rub up against monstrosity if we regard *Carrie* as a horror story?

I WAS A TEENAGED SUBJECT

Simone de Beauvoir (1908–1986) is particularly concerned with how "feminine destiny" shapes women's lives, and her work can help illuminate Carrie White's situation, as well as the "destinies" offered to her by her mother and peers. Beauvoir describes how "femininity" is constructed separately from "humanity." In her view, to be a woman, to assume the constructed particularities associated with "womanhood," one must categorize oneself as something within the realm of the human being yet separate, as our cultural understanding of the human being is conflated with maleness. Beauvoir says, "Nominalism is a doctrine that falls a bit short; and it is easy for antifeminists to show that women are not men. Certainly woman like man is a human being; but such an assertion is abstract; the fact is that every concrete human being is always uniquely situated."[2] At once this poses a problem. If "woman" and "human" are not one and the same category, what is one to do? If one is a woman and wishes to be included in a social grouping that affords such things as "human rights" or "human dignity," where is one? And, if she is not included in the masculine definition of human, does this mean she is monstrous?

The horror film typically explores the categories of "human" versus "nonhuman" through the concept of the monster, "the most unifying element of the horror story." Noël Carroll describes the monster as "any being not believed to exist now according to contemporary science," or anything that constitutes "an aberration of form, since most monsters occupy status between two or more categories of existence."[3] In some ways, Carrie White certainly fits the criteria, since she is a girl with supernatural characteristics and is a social outcast like other monsters before her. However, apart from her telekinetic ability Carrie is remarkably average: she has the same desires and problems of any teenage girl: not fitting in at school, unsure of the changes in her body, trouble reconciling her home life with the expectations of her peers. What makes Carrie's story so tragic is the repeated glimpses of her humanity the reader is privy to: we are meant to sympathize with Carrie's situation. In many ways, she is not monstrous enough. It might be suggested that the real "villain" of the story is the community that fails to support her.

Carrie's identity is significantly tied to the changes in her physical body, changes noted from the outset of both adaptations. Taking a shower, she suddenly realizes she is bleeding between her legs. Unable to recognize what is happening to her, she screams and cries for help, believing she is wounded. As Beauvoir notes, "Blood is for the young girl the manifestation of a wound of the internal organs."[4] Unless she is given fair warning, first menstruation will always be shocking and confusing. Carrie's more knowledgeable classmates pelt her with tampons, crying, "Plug it up!" instead of coming to her aid. Sue Short, in *Misfit Sisters: Screen Horror as Female Rites of Passage*, writes, "As the film's opening sequence makes clear, [Carrie's] first period terrifies her into thinking that she is bleeding to death—a terror that is greeted with mocking humiliation by her female peers."[5] Unfairly punished for her ignorance, Carrie unknowingly lashes out:

> There was a bright flash overhead, followed by a flashgun-like pop as a lightbulb sizzled and went out. Miss Desjardin cried out with surprise, and it occurred to her (the whole damn place is falling in) that this kind of thing always seemed to happen around Carrie when she was upset, as if bad luck dogged her every step. The thought was gone almost as quickly as it had come.[6]

First menstruation may be traumatic. Beauvoir writes that menstruation and the primary sexual encounters of women are an unexpected break from the ease of girlhood into the frightening prospects of womanhood. She says of menstruation, "It is natural for the young girl to be afraid: it seems to her that her life is seeping out of her . . . even if cautious advice saves her from excessive anxiety, she is ashamed, she feels dirty."[7] Beauvoir contrasts this to male adolescence, which is received with some degree of pride within society. However, "the girl is soon disappointed because she sees that she has not gained any privilege and that life follows its normal course. The only novelty is that the disgusting event is repeated monthly; there are children that cry for hours when they learn they are condemned to this destiny."[8]

Menstruation then, according to Beauvoir, plays a large role in determining a young woman's destiny because women are understood almost entirely in terms of their bodies, specifically their reproductive capacities. Women are not granted the same freedom and ease that men have in regard to sexuality, due to the restrictions on birth and childbearing. Margaret White represents a frenzied distortion of the idea of sexual intercourse and childbirth as sinful, forbidding Carrie any knowledge or association with it. Purity in Margaret's world is virginity and asceticism: this likens her to Beauvoir's archetype of the "Mystic" in *The Second Sex*. However, the sexually active lifestyle endorsed by Carrie's peers is hardly affirming, either. In the De Palma film, the gym teacher Miss Collins acts as a liaison between Carrie and the world of her peers. Sue Snell assumes this role in the novel. King describes the dissatisfaction Sue feels in her relationship with Tommy Ross, as well as Chris Hargensen's abusive relationship with Billy Nolan.

Ultimately, Carrie becomes caught between two destinies emphasized by two mother figures: Mrs. White and Sue Snell/Miss Collins. Short writes, "In many ways then, Carrie has two mothers in the film, one who obstructs her journey to adulthood because she is filled with a pathological hatred towards women, as much as patent distrust of the 'unbelievers' in their midst, while the other attempts to encourage her to make more of herself physically and thus 'fit in' better with the other girls at school and their superficial world of dates and dances."[9] If *Carrie* can be interpreted as a coming-of-age myth (Short likens it to Cinderella), the mother plays an important role in determining what course the girl's future will take.

Beauvoir writes, "For the mother, the daughter is both her double and an other, the mother cherishes her and at the same time is hostile to her; she imposes her own destiny on her child: it is a way to proudly claim her own femininity and also to take revenge on it." Like the doll that is both an extension of the self and a foreign object for the little girl, the daughter represents a possibility for the mother who is already fixed in carrying out her own destiny. "Thus, women given the care of the little girl are bent on transforming her into women like themselves with zeal and arrogance mixed with resentment."[10] This explains the fervor that Margaret White has in preserving Carrie's own piety. In a disturbing passage, King describes how Margaret had become pregnant and delivered Carrie by cutting her out of her own womb.

> "I thought God had visited me with cancer; that He was turning my
> female parts into something as black and rotten as my sinning soul.
> But that would have been too easy. The Lord works in mysterious
> ways His wonders to perform. I see that now. When the pains began
> I went and got a knife—this knife—" she held it up "—and waited

for you to come so I could make my sacrifice. But I was weak and backsliding. I took the knife in hand again when you were three, and I backslid again. So now the devil has come home."[11]

Margaret's attempts to murder Carrie, or at least turn her into a purer version of herself, are made quite clear throughout the novel as an exaggerated form of imposed destiny. She never truly claims Carrie as her daughter, only as an extension of herself (and her sexuality) that she must control. As Beauvoir says of the Mystic, "It is not transcendence [she is] aiming for: it is the redemption of [her] femininity."[12] Having found shame in her own sexual desires and feminine body, Margaret projects her feelings onto her daughter. Therefore, any means of assuming femininity in the White household is taboo, lest it become an invitation to sin. Having become entangled in Margaret's own projected shame, Carrie is forced to kill her mother in self-defense, the final foundation of her childhood come apart.

Likewise, the fact that Carrie cannot fit in with her peers at school is also met with a mixture of zeal and hostility. In the De Palma adaptation, Miss Collins takes pity on Carrie and tries to encourage her to embrace femininity by introducing Carrie to cosmetics and encouraging her to go to prom. But this solution is illusory. Short notes, "The prom reveals the fallacy behind the idea that the accouterments of femininity (having the right dress, hair, makeup, and date) are the only desirable goals for a woman—and this is what makes it such an important revisionist fable."[13] The emphasis on the prom or losing one's virginity as the most important event in a teenage girl's life echoes the belief that marriage and children are the ultimate feminine destiny. In other words, the girl's femininity will only be fulfilled through consummation with a man. While Mrs. White's destiny requires abstaining from sexual relations, Miss Collins is asking for Carrie to refine herself into something more palatable to heterosexual men. The result is either death (one could interpret this directly as Mrs. White tries to kill Carrie) or mutilation of her subjectivity (Carrie has to change in order to fit in). As Shelley Stamp Lindsey states, "Carrie's subsequent path to womanhood is presented as a treacherous course which must be cautiously navigated by either two possible routes she is offered: the sexual repression demanded by her mother or the promise of femininity volunteered by her gym teacher, Miss Collins."[14] Woman is in an ambiguous position. She must either reject societal norms and expectations and be outcast, or adopt them and thereby threaten her very subjectivity.

The novel describes this treacherous aspect in more detail, through the perspective of Sue Snell. King writes, "And having something she had always longed for—a sense of place, of security, of status—she found that it carried uneasiness with it like a darker sister. . . . The idea that she had let him fuck her simply because he was popular for instance."[15] The idea that social conformity (in this case, popularity at school) and sexuality are intrinsically linked ties in with previous claims about feminine destiny. In this case, for Carrie to reject femininity altogether would place her in the same strange denial as her mother. At the same time, to assume femininity entails a particular kind of assimilation and "uneasiness." It is not a true affirmation of one's subjectivity; rather, it places woman's sense of self only at the level of embodiment.

DAMNED IF YOU DO...

The true "horror" of the film generates not from the fact that Carrie White is different from her peers, as King himself admits we are meant to identify with her rather than her tormentors. The horror comes from the fact that Carrie cannot live differently; she must change herself in order to become like the very people who demonize her. Like her other monster predecessors, Carrie's story becomes one of resisting assimilation. As Carol Clover states, "At the end, she turns the tables, she herself becomes a kind of monstrous hero—hero insofar as she has risen against and defeated the forces of monstrosity, monster insofar as she herself has become excessive, demonic."[16]

However, Carrie's telekinesis does not come from some monstrous "feminine" that is at the base of her actions and motivations, for which she is consequently punished, like some critics of *Carrie* have suggested. One could describe it in the way Serafina Kent Bathrick does. Carrie White is ultimately punished for failing to conform to either the world of her fundamentalist mother or her sexually active peers. Bathrick argues, "Like all the women in the film, [Carrie] brings on her own destruction, she is punished for being a woman,"[17] collapsing along with her childhood home. Carrie is experiencing a deep frustration from a world that fails to recognize her as a subject in her own right. Thus, "[telekinesis] can be seen as a metaphor of empowerment, for it is in discovering this ability that she takes her first steps in resisting the wrongs that have been made against her."[18] The "monstrous" aspect of Carrie's condition is the fact that her heightened feelings of fear and anger create an externalized physical threat that she uses to fight back against her tormentors. We are not meant to identify with Carrie's oppressors; even King recognizes this when he talks about how any student who has been bullied will "approve" of the film.

Carrie's telekinesis is an extension of her body, rather than a feature of her embodiment. Unlike Buffy Summers in Joss Whedon's *Buffy the Vampire Slayer*, Carrie is not the one throwing the kicks and punches or burning down the school; rather, she is acting through a metaphysical third party. But Carrie only reacts instead of taking conscious, deliberate action. Her passivity becomes problematic for critics like Bathrick, as it reflects a deeper, socialized structure. But does this type of passivity only reflect the kinds of limitations imposed on woman?

Beauvoir suggests, "Woman feels so deeply passive . . . only because she already thinks herself that way."[19] We are given only a small glimpse of Carrie White's childhood, but it's implied that she was meant to assume a passive existence from a young age. The girl is meant to feel alienated from her body as a means of acting within the world. "For girls and boys, the body is the first radiation of a subjectivity, the instrument that brings about the comprehension of a world."[20] These feelings brought about in early childhood begin when the young girl copies the actions of her elders, and also in the toys with which she is meant to play. This might serve to complicate the way in which Carrie's power is mediated because the girl's subjectivity is already mediated in terms of how it is understood. The problem is that Carrie is pushed in so many different directions that in order for her self to emerge she must act in spite of the conditions presented to her. Acting, in this case, would require a way of being that isn't dictated by some external norm, an authentic, radically free activity. Activity not bound by expectations or a context that determines it. This is what the telekinesis represents.

This analysis brings up an important point in regard to both how femininity and subjectivity are constructed from Beauvoir's point of view. For one thing, it raises questions as to what femininity actually does for the female as subject. Carrie White attempts to embrace her femininity, yet it's not enough to mark her as a being worthy of acceptance within her social world. It's implied that no matter how much makeup Carrie wears or how pious she is, she will never fit in to either prescribed sphere, she will never be good enough, she will never attain the ideal. Beauvoir describes how assumption of femininity immediately dooms the female subject to immanence, to being defined and fated to being a woman within a specific historical period with all the expectations and demands that come with being a woman in that historical circumstance. She writes, "In exchange for her freedom, she was given fallacious treasures of 'femininity' as a gift."[21] Once Carrie rejects her femininity as a sign of betrayal at the prom (once the bucket of pig's blood is upturned over her head and she fully embraces her abilities) only then can she act on her own behalf.

DEATH BECOMES HER

In the end, Carrie's death becomes especially poignant since it serves as a cautionary tale for young women who wish to escape the burden that femininity imposes. Whether or not this is the case, the idea of strong heroines committing suicide in the face of a harmful reality is a significant trope of both film and literature. This is true of Ridley Scott's 1991 film *Thelma and Louise* and Kate Chopin's novel *The Awakening*. Yet this is not entirely the case concerning Carrie, as her story is also a revenge fantasy. Bathrick's analysis hardly touches the concept of revenge, while it is a major theme that King discusses in reference to his own work. Yet another way to read *Carrie* might be in light of the destructive aspects of revenge and the nature of tragedy, which would explain Carrie's own self-destruction in part.

In addition, the idea that Carrie is being "punished" for lashing out assumes that horror narratives provide some sort of underlying moral instruction: act accordingly or receive some sort of grisly supernatural fate. Art-horror is fiction, and as such must open itself up to the possibility of multiple interpretations. But to read the horror tale so simplistically runs the risk of reducing it to the level of propaganda. Given the popular appeal as well as the endurance of horror within literature, this charge is unfounded. And *Carrie* also parallels other monster narratives with masculine protagonists who suffer similar fates. In James Whale's adaptation of Mary Shelley's *Frankenstein*, the monster dies at the hands of the villagers because he cannot be assimilated into society. Likewise, in *Bride of Frankenstein*, the monster solemnly acknowledges that "we belong dead" once his created Bride rejects him. Because Frankenstein's monster cannot live among the living, nor be accepted by others like himself, he dies tragically in the same way Carrie White dies at the end of King's novel. In this sense, *Carrie* is similar to its monster movie predecessors in that Carrie White is presented as too different from the world she inhabits. I would thus be reticent to accept that her death serves as punishment for fighting back against her tormentors. As Short notes, "While it may be argued that her death is used to punish female aberrance, it may also be seen as an indictment of those who tormented her, for the true monster of the text is the ignorance of an entire community, including her mother, for treating her as they have."[22] Short, who also reads *Carrie* as a coming-of-age myth, views the destruction of the "wicked stepmother" as necessary for the heroine to overcome her obstacles. Yet, in this particular myth, the "stepmother" has her final say in pulling the heroine down with her, which makes *Carrie* a horror tale, as opposed to a fairy tale.

A better way of understanding Carrie White's situation would be Beauvoir's claim that there is no unified solidarity among women, a failure of a community as opposed to the delinquency of an individual. Beauvoir describes how women regard themselves as the "Other," yet are in no way unified by this fact. She says, "women—except in certain abstract gatherings such as conferences—do not use 'we'; men say 'women', and women adopt this word to refer to themselves; but they do not posit themselves authentically as Subjects."[23] This dynamic is played out multiple times throughout both film and literary versions of *Carrie*. Carrie's mother rejects her daughter's femininity as sin, Miss Collins/Miss Desjardin and Sue Snell attempt to befriend Carrie but ultimately fail, and Chris projects her feelings of powerlessness onto Carrie in the form of abuse. Whether they are well intentioned or malicious, it is predominantly women who fail to help Carrie White. Therefore, when describing the failures of a community, it should be noted that the community in question is a community of women.

However, unlike these women, Carrie is unique. Although we see her wanting to be feminine like the others, she is noticeably more self-reliant. More than telekinesis, in some respects, her power lies in the fact that she experiments and disagrees with both destinies laid out for her. In this respect, she is more like a "Subject" as she determines her own situation as opposed to having her desires mediated through others. However, as Beauvoir notes "no one teacher can shape a 'female human being' that would be an exact homologue to the 'male human being': if raised like a boy, the young girl feels she is an exception, and that subjects her to a new kind of specification."[24] This presents an important note on Beauvoir's conception of female subjectivity: it must exist in a community of others where it can thrive as an accepted possibility.

Which brings us back to the initial point about Carrie White's tragic death. Though she is strong enough to take care of herself, she cannot exist alone. Beauvoir acknowledges this not only when she talks about the Self and Other in terms of Man and Woman as in a dependent relationship where each implicates the other, but also when she discusses how women interact with each other. Even though she critiques female friendships as still being directed under the male gaze (even when there are no men present), there is a sense of urgency she has about developing solidarity among women. This urgency is also present in *Carrie* in the form of Carrie White's death. Though one could argue that the climax of the film was the infamous prom scene, the real denouement occurs when Carrie collapses inside the closet, clutching her mother's body due to her overall sense of helplessness, and the distrust between Carrie and her community.

To respond to King's claim that "any student" could relate to Carrie, I would still say yes, but with the particular experience of teenage girls in mind. As Beauvoir has repeated throughout *The Second Sex*, adolescence for the young girl is fraught with the idea of feminine destiny. In order to affirm one's own subjectivity, Beauvoir asserts that one must renounce femininity to a degree. However, the female subject is at risk of becoming an outcast or a monster within the community if she chooses to do so. *Carrie*, in this sense, is a novel that uses the supernatural as a response to the pressures of feminine destiny, and the horror of losing one's place in the world by choosing to live differently.

NOTES

1. Stephen King, *Danse Macabre* (New York: Berkley, 1981), 12.

2. Simone de Beauvoir, *The Second Sex*, trans. Constance Borde and Sheila Malovany-Chevallier (New York: Random House, 2011), 4.

3. Kellye Byal, *Monsters on the Couch: Art-Horror and Psychoanalysis* (MA thesis, Kingston University London, 2015), 39.

4. Beauvoir, *The Second Sex*, 324.

5. Sue Short, *Misfit Sisters: Screen Horror as Female Rites of Passage* (Hampshire, UK: Palgrave Macmillan, 2007), 74.

6. Stephen King, *Carrie* (New York: Doubleday, 1974), 12–13.

7. Beauvoir, *The Second Sex*, 324.

8. Beauvoir, *The Second Sex*, 326.

9. Short, *Misfit Sisters*, 76.

10. Beauvoir, *The Second Sex*, 295.

11. King, *Carrie*, 210.

12. Beauvoir, *The Second Sex*, 713.

13. Short, *Misfit Sisters*, 75.

14. Shelley Stamp Lindsey, "Horror, Femininity, and Carrie's Monstrous Puberty," *Journal of Film and Video*, 43 (1991): 33–44.

15. King, *Carrie*, 45.

16. Carol Clover, *Men, Women and Chainsaws: Gender in the Modern Horror Film* (Princeton, N.J.: Princeton University Press), 4.

17. Serafina Kent Bathrick, "Ragtime: The Horror of Growing Up Female," *Jump Cut: A Review of Contemporary Media* 14 (1977): 5.

18. Short, *Misfit Sisters*, 75.

19. Beauvoir, *The Second Sex*, 763.

20. Beauvoir, *The Second Sex*, 283.

21. Beauvoir, *The Second Sex*, 757.

22. Short, *Misfit Sisters*, 80.

23. Beauvoir, *The Second Sex*, 8.

24. Beauvoir, *The Second Sex*, 761.

3

"SOMETIMES DEAD IS BETTER"

King, Daedalus, Dragon-Tyrants, and Deathism

Katherine Allen

The Tommyknockers and *Pet Sematary* might seem like an incongruous pairing, superficially quite dissimilar in plot and style, and occupying very different positions in King's oeuvre. *Pet Sematary* is generally well regarded among King fans, cropping up in various "Top Ten"[1] lists and is squarely in the horror genre, complete with spectral signs and ghastly ghouls. It is (for King) unusually short at 368 pages, a spare, surgically plotted tragedy with a decidedly nasty sting in the tail. Meanwhile, *The Tommyknockers* is rambling and richly digressive, going off on a number of interesting tangents about, for example, Gard's adventures in alcoholism or Ruth McCausland's struggles with infertility, and weighs in at nearly a thousand pages. Despite its occasional forays into the horrific (as when Bobbi apparently dispatches her unpleasant sister), it is a science fiction novel first and foremost. And, unfortunately, it is a novel with a reputation; King himself disparaged it as "awful,"[2] and ranks it as one of his least favorite of his own books, and it is frequently (and unfairly) dismissed as a muddled and "mess[y]"[3] work, a casualty of King's own battle with alcohol and cocaine addiction.

Despite these surface differences, I will argue that *Pet Sematary* and *The Tommyknockers* are in fact thematic twins, dark and morally serious works driven by similar preoccupations and tensions. Both are pervaded by a thoroughgoing skepticism about human efforts to better ourselves, and render the universe tame and knowable, through science and technology. King suggests that our easy trust in science's ability to make our world a "clean and well-lighted place"[4] can edge into a dangerous complacency, rendering us especially vulnerable when, like Bobbi and Louis, we happen to stumble into one of the few remaining "pockets of perplexity."[5] Worse, while science can enable us to bend the natural world to our will, it cannot arm us with the ability to judge when it might be more prudent to refrain from doing so: as a species we are clever but not always wise, simultaneously "smart enough to land on the moon"[6] and foolish enough to "blow up the world."[7]

Both novels deal intelligently with important concerns about human nature and our relationship with technology, posing, if not always answering, questions like:

- Are there some things humans are simply not meant to know, some abilities we are never supposed to acquire?
- Would we be better off if we could scientifically "improve" ourselves?
- Is our finitude tragic or fundamental to human nature?
- Would interventions designed to increase our intelligence or extend our life span elevate or degrade us?
- Would something be lost, as well as gained, if death became optional?

I will argue that *Pet Sematary* and *The Tommyknockers* can fruitfully be read as bioconservative fables, thematic enactments of the kind of worst-case scenarios postulated by theorists such as Bill McKibben, Leon Kass, and Francis Fukuyama. King is famously impatient with what he calls "academic bullshit,"[8] the kind of arcane theorizing and inventive close readings that populate literary journals, so it may be best to clarify at this point that I do not mean to suggest that King consciously set out to advance any philosophical agenda or that he had transhumanist theories (or bioconservative ones) in mind while writing either work. However, I would argue that it is no accident that textually prominent themes within each work—the importance of making peace with one's mortality, the allure of forbidden knowledge, our dangerous faith in technology—echo bioconservative anxieties about biotechnologies. Misgivings about the socially transformative powers of new technologies are hardly exclusive to contemporary philosophers; while the labels "transhumanist" and "bioconservative" may be unfamiliar to King (and to many readers), they correspond to very familiar attitudes. Indeed, fiction has long acted as an arena for our warring impulses toward technology, showcasing its attractions and its dangers.

While transhumanism as a movement proper formed in the 1980s, proto-transhumanist themes and aspirations animate many earlier works of fiction and philosophy. Humanity's reach has always exceeded its grasp, so to speak: tales of heroes acquiring superhuman powers or becoming immune to aging/bodily injury and esoteric treatises on methods to extend life or obtain physical immortality abound cross-culturally. Yet, as the philosopher Nick Bostrom observes, the impulse to "transcend our natural confines" is often commingled with an equally strong sense of misgiving, a feeling that "some ambitions are off-limits and will backfire if pursued."[9]

The ancient Greek myth of Daedalus is a classically double-edged account of the career of one "overreacher" who commandeers hitherto superhuman powers, at one point manufacturing artificial wings so that he and his son, Icarus, may escape from imprisonment. The proto-transhumanist J. B. S. Haldane hailed Daedalus as a "modern man" stranded amid the ancients, "the first to demonstrate that the scientific worker is not concerned with gods,"[10] taboos, or sacred mysteries, but systematically applies his ingenuity to any problem that arises. Yet the story is far from a triumphal tale of human innovation: Daedalus succeeds in his endeavors but pays the ultimate human cost, when Icarus plummets to his death after the wax holding his wings together melts. As in later overreacher narratives such as *Frankenstein* and *The Fly*, the stratagems of science prove to be efficacious, yet mortally, and morally, dangerous. Like Daedalus or Victor Frankenstein, Bobbi and Louis are unhappy pioneers, modern people who find themselves at the center of a very old-fashioned tragedy. Both attempt to transcend humanity's biologically endowed limitations—with disastrous consequences for their nearest and dearest—and are ultimately consumed by the forces they presume to harness for their own ends.

The mad scientist whose hubris proves to be his (or her) undoing is a well-worn horror trope, and one with which most horror fans will be familiar. The moral of such tales seems clear: those who get above themselves, who attempt to play God by trying to subvert the laws of nature, will be punished for their ambitions. "Nature" is, if not always especially kind, implicitly presented as the only viable option, since those who attempt to dethrone her are shown to be arrogant, incompetent, and very possibly evil. Before detailing how *Pet Sematary* and *The Tommyknockers* conform to this narrative tradition, however, I will first discuss a philosophical movement that represents the exact inverse of this view, asking: What if the mad scientist were actually the hero of the story, her outsized ambition and disregard for convention inspiring her to change the world for the better? What if our instinctive attachment or deference to the idea of the "natural" clouds our thinking and prevents us from tackling avoidable suffering?

TRANSHUMANISM 101

Transhumanism is a broad (and broadly secular) church, encompassing a variety of views about, for example, when emerging biotechnologies will become viable, the extent to which most people are likely to opt for personal enhancement, or how a "posthuman" society would function. However, transhumanist theorists share an ideological commitment to the development of biomedical technologies designed to enhance our intellectual, emotional, and physical capabilities and extend our life spans, advocate for "morphological" freedom—arguing that each individual has a right to alter or augment herself as she sees fit—and reject the notion that we should "meekly [accept] 'natural' limits"[11] simply because they represent the status quo.

Rather, the majority of transhumanists hold that the human condition is more or less circumstantial, a matter of evolutionary happenstance. We are as we are not because of any overarching scheme dreamed up by an all-knowing deity but due to myriad incremental changes in response to environmental pressures. We are biological accidents rather than divinely crafted likenesses: we are therefore, if not perfectible, at least *improvable*. As the transhumanist theorist Nick Bostrom observes, "Nature's gifts are sometimes poisoned and should not always be accepted."[12] Arsenic, botulism toxin, and cyanide are all eminently "natural" yet few of us would elect to ingest them given a choice in the matter; similarly, aging, susceptibility to physical and mental illness, and a certain propensity for superstition, bigotry, and cruelty may well be naturally occurring features of human life, but it does not follow that they are in any way beneficial. Human nature is, in short, "a work-in-progress, a half-baked beginning that we can learn to remould in desirable ways."[13]

We are, after all, already accustomed to people modifying their bodies and bodily processes, in sometimes drastic ways, in order to improve their physical/psychological functioning and appearance. Deaf and hard-of-hearing people can choose to have cochlear implants fitted, people with poor vision can opt for laser eye surgery, and transplants are regularly used to replace failing organs. Depression, ADHD, and bipolar disorder are commonly treated with psychoactive drugs such as SSRIs, stimulants, and lithium, and many women use the contraceptive pill to control their fertility and manage conditions like polycystic ovary syndrome or dysmenorrhea. More frivolously, those worried about excess hair or adipose tissue, thin lips, or wrinkles can get electrolysis, liposuction, collagen injections, and face-lifts if they so desire. Some of these interventions remain controversial but, broadly speaking, there is widespread acceptance of the idea that at least some planned disruptions of, or alterations to, natural bodily processes and structures are legitimate, that, in certain circumstances, Mother Nature does not know best.[14]

Transhumanists simply argue for a more extensive application of this basic principle; while medical interventions currently act to move or restore people to a typical level of human functioning, future biotechnologies can optimize and reconfigure, allowing their beneficiaries to function at a preternatural, or better-than-human, level. By making careful, informed use of currently available technologies such as embryo screening and selection and psychopharmacology, and developing ones such as germ-line genetic engineering, cryonic suspension, and nanotechnology, we can defeat (or at least defer) death and direct our own evolution, becoming self-made men and women.

NEW IMPROVED PEOPLE?
KING'S POSTHUMAN NIGHTMARES

Transhumanists view the current limitations on our life span, intellect, and capabilities as impediments to human flourishing, a burden from which future technologies will one day liberate us. Their underlying thesis—that life is good and infirmity and death are bad, and to be averted wherever possible—seems unobjectionable. Few of us would turn up our noses at the guarantee of living a longer and healthier life, or of enjoying perpetual youth and good health tempered by the wisdom of experience. However, bioconservatives suggest that we should exercise caution when contemplating removing these constraints. When knocking down a wall, one should first check that it is not load bearing; our limitations may frustrate us, may often cause us great suffering, but they are also central to our identity. By pulling at certain threads— eagerly discarding traits we have identified as bad, and augmenting those we view as desirable—we are in danger of unraveling or "defac[ing]"[15] our nature as a whole. Francis Fukuyama characterizes transhumanism as the world's most "dangerous idea" in part because of this possibility, postulating that we may find out, too late, that "our good characteristics are intimately connected to our bad ones."[16] Similarly, Bill McKibben warns that, while "it's possible [humans] will die" as a result of experimenting with biotechnologies, an even "greater danger" is that they will work as planned and we will become "something else entirely."[17]

If transhumanists envision using new technologies to shed our flaws and emerge as better, fuller versions of ourselves, bioconservatives such as McKibben and Leon Kass argue that any technologically assisted "becoming" would, like Bobbi's, result in a creeping loss of humanity. Setting aside the practical considerations that spur some of transhumanism's opponents,[18] McKibben suggests that, even if biotechnologies go on to be used safely and equitably, and all goes entirely according to plan, we will be the worse for it.

Paradoxically, the "freedom and spontaneity"[19] that we now take for granted—the sense that our passions, our talents, are peculiarly our own, a happy combination of luck and inclination and hard work, that we choose our own path in life—arises from "honoring limits"[20] and allowing the dice to fall where they may. If we somehow managed to genetically engineer our offspring to become, for example, fanatically driven chess champions, their proficiency would be "robot[ic]" and "meaningless,"[21] more akin to Deep Blue's ruthless, programmed efficiency than Garry Kasparov's brilliance. Banishing "nature's unpredictabilities"[22] by writing our hopes and dreams for our children on their DNA would reduce them to dutiful "automat[a]."[23] Like the soma-pacified citizens in Aldous Huxley's *Brave New World*, engineered humans would be akin to "happy slaves"[24] who "do not know they are dehumanised" and "would not care" if they did.[25]

The fear of losing one's identity, one's humanity, is central to the horror of *The Tommyknockers* and *Pet Sematary*. Both novels caution against the lure of getting something for nothing, suggesting instead that abilities that seem miraculous, powers, like raising the beloved dead, that seem "too good to be true" are likely to hide a hefty price tag. After inducting Louis in the secrets of the Pet Sematary, Jud cryptically remarks that "a man grows what he can . . . and he tends it."[26] Once Church returns, with a newfound enthusiasm for murdering small animals, Louis realizes that the "ripped mice" and eviscerated birds the cat leaves in his wake are his harvest, the fruits of Church's unholy resurrection: "he had . . . bought them"[27] and must deal with them alone.

Following Church's return from the grave, he is somehow *different*, inspiring revulsion and even loathing in all those he encounters: Louis breaks out into "gooseflesh"[28] at the cat's touch, and has to restrain himself from kicking it. Church-the-revenant is, more or less, a "poor imitation" of a cat, one that people instinctively *"feel,"* rather than see.[29] While the undead Church in some respects resembles the shambling, vacuous zombies of horror movie fame—slow, lurching, and graceless, "muddled"[30] and smelling of "sour earth"[31]—he also displays alarming flashes of malevolent intelligence, clearly evil insofar as a house cat, dangerous mainly to small animals, can be. After returning from vacation, even Ellie notices that something is different, observing that "Church was better before."[32] Like every creature that returns from the Pet Sematary, Church comes back "fundamentally different and fundamentally *wrong*."[33]

Similarly, the "New Improved Bobbi"[34] displays astonishing abilities but has lost some essentially *human* quality—on their reunion, Gard immediately perceives that there is something evasive, something "off-note and off-key"[35] about her, like a bad actress stumbling through her best Bobbi impression. As she progresses in her becoming, Bobbi grows increasingly indifferent to everything she valued during her human life, first using her (previously beloved) beagle Peter as a living battery and eventually attempting to murder Gard. By the end, she is barely a "strange parody"[36] of the old, unimproved Bobbi; sans teeth, sans hair, and almost entirely without conscience.

Even the gifts the Tommyknockers' ship bestows have an alarmingly compulsive effect, working *through* their recipients and driving them to invent ceaselessly and often indiscriminately, their ingenuity a chronic way of being rather than a conscious choice. On his arrival in Haven, Gard finds Bobbi working herself quite literally to death, a "shambling, dirty, stumbling skeleton" reminiscent of a drunk "at the end of a jag."[37] Bobbi has used her newfound knack for "home improvement"[38] in some genuinely useful ways, fixing the dangerous stairs in her basement and changing its lightbulbs, but her urge to invent also spills over into superfluous and uncharacteristic side projects such as a "doorbell with a built-in microchip."[39] Echoing McKibben's vision of genetically engineered athletes or musicians or scientists too well programmed ever to question their vocation, the Haven Tommyknockers are compulsive, and in some ways mindless inventors, full of know-how but seldom asking why. They are "builders, not understanders,"[40] "idiot savant[s]"[41] who excel at applied science while lacking any real comprehension of the underlying principles.

The Tommyknockers and *Pet Sematary* function as cautionary tales, chilling enactments of bioconservative concerns about the technological refashioning of human nature. Each novel acts as a kind of thought experiment, invoking long-standing human fantasies of mastery over nature—What if we could bring dead loved ones back to life? What if we could acquire supernatural powers that would enable us to shape the world to our liking?—and exploring some of the (more nightmarish) consequences that might ensue if they actually came to pass. As with any fiction, and especially any horror fiction, this emphasis on conflict and negative outcomes is probably at least partially pragmatic or story driven: a tale recounting how "I Raised My Son from the Dead and It All Went Splendidly" is unlikely to raise goose bumps or bring many readers to the edge of their seats. However, the fact that certain subjects reliably crop up in horror fictions, reliably *work* as horror tropes, does suggest that we are already attuned to their horrifying possibilities. In other words, mad scientists and vengeful zombies strike us as frightening because they resonate with a preexisting cultural ambivalence about efforts to transform our world, and ourselves, using technology.

DEATHISM; OR, THE ART OF MAKING A VIRTUE OF A NECESSITY

Death is the undisputable cause of an "unfathomable amount of human suffering."[42] Death can be relatively kind, offering solace to those in the final throes of terminal illness or debilitated by extreme old age. All too often, however, death arrives prematurely, pointlessly, and painfully— "a sudden dive-bombing from a clear blue sky"[43]—racking those left behind and leaving a decedent-shaped hole in the world. Conventional thought recognizes deaths of the latter sort as undesirable, but views a dignified "natural" death in old age as a more or less fitting end to life— perhaps not an especially pleasant or personally appealing prospect, but far from a tragic one. That is to say, many people, including many philosophers, think that "death is not necessarily an evil,"[44] although individual deaths may well be.

Transhumanists such as Nick Bostrom differ, however, arguing that death's very inescapability, its status as an implacable "fact of life," has dulled our sense of its enormity. Bostrom devised a fable to press this point, casting death not as the elephant, but the dragon, in the room, an obstacle we are so used to negotiating that we have ceased even to recognize it as a problem.

Bostrom's "Fable of the Dragon-Tyrant" depicts a land terrorized by an insatiable dragon who exacts a daily, "blood-curdling tribute":[45] every evening, ten thousand people must be delivered to the foot of the dragon's mountain lair to be devoured at its leisure. The dragon is impervious to even the most advanced weaponry, apparently "invincible to any human assault,"[46] and most denizens of the land resign themselves to remaining under its bloody reign forever. Prominent thinkers issue impressive-sounding apologetics for the dragon's diet, arguing that its dietary demands help to control overpopulation or appealing to its place in the "natural order."[47] Others attempt to mitigate the horror by offering consoling visions of a dragon-free afterlife. This undesirable state of affairs continues for centuries, while the dragon flourishes and its appetite grows.

The few intransigent "anti-dragonists" who continue to propose various methods of exterminating the beast are widely regarded as cranks; after all, everyone knows that the dragon is "a fact of life":[48] to rage against its monstrous appetites is akin to railing against the tides. The

eminent "chief moral advisor" even suggests that, in the unlikely event
that defeating the dragon does prove possible, it would serve to debase
rather than to preserve humanity, whose "species-specified nature is
truly and nobly fulfilled only by getting eaten."[49]

In Bostrom's fable, of course, the dragon is eventually vanquished
and common sense prevails: while the moral advisor's lofty-yet-
insubstantial pronouncements initially impress the people of the land,
his "rhetorical balloon"[50] is punctured, in true fairy-tale fashion, by a
child who, unafraid of looking stupid, protests that "the dragon is
bad!"[51] Analogically, Bostrom suggests, death as we currently know it is
a thoroughly "bad" thing, undignified by any higher meaning or purpose, and the "deathist" bioethicists and theorists who counsel acceptance of our mortality deal, like the pompous moral advisor, in elegantly
phrased nonsense.

BETTER THE DRAGON YOU KNOW ...

Like the dragon defenders in Bostrom's fable, bioconservatives such as
Bill McKibben and Leon Kass argue that, despite appearances, death is
a feature, rather than a bug, of human existence. Throughout our history as a species, they note, we have known ourselves as "'mortals,' literally defined by the fact that we perish,"[52] that we are embodied, vulnerable, and finite. While we may chafe at the indignities and infirmities
that attend our creaturely existence, were such limitations to be removed, we might find the value drained out of things, that "meaning
and pain, meaning and transience, are inextricably intertwined."[53] Limits define as well as restrain, giving shape and context to our lives and
stopping us from drifting away into "the vacuum of meaninglessness."[54]
Transhumanism's critics argue that our mortality, our frailty, may well
be "the ground of our taking life seriously and living it passionately":[55]
were we untroubled by any consciousness of a final "deadline," life
would lose its sense of urgency and intensity, lacking the "necessary
spur to the pursuit of something worthwhile."[56] Uniquely human endeavors such as art, philosophy, and even science itself are, they argue,
the legacy of our awareness of our own mortality, whether due to a
"search for the imperishable and unchanging"[57] or a means of memori-

alizing life's "evanescent glories,"[58] and would wither and die in the absence of this impetus.

Similarly, those who seek to avert aging and tame death might irrevocably alter the arc and rhythms of human life, the relationship between generations. Kass argues that the desire to vanquish death is a fundamentally "childish" one, intrinsically "hostile" to future generations.[59] On a purely logistical level, radical life extension promises to at least complicate kin relations: as overpopulation becomes an even more urgent issue, perpetually youthful parents might find themselves clashing with their offspring in the workforce or even the romantic marketplace, their children no longer successors but competitors for ever-dwindling resources.

Our understanding that our offspring will grow up to replace us, flourishing and prospering as we decline and eventually die—that we are, in effect, raising our replacements—has always been at the heart of the parent-child relationship. Children are a kind of living reminder of our mortality, evidence that we no longer belong to the "frontier generation."[60] Once everyone has the capacity to live a posthuman life span, however, our children may become "one more figure in the sea of figures, owing [us] little and owed nothing in return."[61] Such theorists argue, in short, that delayed/elective mortality would not be "just *more* [but] *different*,"[62] radically transforming the shape and meaning of human life, in potentially undesirable ways.

According to these theorists, the promise of "more" is a fantasy and a trap. While few of us would balk at the prospect of living longer, healthier lives, they suggest that if we finally managed to slay the dragon Death, it would not be humanity, as we currently know ourselves, who benefited. The beings who flourished following this victory might resemble humans but would be fundamentally alien, shaped by very different experiences and values.

"SOMETIMES DEAD IS BETTER":[63]
PET SEMATARY AS DEATHIST FABLE

While the horror genre as a whole is unavoidably preoccupied with death, and the "bad death" in particular, *Pet Sematary* is unusual in its unflinching focus on the brute *physical* fact of death and the bodily

disintegration that awaits us all; beneath the novel's supernatural trap-
pings, the Micmac burial ground and malevolent Wendigo, death itself,
mundane and terrible, is the true antagonist.

King refuses to sentimentalize death or to permit readers to avert
their gaze from the genuine horrors associated with our mortality.
Gage's exhumation, rather than the supernatural terrors that follow, is
at the dark heart of the novel, forming the apotheosis of "horror and
pity and sorrow."[64] King describes the condition of Gage's remains in
implacable, unsparing detail, evoking a grotesque mixture of artifice
and decay. Gage's carefully reconstructed, cotton-stuffed face resembles a cross between a "badly made doll" and a sunken-cheeked "old
man," his head held precariously on by a "grinning circlet of stitches."[65]
His body, malodorous and "miserably smashed,"[66] is stuffed into a suit
and new shoes, and there is moss growing on his face. Significantly,
there is nothing obviously spooky or otherworldly about the *manner* of
Gage's demise—while the truck driver who hit him later reports that,
for some unknowable reason, he "just felt like putting the pedal to the
metal"[67] along the fateful stretch of road, Gage's death is due to the
thoroughly natural and utterly predictable physical laws of mass and
acceleration, of hard steel barreling into soft flesh.

Similarly, King provides readers with a wealth of seemingly prosaic
and inconsequential details about the aftermath of Gage's death—the
layout of the funeral home, the selection of Gage's coffin, the book for
attendees to sign in the viewing room—which he might have chosen to
brush past in favor of more obviously plot-driving scenes. I would argue
that, for King's purposes, every one of these mundane details matters,
because the deepest horror lies in Gage's death rather than his later
resurrection. By so thoroughly grounding Louis and his family in the
real world, furnishing their fictional grief with the banal and bureau-
cratic minutiae that must be attended to after any bereavement, King
insistently reminds readers that death—even sudden, violent, and
heartbreakingly premature death—is not just the stuff of stories.

Yet throughout the novel, an inability to reconcile or come to terms
with death is linked to immaturity at best, and, in the story's final act, to
madness and calamity. Louis reflects that those who cannot arrive at a
"nodding acquaintance"[68] with death are doomed to end up "in a small
room writing letters home with Crayolas,"[69] a maxim that proves grimly
apt in his case. After Gage's accident, Louis realizes that, for all his

trying to explain and justify the "facts of death" to Ellie, he too finds these facts "ultimately unacceptable"[70] when encountered in the personal, rather than the abstract. Louis's refusal to accept Gage's demise compounds the original tragedy, heaping loss upon loss as the Pet Sematary takes Jud, Rachel, and, in the end, Louis's sanity.

Even routine biomedical interventions designed to postpone the inevitable prove to be fallible and corrosive to the subject's dignity. It is Jud, the architect of Church's later revival, who first urges Louis to have his pet neutered, since "a fixed cat don't tend to wander as much."[71] Louis initially hesitates because of his "vague but strong" intuition that the procedure would destroy something of value in Church, extinguishing the "go-to-hell look in the cat's green eyes."[72] Ellie's terror at the prospect of Church dying finally prompts Louis to schedule the operation, despite his feeling that it will somehow "lessen the cat, turn[ing] him into a fat old tom before his time."[73] Louis's misgivings are textually vindicated—the neutered Church is "fat and slow" and leads a sorry, circumscribed life, waddling with "placid stupidity" between his food dish and the couch, and nonetheless meets with a violent and premature end.[74] The procedure ultimately fails in its objective as, owing either to some feline whim or the malign influence of the Pet Sematary, Church manages to wander into the road and get struck by a car. Louis's attempt to extend the cat's life through biomedical means serves only to diminish him and thwart his "real nature,"[75] depriving him of the feral pleasures that a tomcat properly enjoys. The narrative implication is clear—an artificially prolonged life may be a tame and toothless one, lacking in its former dignity and meaning. Worse, our efforts to outmaneuver fate may fail or backfire spectacularly, subverted either by mischance or forces beyond our comprehension.

As discussed previously, Church's second transformation is less benign, effected by the dark magic of the Micmac burial ground. The transformation is even more evident in Gage's case. While deliberating about what to do, Louis reflects that if Gage came back altered in the same intangible way "it would be an obscenity."[76] Like the resurrected Timmy Baterman, the returned "Gage" *is* obscene, both less and more than human. While the creature that stalks Jud and Rachel uses Gage's mangled body to do so, the original occupant is obviously no longer home: the body's new owner speaks in full, and somewhat scatological, sentences, and uses its uncanny knowledge to manipulate those it encounters, a "demented parody of [Gage's] former self"[77] filled with "stupid hate."[78] Worse, the awakened Gage demonstrates "unspeakable appetites,"[79] partially cannibalizing Rachel's corpse. Defying nature by bringing the dead back to life leads to the vicious perversion of familial norms, a shambling travesty of a child feeding not on his mother's milk but her flesh and blood.

This nightmarish image exceeds even the most fevered bioconservative imaginings of a posthuman future, yet the preoccupations that drive the novel are not so far removed from those of theorists such as Kass and McKibben. Within the narrative world of *Pet Sematary*, attempts to outwit one's biological destiny—whether through mundane methods, such as Church's sterilization, or magical ones—are worse than futile; at best one will live on, diminished, like a complacent, waddling tomcat. At worst, someone, or some*thing*, else might take up residence in one's body and return to wreak havoc among the living. When death is denied and kept a secret, reviled and hidden from view, like Zelda dying miserably in a back bedroom, it becomes a "monster"[80] bent on "supernatural vengeance."[81] Or, in real-world terms, we make a monster of death when we lose our "nodding acquaintance" with it, and we risk making monsters of ourselves by trying to deny it at any cost.

"SOME THINGS IT DON'T PAY TO BE CURIOUS ABOUT":[82] FORBIDDEN KNOWLEDGE AND DANGEROUS IDEAS

Most transhumanists would agree that, in principle at least, "no mysteries are sacrosanct [and] no limits unquestionable."[83] While, in individual cases, knowledge may be obtained or used in imprudent and unethical ways, there is nothing intrinsically wrong with trying to understand, control, and alter our biological and psychological processes, even in ways that seem intuitively "unnatural."

In contrast, bioconservative theorists such as Leon Kass, Francis Fukuyama, and Bill McKibben suggest that there are areas of life that should not be subjected to science's impersonal gaze. They argue that the transhumanist precept that any area of human experience is up for grabs, scientifically speaking, amenable to intellectual scrutiny and biotechnological tinkering, is ultimately a dangerous and dehumanizing one. Some knowledge, some capabilities, *should* remain off limits, and attempting to venture beyond these frontiers is both ethically suspect and deeply unwise.

Even engaging in reasoned argumentation regarding the possible pros or cons of controversial biotechnologies such as human cloning is, in a sense, beside the point: coolly analytical discourse of the sort in which philosophers typically engage excludes the most damning evidence against cloning—many people's instinctive revulsion at the prospect. Kass argues that this widespread "yuck" reaction "is the emotional expression of deep wisdom," a visceral internal alarm system "warning us not to transgress what is unspeakably profound." By viewing the "wondrous mysteries" of human procreation through "the lens of our reductive science," proponents of cloning and similar technologies display a dangerous and "Frankensteinian hubris."[84]

King too suggests that there are lines of inquiry that humans should not pursue—areas of forbidden knowledge that, once trespassed, can consume our lives or sanity—and gives them physical embodiment in the form of forbidden *places*. Louis and Bobbi literally walk into trouble, unwittingly coming under the influence of immense and malevolent superhuman forces when they stray too far from the "*safe* path."[85] At the beginning of *Pet Sematary*, Jud cautions Louis and his family against wandering freely through the woods, lest they stray too near the land "the [Micmac] Indians want back":[86] "you keep on the path and all's well."[87] Similarly, it is Bobbi's decision to venture off the beaten track in pursuit of firewood that leads her to the Tommyknockers' ship—"for the choice of a path, the ship was found."[88] Those wayward souls who leave the confines of the familiar, who breach boundaries, like the treacherous "deadfall,"[89] which "are not meant to be broken," risk "the destruction of all [they] love."[90]

Pet Sematary and *The Tommyknockers* act as warnings to the curious, the fates of their unfortunate protagonists serving as object lessons in what Kass terms the "wisdom of repugnance."[91] Both Bobbi and Louis fail to heed their instinctive (and prescient) sense of unease, their "rational minds reject[ing]"[92] the supernatural dangers to which their guts alert them. Instead, each takes a determinedly "scientific" stance, ignoring, or rationalizing away, the ill omens and darkly prophetic dreams that might otherwise repel them.

From the moment Bobbi discovers the Tommyknockers' ship, she shares her dog Peter's sense that there is something very *"wrong"*[93] with it. The night of her discovery, she dreams of "poisonous green light . . . and her teeth all falling painlessly out of her gums,"[94] but daylight dispels the nightmare, and its warning.

Like his literary antecedents, Louis is a man of science, accustomed to dealing in problems rather than mysteries. A doctor by profession, he approaches the world as a hardheaded empiricist, having "pronounced two dozen people dead [and] never once felt the passage of a soul."[95] King characterizes him as a "man with no deep religious training, no bent towards . . . the occult."[96] He is, therefore, ill equipped to mark the misty presentiments and portents that might forewarn a more superstitious man: when, while holding Gage, he is gripped by a sudden "premonition of horror and darkness," he dismisses it as "one of those psychological cold-pockets people sometimes passed through," physiological rather than psychical in origin—"more gravy than grave."[97]

Even as Louis succumbs to the sick "glamor"[98] of the Pet Sematary and begins contemplating Gage's resurrection, he proceeds according to a parody of scientific ratiocination and hypothesis forming, "trying to place all the known components in an order as rational and logical as [the place's] dark magic would allow."[99] Louis willfully ignores his intuitive knowledge that returnees from the Pet Sematary come back wrong, his experience of people *"feel[ing]"* (rather than seeing) through the new Church's "poor imitation" of a cat.[100] He even rationalizes away his gut-level revulsion at the idea of a similarly changed Gage—the "obscenity"[101] of even contemplating such a transformation—conceiving of it as an experiment of sorts, a diagnostic exercise. If, after an adequate "examination period,"[102] Louis determines that Gage has come back irrevocably damaged or altered—a "thing of evil"[103] like Timmy Baterman—he will terminate the "failed experiment"[104] with suitably scientific apparatus, euthanizing his subject if necessary. King's depiction of Louis's poignant, and ultimately doomed, efforts to cling to "the balance-beam of rationality"[105] in a situation that defies reason—attempting to accommodate and interpret the occult mysteries of the Pet Sematary within a humanly rational framework—evokes Kass's critique of contemporary bioethics.

Like many of King's works, both novels touch upon themes of addiction and compulsion, but in each narrative the most potent—and dangerous—intoxicant is knowledge, rather than any cruder substance. The Micmac burial ground and the alien ship each exude a seductive glamor, calling to those, like Louis and Bobbi, who may be susceptible to their enticements. Contact with either place confers a kind of high: when first venturing into the "real" Pet Sematary to bury Church, Louis is buoyed by a strange (and contextually jarring) feeling of "contentment," the "magnetic" promise of some "secret," just out of sight, drawing him onward.[106] Before Gard's arrival, Bobbi tries to abort her excavation of the ship, but finds herself gripped by a "physical craving" to uncover more—akin to an addict's itch for "coke or heroin or cigarettes or coffee."[107]

As the addiction motif suggests, both novels are imbued with a profound skepticism about humanity's ability to "put away *any* knowledge once they've seen the edge of it,"[108] however incendiary. In an unsettling coda, while the Tommyknockers are vanquished, the U.S. Army seizes control of the dangerous new technologies they created and, it is implied, will go on to weaponize them. Similarly, even after Louis's family is (mostly) dead and gone, the narrator predicts that their house will be go on to be claimed by a new family, equally vulnerable to the fatal lure of the Pet Sematary—"bright young marrieds [who] will congratulate themselves on their lack of superstition" and, perhaps, "have a dog."[109] Once the atom bomb—or designer baby—has been perfected, there is no putting the genie back in the bottle.

In interviews, King has expressed the concern that "our technological expertise has far outraced our ability to manage our own emotions."[110] In this respect at least, one can read the Tommyknockers as souped-up or augmented humans, enhanced yet deeply fallible in recognizably human—if inhumane—ways. Indeed, King implicitly encourages us to do so, characterizing the "original" Tommyknockers as "people smart enough to capture the stars [who] got mad and tore each other to shreds with the claws on their feet"[111] and "cavemen from space."[112]

While the Haven Tommyknockers can appear chillingly alien—utterly devoid of any concern or fellow feeling for those who have not become—they are prey to the same petty irritations and irrationalities as their human neighbors, capable of starting "terrible, world-ripping conflict[s]" over "whose turn it had been to pick up the coffee-break check."[113] Despite their enhanced abilities, their superlative knack for invention, the Tommyknockers are no more "evolved," in a colloquial sense, than humans; their ready access to advanced technology merely serves to ensure that their temper tantrums have galactic repercussions. Armed with a little knowledge, they know just enough to be dangerous, toying with immense and hazardous natural forces with the breezy unconcern of "a baby with a loaded pistol."[114]

The Tommyknockers is packed with references to real-life scientific blunders and ethical lapses, a bread-crumb trail of human incompetence and depravity designed to lead the attentive reader to one conclusion: in light of such staggering historical missteps, how can we trust that, this time, the "Dallas police"[115] (Bobbi's mental shorthand for all dubiously competent and morally dubious authorities) really know what they're doing, really have our best interests at heart? Our faith in achieving better living through science—in our ability to use technology to become better, even "posthuman," people—is founded in the (historically and psychologically naïve) belief that the "new boss" is meaningfully different from the "old boss."[116]

Some of these allusions are glancing and open to interpretation—King may or may not have intended to reference the beagles famously used in laboratory tests in the mid-1970s when he specified Peter's breed[117]—while others are more explicit and sustained. Like *Pet Sematary*, *The Tommyknockers* is, despite its fantastical subject matter, firmly situated in the real world. King introduces Bobbi as a woman keenly aware that she is living through the last dregs of a century marked by astounding technological innovations and disasters, in a "world hurtl[ing] down Microchip Alley towards the unknown wonders and horrors of the twenty-first century."[118] Like Gard, she begins the novel preoccupied by the possibility of an imminent, and technologically assisted, apocalypse, making future plans with the mental proviso "if someone didn't blow up the world in the meantime."[119]

The threat posed by nuclear power looms large throughout the novel, and King draws insistent parallels between the becoming and the effects of acute radiation exposure. Those living in Haven experience the effects of fallout from the ship, whose dispersal is unpredictable and affected by atmospheric conditions. By the end of their transition, Gard reflects that the Haven Tommyknockers resemble nothing so much as "someone who got caught in a great big messy atomic meltdown,"[120] their teeth and hair the first sacrifices to the becoming. The theme is given its fullest articulation during the second section of the novel, which follows Gard's tragicomic progress through a poetry reading, career-ending party, and binge-to-end-all-binges. At the postreading party, Gard is unable to resist "holding forth," [121] and gives an impassioned lecture about his abiding obsession: the perils of nuclear power. Gard informs startled partygoers (and readers) of a number of alarming facts, detailing the "death march" from Marie Curie's discovery of radium to the modern proliferation of nuclear power plants, and raging at the hubris of those who *"assumed . . .* and played with the lives of living human beings." [122]

"THE DEVIL YOU KNOW IS ALWAYS BETTER THAN THE DEVIL YOU DON'T" [123]

Although the transhumanist project promises total "liberation"—from the depredations of time and nature, from the "limitations of our DNA" [124] —bioconservatives argue that we are, in many ways, "the sum of our limits." [125] In other words, the distinctively human forms of flourishing we now enjoy emerge from—and are contingent upon—our frailties. A "default assumption that more is better" [126] animates our desire to remove all checks on human life and power, to attain more perfect mastery over nature. Yet bioconservatives warn that efforts to "save mankind from itself" may work only at the cost of our "humanness," [127] a kind of soft annihilation. We might gain certain powers only by first surrendering our souls, becoming as alien, as removed from our old ways of life, as the Tommyknockers.

In *The Tommyknockers* and *Pet Sematary*, King makes a case for embracing the devil we know and learning to live with our limitations. Bobbi and Louis are, to begin with at least, thoroughly likable protagonists and King is not wholly unsympathetic to their Promethean aspirations. Yet the narrative arc of each novel is unmistakably that of the cautionary tale: like the man who unwisely wishes on a monkey's paw or the young doctor who decides to build a man from spare parts, Louis and Bobbi defy the natural order and pay a heavy price.

Both begin with humanitarian ends in mind: Bobbi wants an antidote to business as usual, the corruption and thoughtless greed of the Old Bosses. As a doctor, Louis is professionally bound to do battle with death and debility but remains firmly within the boundaries of medical orthodoxy until death infiltrates his family, first through Church and then his son, Gage. Neither bears much resemblance to the mad scientist of horror movie fame, driven by an arrogant lust for power. But just as the proverbial road to hell is paved with good intentions, a devil's bargain can come disguised as a godsend. Like the "techno-utopians"[128] bioconservatives criticize, Bobbi and Louis attempt to refashion the world—and human nature—to their liking, making the world a kinder, fairer place. And, as bioconservatives predict happening if the transhumanist project ever comes to fruition, they succeed only in eroding human *meaning*, populating their corners of the world with New Improved People who behave and feel and think nothing like people at all, "abomination[s]"[129] with nothing in common with their former selves.

NOTES

1. Jake Kerridge, "Top Ten Stephen King Books," *Telegraph*, September 19, 2013, accessed September 11, 2015, http://www.telegraph.co.uk/culture/books/booknews/10321006/Top-ten-Stephen-King-books.html.

2. Andy Greene, "Stephen King: The *Rolling Stone* Interview," *Rolling Stone*, October 31, 2014, accessed September 11, 2015, http://www.rollingstone.com/culture/features/stephen-king-the-rolling-stone-interview-20141031?page=5.

3. James Smythe, "Rereading Stephen King, Chapter 25: *The Tommyknockers*," *Guardian*, August 28, 2013, accessed September 11, 2015, http://www.theguardian.com/books/booksblog/2013/aug/28/the-tommyknockers-stephen-king-rereading.

4. Stephen King, *Pet Sematary* (London: Hodder and Stoughton, 1983), 177.

5. King, *Pet Sematary*, 177.

6. Stephen King, *The Tommyknockers* (London: Hodder and Stoughton, 1988), 78.

7. King, *The Tommyknockers*, 5.

8. Greene, "Stephen King."

9. Nick Bostrom, "A History of Transhumanist Thought," *Journal of Evolution & Technology* 14, no. 1 (April 2005): 2.

10. J. B. S. Haldane, "Daedalus; or, Science and the Future" (paper presented to the Heretics, Cambridge, February 1923): 12.

11. Max More, "The Extropian Principles 2.5," July 1993, accessed September 11, 2015, http://www.aleph.se/Trans/Cultural/Philosophy/princip.html.

12. Nick Bostrom, "In Defense of Posthuman Dignity," *Bioethics* 19, no. 3 (2005): 204.

13. Nick Bostrom, "Human Genetic Enhancements: A Transhumanist Perspective," *Journal of Value Inquiry* 37, no. 4 (2003): 493–506, accessed September 13, 2015, http://www.nickbostrom.com/ethics/genetic.html.

14. Significantly, there is also (albeit more qualified) acceptance of parents making such choices on behalf of their children and future children. Parents can opt for preimplantation genetic screening in order to lessen the risk of their offspring being born with life-limiting conditions such as cystic fibrosis and muscular dystrophy. Once children are born, parents remain legally empowered to make life-altering, and often irreversible, decisions regarding their medical care, for example, determining that an infant born with a cleft lip should receive reconstructive surgery.

15. Francis Fukuyama, "Transhumanism," *Foreign Policy*, no. 144 (September–October 2004): 43.

16. Fukuyama, "Transhumanism," 43.

17. Bill McKibben, *Enough: Genetic Engineering and the End of Human Nature* (London: Bloomsbury, 2003), 7.

18. For example, theorists such as Francis Fukuyama and Lee Silver have voiced the concern that wide-scale use of new (and therefore expensive) biotechnologies by rich "early adopters" might reduce social mobility and entrench existing inequalities, creating a kind of genetic caste system.

19. Leon R. Kass, "Triumph or Tragedy? The Moral Meaning of Genetic Technology," *American Journal of Jurisprudence* 45, no. 1 (2000): 5.

20. McKibben, *Enough*, 218.

21. McKibben, *Enough*, 49.

22. Kass, "Triumph or Tragedy?," 16.

23. McKibben, *Enough*, 52.

24. Kass, "The New Biology: What Price Relieving Man's Estate?" *Science* 174, no. 4011 (1971): 785.

25. Kass, "New Biology," 785.

26. King, *Pet Sematary*, 123.

27. King, *Pet Sematary*, 215.

28. King, *Pet Sematary*, 133.

29. King, *Pet Sematary*, 225.

30. King, *Pet Sematary*, 256.

31. King, *Pet Sematary*, 133.

32. King, *Pet Sematary*, 157.

33. King, *Pet Sematary*, 141.

34. King, *The Tommyknockers*, 256.

35. King, *The Tommyknockers*, 237.

36. King, *The Tommyknockers*, 735.

37. King, *The Tommyknockers*, 174–75.

38. King, *The Tommyknockers*, 191.

39. King, *The Tommyknockers*, 193.

40. King, *The Tommyknockers*, 845.

41. King, *The Tommyknockers*, 256.

42. Nick Bostrom, "The Fable of the Dragon-Tyrant," *Journal of Medical Ethics* 31, no. 5 (2005): 277.

43. King, *Pet Sematary*, 321.

44. Bernard Williams, "The Makropulos Case: Reflections on the Tedium of Immortality," in *Problems of the Self: Philosophical Papers 1956–1972* (Cambridge: Cambridge University Press, 1973), 83.

45. Bostrom, "Dragon-Tyrant," 273.

46. Bostrom, "Dragon-Tyrant," 273.

47. Bostrom, "Dragon-Tyrant," 273.

48. Bostrom, "Dragon-Tyrant," 274.

49. Bostrom, "Dragon-Tyrant," 275.

50. Bostrom, "Dragon-Tyrant," 275.

51. Bostrom, "Dragon-Tyrant," 275.

52. McKibben, *Enough*, 162.

53. McKibben, *Enough*, 164.

54. McKibben, *Enough*, 48.

55. McKibben, *Enough*, 183.

56. McKibben, *Enough*, 183.

57. Leon R. Kass, "Problems in the Meaning of Death," *Science* 170, no. 3963 (December 1970): 1235.

58. McKibben, *Enough*, 219.

59. Leon R. Kass, "The Case for Mortality," *American Scholar* 52, no. 2 (Spring 1983): 189.

60. Kass, "The Case for Mortality," 190.

61. McKibben, *Enough*, 164.

62. McKibben, *Enough*, 165.

63. King, *Pet Sematary*, 146.

64. King, *Pet Sematary*, 306.

65. King, *Pet Sematary*, 305.

66. King, *Pet Sematary*, 305.

67. King, *Pet Sematary*, 260.

68. King, *Pet Sematary*, 51.

69. King, *Pet Sematary*, 26.

70. King, *Pet Sematary*, 333.

71. King, *Pet Sematary*, 23.

72. King, *Pet Sematary*, 23.

73. King, *Pet Sematary*, 53.

74. King, *Pet Sematary*, 108.

75. King, *Pet Sematary*, 108.

76. King, *Pet Sematary*, 225.

77. King, *Pet Sematary*, 353.

78. King, *Pet Sematary*, 359.

79. King, *Pet Sematary*, 358.

80. King, *Pet Sematary*, 179.

81. King, *Pet Sematary*, 185.

82. King, *Pet Sematary*, 149.

83. Max More, "The Overhuman in the Transhuman," *Journal of Evolution & Technology* 21, no. 1 (January 2010): 1–4, accessed September 11, 2015, http://jetpress.org/v21/more.htm.

84. Leon R. Kass, "The Wisdom of Repugnance: Why We Should Ban the Cloning of Humans," *Valparaiso University Law Review* 32, no. 2 (1998): 687.

85. King, *Pet Sematary*, 31.

86. King, *Pet Sematary*, 31.

87. King, *Pet Sematary*, 33.

88. King, *The Tommyknockers*, 7.

89. King, *Pet Sematary*, 112.

90. King, *Pet Sematary*, 75.

91. Kass, "The Wisdom of Repugnance," 687.

92. King, *The Tommyknockers*, 20.

93. King, *The Tommyknockers*, 21.

94. King, *The Tommyknockers*, 29.

95. King, *Pet Sematary*, 28.

96. King, *Pet Sematary*, 63.

97. King, *Pet Sematary*, 28.

98. King, *Pet Sematary*, 225.

99. King, *Pet Sematary*, 255.

100. King, *Pet Sematary*, 225.

101. King, *Pet Sematary*, 225.

102. King, *Pet Sematary*, 276.

103. King, *Pet Sematary*, 275.

104. King, *Pet Sematary*, 276.

105. King, *Pet Sematary*, 275.

106. King, *Pet Sematary*, 110.

107. King, *The Tommyknockers*, 70.

108. King, *The Tommyknockers*, 736.

109. King, *Pet Sematary*, 354.

110. Greene, "Stephen King."

111. King, *The Tommyknockers*, 810.

112. King, *The Tommyknockers*, 961.

113. King, *The Tommyknockers*, 597–98.

114. King, *The Tommyknockers*, 843.

115. King, *The Tommyknockers*, 71.

116. King, *The Tommyknockers*, 715.

117. In the 1975 article "The Smoking Beagles," the investigative journalist Mary Beith detailed the now-notorious experiments in which forty-eight beagles were restrained in stock-like devices and forced to smoke up to thirty cigarettes per day, in order to test the safety of a new and allegedly healthier cigarette. Roy Greenslade, "Mary Beith, the Journalist Who Broke the 'Smoking Beagles' Story," *Guardian*, May 20, 2012, accessed September 11, 2015, http://www.theguardian.com/media/greenslade/2012/May/20/thepeople-investigative-journalism.

118. King, *The Tommyknockers*, 15.

119. King, *The Tommyknockers*, 5.

120. King, *The Tommyknockers*, 715.

121. King, *The Tommyknockers*, 116.

122. King, *The Tommyknockers*, 120–21.

123. King, *The Tommyknockers*, 849.

124. McKibben, *Enough*, 48.

125. McKibben, *Enough*, 214.

126. McKibben, *Enough*, 162.

127. Kass, "New Biology," 785.

128. McKibben, *Enough*, 162.

129. King, *Pet Sematary*, 237.

4

"GAN IS DEAD"

Nietzsche and Roland's Eternal Recurrence

Garret Merriam

What, if some day or night a demon were to steal after you into your loneliest loneliness and say to you: "This life as you now live it and have lived it, you will have to live once more and innumerable times more; and there will be nothing new in it, but every pain and every joy and every thought and sigh . . . all in the same succession and sequence. . . . The eternal hourglass of existence is turned upside down again and again, and you with it, speck of dust!" Would you not throw yourself down and gnash your teeth and curse the demon who spoke thus? Or have you once experienced a tremendous moment when you would have answered him: "You are a god and never have I heard anything more divine."—Friedrich Nietzsche, *The Gay Science*[1]

How many times had he climbed these stairs only to find himself peeled back, curved back, turned back? . . . How many times had he traveled a loop . . . ? How many times would he travel it?

"Oh no!" *he screamed.* "Please, not again! Have pity! Have mercy!"

The hands pulled him forward regardless. The hands of the tower knew no mercy.

They were the hands of Gan, the hands of ka, and they knew no mercy.—Stephen King, *The Dark Tower* [2]

After proclaiming the death of God, Friedrich Nietzsche (1844–1900) proposed a new way for each of us to assess and evaluate our own lives. Without God's judgment to serve as an objective assessment of our lives, Nietzsche invokes the ancient concept of "eternal recurrence" to force us to fill God's shoes in judgment of ourselves. As presented in the quote above, the question that each of us must ask ourselves is "Am I so committed to my life that I would relive it all over again, not once, but an infinite number of times?" In order to truly judge your life a success you must *amor fati*—love your fate. Nietzsche, having rejected the linear, teleological ("purpose-driven") metaphysics of Christianity, has replaced it with a cyclical metaphysics, which makes each of us the ultimate judge of our own existence.

At the end of *The Dark Tower*, Roland scales the Tower and ascends to the room at the top, only to learn that it contains the very quest he believed himself to have just completed. Rather than finding the end of his quest, Roland returns to the Mohaine Desert, where we first encountered the gunslinger at the very beginning of the first book in the cycle. The linear image of the beam (Roland's quest terminating at the Tower) is replaced by the image of the wheel, with the Tower as its axis around which all of existence—Roland's life especially—continually rotates. By saving the Tower, Roland condemns himself to repeat the cycle in perpetuity, his quest unending. Based on the quote above, it looks like Roland fails Nietzsche's test; at the moment of truth Roland most certainly does not love his *ka*.

Questions about the relationship between man and God, fate and free will, nihilism and the meaning of life abound in Nietzsche's work, and by looking at *The Dark Tower* through Nietzsche's eyes we can come to a better understanding of both the philosopher and the gunslinger. This chapter will explore how Roland's quest serves as an illustration of Nietzsche's philosophy and what *The Dark Tower* can teach us about living a meaningful life.

FATALISM AND THE HORN OF ELD: COULD ROLAND CHANGE HIS KA?

Unlike Nietzsche's thought experiment above, there is a hint that Roland might change his fate: the Horn of Eld. In contrast to the first time we encounter Roland in the Mohaine Desert at the beginning of *The Gunslinger*, at the end of the seventh book Roland carries the horn of his ancestor with him as he follows the man in black once more. Whereas in the previous cycle Roland left the horn in the dying hands of Cuthbert Allgood at the Battle of Jericho Hill, it seems that in this iteration, "Roland had paused just long enough to pick it up again, knocking the death-dust of that place from its throat."[3] Assuming he carries it with him the length of this next iteration of his quest, Roland will no doubt blow the horn once he reaches the scarlet fields of Can'-Ka No Rey.

While it is not exactly clear what effect, if any, this will have on Roland's fate, it at least holds out the prospect of hope for the beleaguered gunslinger. As he sets out, once again, across the desert at the end of the seventh book, the voice of Gan says, "This [the Horn of Eld] is your promise that things may be different, Roland—that there may yet be rest. Even salvation."[4] In *Stephen King's The Dark Tower: A Concordance*, Robin Furth interprets this to mean that "Roland's journey must endlessly repeat because he does not have the Horn of Eld with him. . . . This lack of foresight, and Roland's inability, at times, to see the long term consequences of his actions is one personal fault which Roland must correct before he can reach the true end of his quest. . . . Perhaps, then, the story we read in the Dark Tower series is Roland's penultimate journey to the Tower."[5] Maybe this time around Roland might just manage to save himself from the cursed fate in store for him. Furth (and possibly King himself) views this as the silver lining, a glimmer of hope in the otherwise grim, fatalistic end to the tale.

At first glance, the fact that Roland has at least a chance to change things suggests an incompatibility with Nietzsche's eternal recurrence. As Nietzsche presents the idea of eternal recurrence, you can't change your fate (that is, after all, why it's called "fate"). Nietzsche was rather direct in his statement that "there will be nothing new in it [your life], but every pain and every joy and every thought and sigh . . . must return to you all in the same succession and sequence."[6] Taken at face value, this would seem to nullify any application to Roland's quest, since it implies the very fatalism that Furth rejected above. In Nietzsche's thought experiment, you have no free will since everything you do is dictated by the inexorable hands of fate. Yet Roland has, this time around, exercised his free will and made a minor (but significant) change in the cycle by picking up the Horn of Eld. If he can exercise at least that small measure of control, then perhaps Roland may yet break the cycle and find peace.

Yet this seems to be taking Nietzsche too literally (something that Nietzsche himself warns us not to do.) While he was something of a fatalist, Nietzsche maintained that we are nonetheless responsible for who we are. This seemingly contradictory position—called "compatibilism"—is important to our reading of both Nietzsche and the Dark Tower series. The notion of amor fati can be read, not as an attempt by Nietzsche to deny that we have free will so much as it is an attempt to encourage us to embrace our lives, both those things that we can control and those things that we cannot.[7] Furth seems to acknowledge this when she emphasizes Roland's responsibility for his predicament. "Like so many of us, Roland is caught in a trap. To escape that trap, Roland must first understand that it is of his own creation."[8] This mix of responsibility and lack of control are characteristic themes of Nietzsche's philosophy.

NIETZSCHE, NIHILISM, AND THE CRIMSON KING

At the same time, however, Nietzsche would probably reject Furth's goal of "escaping the trap." If our only hope for Roland is that this time he will exercise enough foresight to hold on to the Horn of Eld, then we're missing the more profound lesson the Dark Tower has to teach us. Let's say that the next time around Roland holds on to the Horn of Eld and blows it when he reaches the fields of Can'-Ka No Rey. What happens next? He scales the Tower again and . . . then what? He opens the door at the top and is not catapulted backward, but is instead . . . ? What could possibly happen the next time around that would satisfy Roland (to say nothing of the reader)? Roland's true curse is not eternal recurrence, but rather his vision of his life as a linear quest, a means to be justified by the end.

Strangely enough, there is another character who also views his quest in the same linear fashion as Roland: the Crimson King. Whereas Roland's quest is to protect the Tower, the Crimson King's goal is to destroy it. While their goals are opposite in nature, they both fail to appreciate the cyclical nature of ka and both are undone by that mutual failure. There is a perversity in this observation: since saving the Tower didn't save Roland, it may be that his only true peace will come if the Tower falls. Is that not the heart of the cruel irony inherent in Roland being cast back to redo his quest yet again? By being successful, he must continue to struggle; were he to fail he would find peace.

One can see in this suggestion a view known as nihilism, which has often been associated with Nietzsche and was an idea he wrote about frequently. Nietzsche could very well have been referring to the Crimson King when he said that "a nihilist is a man who judges of the world as it is that it ought *not* to be, and of the world as it ought to be that it does not exist. According to this view, our existence (action, suffering, willing, feeling) has no meaning."[9] Could it be, then, that the best outcome for Roland would be oblivion, the simple end to his (and all of the rest of) existence? Might the Crimson King not be a villain, but rather the only person who can deliver Roland from the merciless hands of ka? Is *The Dark Tower* fundamentally a nihilistic text?

ROLAND STARES INTO THE ABYSS

Once Roland reaches his goal and climbs the Tower, he anticipates vindication, something at the top that will make sense of his quest. But what could possibly fit this bill? What could Gan place at the top of the Tower that would do this? If Roland were to see the face of Gan himself, would this not leave him (and the reader) horribly disappointed? Or what if Roland were to find that the room was empty, as he wonders it may be at various points in his quest? How long would Roland stand at the door, starring into the emptiness? After having climbed the Tower, Roland finds his own brutal, bloody life laid out before him: *"This is a place of death. . . . All these rooms. Every floor. Yes, gunslinger,* whispered the Voice of the Tower. *But only because your life has made it so."*[10]

Nietzsche would have some pointed advice: "Whoever fights monsters should see to it that in the process he does not become a monster. And when you gaze long into the abyss, the abyss gazes also into you."[11] Taking the first half of that quote into consideration, we must ask if Roland has become a monster. Roland is often described as an "antihero," but perhaps this is a major understatement. Shortly after we first meet him in *The Gunslinger* we are told of how he slaughtered the entire town of Tull—all fifty-eight people, including five children. Even recognizing that this action was in self-defense, it nonetheless seems a rather monstrous thing to do (especially given the fact that Roland sees it coming; he could have avoided the slaughter by leaving Tull after Sylvia Pittston's sermon, in which she all but directly threatened Roland with violence). Over the course of the eight-book cycle Roland kills hundreds of people (counting Slow Mutants, taheen, can-toi, and other assorted demons and creatures). Depending on how many iterations of his quest he's gone through, he may have killed infinitely more. Through his actions Roland has made the Tower, the nexus of all existence, the body of Gan himself, into a Golgotha, a place of death. What could be more monstrous than this? We are again drawn back to the question of whether it would have been better off had Roland simply let the Tower fall. While this would still have resulted in as many deaths (and more) when the Tower fell, it would perhaps at least have kept Roland from becoming a monster and corrupting the Tower in the process. To paraphrase the book of Mark, what does it profit Roland to gain the Tower and lose his soul?

Roland stares into the abyss many times over the course of the cycle, but never more literally than when he drops Jake at the end of *The Gunslinger*. This sacrifice to the abyss is a necessity (at least in Roland's mind) in order to continue his quest for the Tower. But Jake's death is not the final word, since as he prophetically states, "there are other worlds than these." Jake is returned to Roland in *The Waste Lands*, only to be ripped from him in *The Dark Tower*. Jake's second death is also a sacrifice, this time to save Stephen King.

And of course, the whole cycle must then repeat itself again, Roland forced to forever sacrifice his surrogate son. We have to wonder if Roland would perhaps have preferred the emptiness of the void to this eternal recurrence. Or perhaps it amounts to the same thing, since either way Roland is denied satisfaction, the salvation for which he has quested. Given the choice between perpetual, unchanging life and nothingness, which would Roland prefer? Given the horror with which he greets the prospect of recurrence Roland may actually choose nothingness. And what does this say about how he has lived his life? Would he have done things differently if he had known at the outset that the top of the Tower was empty?

LOVE YOUR KA

These questions point us toward a nihilistic reading of *The Dark Tower*. While a case could certainly be made for such a reading, as is always the case with Nietzsche (and perhaps all literature) cases can be made for other, less extreme readings. While Nietzsche himself certainly flirted with nihilism, seeing him as a nihilist relies on a narrow reading of his texts. Likewise, reading *The Dark Tower* through a nihilistic lens misses some of the more important lessons King's epic has to teach us. The antidote to these considerations is to return to the notion of amor fati ("There will be water if God wills it"). If Roland can learn to love his ka, then nothingness will no longer seem a preferable alternative.

While Nietzsche is often mistakenly thought to be a nihilist, he only used nihilism as a foil, a point of contrast that he considered in an attempt to underscore the crisis of modern humanity in the wake of what he called "the death of God" (something we'll return to momentarily). Nietzsche wants us to embrace our fate, our existence, to "say yes to life" and redeem ourselves from the meaninglessness of nihilism.

The same theme arises in the Dark Tower cycle, and Furth seems to recognize this when she comments, "The second lesson that Roland has to learn before he finds peace is that life itself, not just the blind pursuit of the quest, is valuable. We often think that the ends justify the means, but what Roland finds when he reaches his life's goal is that the means can taint the end."[12] When given the chance to take his focus off the Tower, Roland finds he has much in his life that is valuable: he has friends he cares about deeply, he knew love with Susan Delgado, and he dances the Commala. (It's worth noting that the same cannot be said for the Crimson King; he has nothing in his life beyond his dream of destroying the Tower.) But by and large, all these things are subservient to the Tower. When Flagg implores him, at the end of *Wizard and Glass*, to "cry off" his quest for the Tower, there isn't even a hint of dramatic tension—the reader doesn't think for a moment that Roland will actually do it. He is willing to risk and even surrender the lives of everyone he loves to make it to the Tower.

Yet, despite this recognition, there is a tension here that seems to elude Furth, between this second lesson and the first one quoted above: if Roland learns that life itself is valuable, then he would not view his life as a "trap" and he would have no desire to "escape" it. Roland's problem isn't whether or not he will manage to break the cycle that has heretofore recapitulated his quest. As long as he expects to find redemption by reaching some end goal he is destined for disappointment. The problem is that Roland does not really embrace his life; he does not love his ka. Even though he says it many times, Roland still does not truly understand that "ka is a wheel." If he insists on thinking of his quest as a line with a specific end point, Roland will never find peace, for he will never understand his ka, much less be able to love it. This is precisely the consciousness that Nietzsche is trying to inspire in us when he asks us to love our fate.

GAN IS DEAD?

Perhaps another way to understand this is by taking a closer look at Nietzsche's famous statement that "God is dead." This famous (and famously misconstrued) proclamation is not to be taken literally— Nietzsche is not saying that the eternal, all-knowing, all-powerful creator of the universe has perished. Rather this statement refers to the role that the *idea of God* has played in Western civilization—as the foundation of meaning, value, and morality—and how that idea is no longer adequate for that task. Nietzsche believed that humanity can no longer honestly believe in a God that justifies our existence in this way. Hence if our lives are to have any meaning at all we must figure out a new source of meaning, a new foundation for our lives. Nietzsche thought the death of God, rather than being a cause for mourning, was actually liberating, and that embracing our emancipation was the first step toward living a life that is truly our own.

The Dark Tower serves as an excellent illustration of Nietzsche's point. Gan is the creative force of all reality in the Dark Tower mythos, akin to God in the Judeo-Christian mythos, which Nietzsche was critiquing. As with the Judeo-Christian mythos, Gan is not dead in the literal sense; the Tower is the body of Gan, and we hear the voice of Gan speak to Roland when he enters (which, Nietzsche would surely note, is more than most can say of the Judeo-Christian God). And much like in the Christian mythos, Roland derives the meaning of his existence from Gan, from his quest to persevere and climb the Tower. Just as the Christian life is defined by a desire to propitiate God and join

Him in heaven, the beckoning call of the Tower defines Roland's purpose. Gan promises Roland "salvation" if he simply obeys that call, and all it will cost him is his perpetual existence. The Tower was the meaning of Roland's life: it bestowed meaning "on high" to his existence. So when it thrusts him back to repeat his cycle again, it's a cruel irony. Eternal recurrence was Nietzsche's attempt to force us to find our own meaning, one that is not given to us from on high. Perhaps Roland's torment at the last minute is his punishment, not for a lack of faith, but rather for the presence of it. Instead of finding something that would make all of his sacrifices (Susan, Cuthbert, Alain, Jake, Eddie, Jake again) worthwhile, he found that he was condemned to make those sacrifices all over again.

Nietzsche would likely maintain that despite such a horrific prospect and despite Gan's promise of salvation, Roland has no need of any such deliverance. Roland, like so many of us, saw his life as teleological ("all things serve the beam"), when in fact it was cyclical ("ka is a wheel"). It is because he invests himself in the idea of finding salvation through the Tower that Roland finds the prospect of eternal recurrence so horrifying. He did not see his life as having meaning in its own right, beyond what he hoped to find in the Tower. Once Roland accepts the fact that Gan is dead—that the only salvation worth its salt is the kind Roland can provide for himself—he will be able to open the door at the top of the Tower, hear the voice of ka beckoning, and reply (with appropriate irony), "You are a god and never have I heard anything more divine!"[13]

CONCLUSION: ROLAND AND SISYPHUS

The existentialist Albert Camus (1913–1960), who was deeply influenced by Nietzsche, offered a meditation on eternal recurrence in his classic essay *The Myth of Sisyphus*. Camus retells the story of the mythical Greek figure Sisyphus, who was condemned by the gods to spend all of eternity pushing a rock up a hill, only to have it roll back down again when he got it to the top. Camus used this story of endless, meaningless toil as an allegory for our lives; no matter how hard we work, no matter what we accomplish, the inexorable march of time will eventually undo everything we achieve. Now that God is dead, how can we find meaning in our lives, since all of our futile endeavors will eventually be plowed under and forgotten? If our labors are ultimately fruitless, then what possible value, purpose, or point can there be to them? The redemption of Sisyphus comes not from the forgiveness of the gods, nor from escaping his fate, but rather from simply recognizing the absurdity of his situation and embracing it as such. At the end of the essay Camus tries to reconcile our lives with their ephemeral brevity: "The struggle itself towards the heights is enough to fill a man's heart. One must imagine Sisyphus happy."[14]

The same moral can help us make sense of the gunslinger: his struggle itself has filled our hearts. It may be difficult to imagine Roland happy—it is not generally in his nature, and our final vision of him on the last pages of book 7 make this a challenging task. But when Camus makes this suggestion with regard to Sisyphus it is meant to be challenging, a transformative reading of an ancient text. If our options are to read *The Dark Tower* as a nihilistic text or an existentialist one, then the takeaway is clear: we must imagine Roland happy.

NOTES

1. Friedrich Nietzsche, *The Gay Science*, trans. Walter Kaufmann (New York: Vintage, 1974), §341.

2. Stephen King, *The Dark Tower* (New York: Scribner, 2004), 847.

3. King, *The Dark Tower*, 829.

4. King, *The Dark Tower*, 829.

5. Robin Furth, *Stephen King's* The Dark Tower: *A Concordance, Volume II* (New York: Scribner, 2005), 297–98.

6. Nietzsche, *The Gay Science*, §341.

7. For more on Nietzsche's "compatibilism," see Robert C. Solomon, "Nietzsche on Fatalism and 'Free Will,'" *Journal of Nietzsche Studies* 23 (Spring 2002): 63–87.

8. Furth, *Stephen King's* The Dark Tower, 297.

9. Friedrich Nietzsche, *The Will to Power*, trans. Walter Kaufmann (New York: Vintage, 1968), §585.

10. King, *The Dark Tower*, 825.

11. Friedrich Nietzsche, *Beyond Good and Evil*, trans. Walter Kaufmann (New York: Vintage, 1966), §89.

12. Furth, *Stephen King's* The Dark Tower, 297.

13. Nietzsche, *The Gay Science*, §341.

14. Albert Camus, The Myth of Sisyphus *and Other Essays*, trans. Justin O'Brien (New York: Vintage, 1991), 122.

5

RĀMA OF GILEAD

Hindu Philosophy in *The Dark Tower*

Matthew A. Butkus

You are what your deep, driving desire is. As your desire is, so is your will. As your will is, so is your deed. As your deed is, so is your destiny.—Brihadaranyaka IV.4.5

The Dark Tower series offers a sampling of a number of different stories, incorporating not only Stephen King's literary multiverse, but also drawing from Marvel Comics, Harry Potter, Star Wars, and other sources. This tableau synthesizes a number of different literary traditions, making connections between very divergent storytelling media and themes. While the pop culture parallels are evident—it is difficult to miss Doctor Doom riding mechanical horses armed with light sabers and killer snitches—there are also deeper connections to be found. For instance, the links to the Arthurian legends and other epic tales are evident in the nature of Roland's particular Grail quest, the Mordred story line, and so on.

Even these callbacks to Arthurian legend don't plumb the depths of literary connection, however. The narrative itself goes even further back, drawing parallels to epic heroes in the Hindu tradition—Roland himself parallels characters found in the Rāmāyana and Mahābhārata. The cyclical nature of his existence, his role as protector (of both his world and, by extension, all worlds), and his efforts to expunge the guilt of past actions offer strong parallels to core elements in Hindu philosophy: *karma* (causation), *dharma* (duty), *samskāra* (character), and *samsāra* (the cycle of death and rebirth).

Roland parallels two people in particular—Rāma, the titular character in the Rāmāyana, and Arjuna, the reluctant hero of the Bhagavad Gītā (part of the much larger Mahābhārata). Rāma is seminal in Hindu myth as both an *avatār* of Vishnu as well as a paragon of proper attention to one's duty. Arjuna is a warrior who is reluctant to shed the blood of his cousins, requiring intervention and education from Krishna (a Hindu deity) on the nature of karma and its repercussions in the cycle of samsāra. While Roland does not face identical challenges, he becomes a vehicle through which we learn of Eastern concepts like karma, dharma, samskāra, and samsāra. Once Roland sets his mind to attaining the Tower, once his will is set, so too is his destiny.

In this chapter, I will explore several topics, focusing first on parallels between Roland, Rama, and Arjuna and how Roland's life as hero and avatār are governed by expunging the negative consequences of his past actions. This provides evidence for the second element of this chapter—Roland as role model for moral agents seeking to escape cycles of death and rebirth. The Bhagavad Gītā instructs that each of us "must discover and earnestly follow his or her own path or perish spiritually."[1] Using literary characters as role models is common in Western approaches to ethics, as we can trace role models and hero emulation at least as far back as Plato and Aristotle's systems of virtue-based ethics. As a modern and relatable character, Roland serves as a vehicle for a contemporary audience to understand the role of dharma in their lives.

ROLAND'S CYCLICAL FATE

"The man in black fled across the desert, and the gunslinger followed." This is the image that opens and closes the Dark Tower series: Roland, our protagonist and semiwilling hero, pursues the man in black, who will give him the answers he needs to complete his quest for the Dark Tower. But will he really?

At the end of the series, we learn that this pursuit is part of a cycle. Roland has traveled this path before—many times before, in fact, and many more times to come. It promises him more hardship, an apparent cyclic cruelty of exposure, thirst, starvation, disease, maiming, violence, and death. But it is also potentially redemptive—the voice fading in his head promises him that things may be different, that salvation is possible. By working through this cycle, by upholding his principles, he may finally attain an end to his wanderings and escape this repetitive path. This is not an ephemeral promise—at the end of the series, something is different. This time around Roland possesses the Horn of Eld, which he had lost much earlier in life.

The horn is not the only clue that things are different. We are told that Roland does not remember previous cycles—he forgets his past to be "born anew," as much as one can when sent back to an arbitrary point in his life. During Roland's ascent of the Tower, he notes faces on the wall that he does not recognize—signs of past actions that he does not remember yet that impact and affect him and his station in life.[2] This ties his current existence to previous lives—indicating that the unremembered actions are still a part of him. His existence isn't limited to the life put forth in the novels—his Dark Tower is the sum total of all of his lives and actions, both those for good and ill.

This cyclical existence is highly reminiscent of the concept of karma in Hindu philosophy, the central theme of this chapter. This is not the only parallel to Hindu philosophy—the character of Roland himself is reminiscent of Rāma, hero of the Rāmāyana and avatār of Vishnu. The avatār restores balance to the world, saving it from descending into chaos, and preserving dharma. Such a rescue is the underlying plot of the Dark Tower series, as Roland seeks to prevent the destruction of the beams that hold the world together.

Ultimately, the picture we are given of Roland's existence is that of samsāra—a cycle of death and rebirth that is potentially redemptive. Samsāra is not isolated; it cannot be understood without simultaneously exploring concepts like karma, dharma, and samskāra. These concepts weave a fabric of one's life that shows how our actions shape our character, which in turn shapes our actions, and so on. This interplay of action and character is contained within a system of causation, and our actions and intentions have effects on us that might not be washed away during one life. As such, we must live multiple lives to make up for misdeeds, allowing us to escape from this cycle of death and rebirth.

Roland cannot escape this lesson—his karma requires him to relearn it again and again. What is not clear is whether this is a finite or infinite process—he is tantalized by the prospect of ultimate redemption and release, but it is conditional. The Tower tells him he must stand, that he must be true.[3] If he fails to do so, he will not be released, extending his quest indefinitely.

LITERATURE, ROLAND, AND RĀMA

The Rāmāyana is seminal in the collection of beliefs referred to as Hinduism.[4] Along with the Mahābhārata (and especially the section comprising the Bhagavad Gītā), it has been a key to understanding the complex interaction of human action, cosmic order, and the cycle of life and death. The impact of these texts cannot be overstated—both the Rāmāyana and the Gītā are seen as examples of idealized humans and their behaviors. They serve as examples of how believers should live their lives and face adversity. They impact Hindus and non-Hindus alike[5]—examples of heroism in both combat and personal behavior resonate with readers. Enduring literature speaks to the human condition, in many cases transcending the specific cultural context in which it is written. One does not need to be Russian to appreciate the profundity of the theological question of evil in *The Brothers Karamazov*. One does not need to be German to appreciate the malaise and desire for understanding and stimulation that drive *Faust*. One does not need to be American to appreciate the monomania of *Moby-Dick*. Similarly, a variety of cultures can appreciate, identify with, and learn from *The Odyssey*, the *Epic of Gilgamesh*, and similar works.

While not elevating Stephen King's Dark Tower series to that pantheon, it is accessible to readers in a way that the others might not be. Despite the fantasy setting, Roland's world is somewhat relatable to our own, especially as the world's blend of pop culture elements creep in, which also serve as a launching point for the reader to appreciate some of the deeper textual elements and parallels in other religions and systems. *Ka*—a mystical force pushing the characters toward action— runs throughout the series, injecting a mythic and religious unifying element to the wide variety of events that unfold in the worlds through which Roland travels.

Much of the discussion of Roland's moral character and his cyclical life is dependent upon his dharma, from the root *dhṛ-* ("to sustain").[6] While I suggest that it be understood as "duty" above, this is only a single, simplified facet of a much larger concept in Hindu philosophy. Dharma actually reflects a number of concepts, including religion, morality, conduct, duty, ethics, law, truth, and social structure, which collectively produce cosmological order.[7] It prescribes how we are to behave but does not mandate that we all act in the same way—it adapts itself to context and situation, recognizing that the duties and conduct of a philosopher are not the same as those of a warrior. This individualized set of requirements is referred to as *svadharma*. There are parallels in Western philosophy; natural law ethics, such as that found in Catholic catechism, introduces concepts like an unchanging divine law in which different creatures participate according to their different natures (producing a different natural law for humans than for cats, for instance).

In creating order, dharma also considers social position. This plasticity creates unique obligations and proscriptions—an action that is required of one person may be forbidden for another (performing the duties outside one's station produces *adharma*—disorder and destruction). Failure to uphold svadharma creates karma, which must be removed before one can escape the cycle of death and rebirth. Simply put, in order for moral agents to be redeemed, they must fulfill the duties of their stations and positions in life, even if they find them burdensome, worrisome, or terrifying. They must stand and be true, regardless of their reservations.

This vigilance is appropriate—the dharma of the warrior class (the Kshatriya) explicitly includes protecting dharma and the world against violence, killing foes both natural and supernatural. War was constant in the historical Indian city-states, so fighting and subjugating enemies became their explicit duty in both history and literature. Dying in bed was seen as dishonorable and an affront to Kshatriya dharma.[8] A warrior is meant to fight, to protect, to risk death in battle for the good of others. And so Rāma takes up arms against the demons (*rakshasas*) as Roland takes up arms against the servants of the Crimson King.

In the Rāmāyana, the life of Rāma is established as a model of living according to dharma. Rāma is described as being the perfect son (fulfilling all of his responsibilities toward his family, respecting his elders, being obedient, etc.), accepting his banishment at the hands of his stepmother, who favored her own son, Bharata. Accompanied by his wife Sita (also established as a paragon of living according to dharma), he remains in the forest, obeying his father even when Bharata encourages him to return to take the throne. Later in the narrative, Sita is abducted by Ravana, a demonic figure (rakshasa), who desires Sita for himself. Rāma frees Sita with the assistance of Hanuman, a monkey-like being with magical powers, but does not accept her back before she can prove her purity. In each of his life challenges, Rāma accepts his fate and the responsibilities of his role as son and warrior and follows his dharma, setting an example that has been instructive for generations of believers.

Rāma is not simply a good character to emulate—he is also an incarnation (avatār) of Vishnu, the preserver of the universe. By upholding dharma, Rāma preserves reality as a whole. Importantly, Rāma follows dharma naturally—he does not need to be coerced into doing so. In fact, his adherence to dharma is indicative of his character—he is naturally predisposed to doing his duty.

Roland's life revolves around violence—while we sometimes see him happy (even dancing), he is consistently a guiding father figure and leader, and never sways from his calling to the Tower. As a gunslinger, he has taken on a role mythologized in his world—the gunslingers are not mercenaries or ruffians, but rather protectors who treat protection of the innocent and vulnerable as a sacred calling. There is a formal ritual of asking for help (witnessed in the *Wolves of the Calla*), which binds him to his supplicant. Like Rāma, he fights supernatural evils like Mordred and the Crimson King, those who would destabilize the world and bring chaos like Walter (in all of his aliases), as well as those who would aid and abet evildoers, such as the town that fell under Walter's sway in *The Gunslinger* or the Breakers. This sense of purpose is not simply imposed on him from external agents—it is indicative of his character, his defining nature.

Aside from both Rāma and Roland having a strong sense of duty, they both are, at their most fundamental essence, protectors of the universe. Roland's quest for the Tower simultaneously becomes a quest to repair the damage being done to the beams supporting existence (much like the spokes of a wheel). Both Rāma and Roland are avatārs— protectors who appear "when *dharma* is threatened by subversive forces disturbing the order of things and there is a risk that the world will come to ruin."[9] It is this disruption that produces the coming of the avatār, who has a very specific role: protect the good, destroy the bad, and restore cosmic order.[10]

Rāma is cast as a moral ideal and a model for others to follow.[11] He fulfills his obligations to his parents and accepts banishment as well as his obligation to rescue his wife and fight the rakshasa, despite its occasionally unpleasant nature, because it was his dharma—his duty—and to fail to do so would incur negative karma. This interaction hints at a larger underlying theme—the actions of mortals represent a complex interweaving of human action (karma) and cosmic order (*niyati*).[12] The Hindu belief system assumes an apparent paradox—our actions are the products both of our own free will as well as their place within a larger framework of dharma.[13] Ultimately, our lives must fit into niyati—which suggests that mortal agents do not have supreme power over their actions. Rather, this supreme power shapes and guides us, giving us a sense of constrained freedom. This niyati strongly parallels ka, a supreme and guiding force in the Dark Tower series, and ultimately shapes the dharma of everything in existence.

Each element of the cosmos has its own dharma as a means of interacting with and maintaining the universe. So long as these elements follow their dharma, the universe is maintained and stabilized. When these elements stop following their dharma, this stability is disrupted. Our particular dharma is influenced by a number of things, including our karma (which can place us into particular roles with particular duties) and our samskāra, which is the sum total of our past lives and actions, which shapes our character in this life.

These ideas have immediate parallels in the character of Roland—his existence is cyclical and shaped by the actions of his current and previous lives. Further, his life is governed by ka, a transcendent combination of force and will that guides actions and circumstances that appears in many of King's books in and out of the Dark Tower series. Happenstance and apparently coincidental events (both good and ill) are explained as manifestations of ka. The group is bound by a common purpose (*ka-tet*), which guides their actions and frames the larger quest for the Tower. In fact, their experiences from the beginning of the series to the end are entwined with a quasi mysticism in which actions have immediate and future impact, both in their world and in others. This interrelationship is a type of mystical causation, strongly reminiscent of karma.

So what is karma? The concept appears in many different guises in many different religions (a derivative of the Hindu concept is found in Buddhism; a related but separate idea is found in Wicca, in which actions are repaid threefold, etc.), and there are underlying similarities between them. At its heart, karma is essentially a causative relationship—the root of the term is *kri* (meaning "to do") tying the concept to action.[14] The actions and intentions of moral agents that violate dharma can accumulate negative karma, which must be worked off by actions appropriate to one's dharma. Sometimes this karma cannot be accounted for in one lifetime, necessitating multiple lives. Both short-term and long-term karma are seen in the Dark Tower series.

There are a number of actions in the series that acquire negative karma and require it to be expunged. Roland's coupling with the demon in *The Gunslinger* is responsible for the Mordred story line in the final three books. Roland's willful failure to save Jake in *The Gunslinger* and his rescue in *The Drawing of the Three* produces his near madness in *The Waste Lands*. Jake, in fact, has the dubious distinction of dying two and a half times in the series overall, by three different hands.[15] It is unclear whether Roland's eventual rescue of Jake was sufficient to work off the stain of allowing him to fall to his death.

These are all isolated incidents, however. The larger concern is the pattern of Roland's behavior—more specifically, what is the content of his character? What does the pattern of his life reveal about who he is at his core? The series offers some veiled insights into his past, either through direct relation or through hints and suggestions. We know the Dark Tower holds a record of his life, and that he does not remember all the faces contained therein, but he feels guilt about his past misdeeds—he describes these actions as "sacrifices to the Dark Tower" and "old times and old crimes."[16] But when were these old times? What were these old crimes?

Obviously, some of them are contained within the narrative of the Dark Tower series, either occurring explicitly on the pages or related in narrative flashbacks. But we also know that Roland doesn't recognize some of the faces decorating the walls of the Tower, and we know that he always forgets his previous cycles in the Dark Tower quest. It would seem, then, that we have faces appearing that were from previous cycles, suggesting that he is working off past deeds (his karma and samsāra). But this isn't the only relevant issue—when he begins a new cycle at the end of the series, he has the Horn of Eld, which he did not possess at the beginning of the narrative's cycle, and a topic we will visit again. This suggests that his actions on the current quest cycle have set the stage for the next one—this goes beyond karma and samsāra, and introduces the concept of samskāra, which states that one's current state (physical, psychological, etc.) is the result of all previous lives. The choices we made in previous lives affect our future just as the choices we make in this life. Consequently, we are more than simply the sum of the actions and desires we remember in this life, but rather the sum total of *all* of our actions and desires in *all* of our past lives.

We don't have the full details of Roland's past life—we are presented with his story in media res, and only get slices of his backstory. However, we do get insight into those events that have shaped his current psyche: his childhood training with Cort, his love affair with Susan Delgado, his adventures with Alain and Cuthbert, and so forth. A recurring theme in these events is the taking on of adult responsibilities—by the time most people are in high school, he has fought and beaten his childhood instructor, seen his true love burned at the stake, killed friends directly and indirectly, and killed men twice his age while foiling a larger conspiracy against his father. These events should not be glossed over—current psychology notes that undergoing traumatic events and taking on adult responsibilities at a young age has a tendency for various psychopathologies. Regardless of whether we consider Roland's experiences as scarring or transformative, the lessons they taught him have been internalized and play out throughout the narrative. He has become desensitized to killing and has developed a single-mindedness in his quest.

This single-mindedness is important. The cyclical nature of Roland's existence does not take him back to his birth or the events he regrets most, but to "that moment in the Mohaine Desert when he had finally understood that this thoughtless, questionless quest would ultimately succeed".[17] —the moment of certainty that set his deep, driving desire, and thereby his will. It is this will that drives him on, despite hunger and thirst. It is this will that drives him on, despite the deaths of his friends. And it is this will that drives him to his final confrontation with the Crimson King and up the Tower stairs. His character is set by his experiences, and while the circumstances of each cycle may be different, that underlying will remains the same. He sees it as essential to his duty, his obligation, and his part in the universe. It is essential to his dharma.

ROLAND'S DHARMA AND ARJUNA

What is Roland's dharma? What seems to be his particular nature and role in the universe? He protects, he dispenses justice, he fights evil, and he kills. The gunslinger dispenses death frequently—in fact, in *The Gunslinger*, he kills an entire town, and many more violent acts follow in the series. But Roland is accustomed to death, killing, and violence—as we have seen, his life to that point has been difficult, filled with violence, deceit, and the worst part of human nature. It would seem that each of these experiences takes away some of his innocence and taints his soul. It would seem that he leaves a part of himself with each friend who dies, stripping away his sense of self until nothing but raw will remains.

Because of all this, Roland has become the gunslinger: an amalgam of knight-errant, *ronin*, and Texas Ranger. He is the protector of the weak, sometimes willingly and sometimes unwillingly, and guardian of reality. By protecting the beams and preventing their destruction he holds together the nature of reality. All of this wears at his soul—he is already weary and haggard when we first meet him set upon his quest with remarkable single-mindedness. He is eager to finish his quest, to stop his wandering and give up this life. He does not relish the task set before him.

This draws a parallel to a similar conundrum faced by the hero of another seminal work of Indian literature, Arjuna in the Bhagavad Gītā. Arjuna is bidden by his king to fight his cousins, with Krishna (an incarnation of Vishnu) himself driving his chariot. Upon realizing the magnitude of the death and destruction to follow in the battle (and the karmic repercussions thereof), Arjuna throws down his weapons and refuses to fight. Krishna then explains to him the nature of his duty as a warrior, explaining his obligation to preserve dharma and stability despite the apparent personal costs, countering each of his arguments about karmic repercussions. This conversation is meaningful for several reasons; for instance, it establishes the desirability of devotion to a particular deity (seen in some sects as a vehicle of liberation from samsara) as well as the importance of divorcing action from desired outcome, as this elevates one's soul toward Krishna consciousness and ultimate liberation.[18] Ultimately, Krishna instructs Arjuna in devotional action—performing one's dharma without succumbing to personal desires. This requires him to fight, despite his personal misgivings, because that is his duty. Refusing to do his duty as a warrior (i.e., refusing his dharma) is what incurs karma.[19]

Like Arjuna, Roland would prefer not to fight—he tires of the death and destruction, tires of the killing, and tires of the personal loss and misery. But it is his duty to carry on, his dharma is to stand as gunslinger, as the last line of defense against the destruction of the world. He is the avatār, the protector of dharma. It is his effort, and that of his ka-tet, that will prevent the dissolution of the universe.

ROLAND AND SAMSĀRA

This would seem to raise a bit of a problem—if negative karma must be worked off to escape samsāra, it would be reasonable to suspect that continuing to kill people would simply accumulate more negative karma, ensuring that Roland remain trapped eternally. But this isn't necessarily so.

It is a given that Roland kills a lot of people, but this isn't done arbitrarily or for selfish ends—even when Roland kills the entire town in *The Gunslinger*, he does so in self-defense. In later killings, Roland is a vehicle of justice and the quasi-divine will of ka. He protects the beams, and thereby reality, by serving as an avatār, much as Rāma had done. Just as Arjuna learns that his dharma is to fight, Roland's dharma is to stand as gunslinger. In fact, Roland's attention to his duty is precisely the mechanism of his own potential redemption—he is told that if he stands and stays true, he could be released. "Could be," however, is important as this release is uncertain, just as it is in the cycle of samsāra.

The reappearance of the Horn of Eld is symbolic of this uncertainty. The horn was lost much earlier in Roland's life (at the Battle of Jericho Hill), an event that profoundly affected him, as it also involved the death of his closest friends. Its return suggests several different things. It is entirely possible that this is a sign of having expunged past guilt or negative karma; it is also possible, however, that it will simply give him the chance to make a different choice in his current life—there is no guarantee that he is closer to release, just that things are different. In fact, the nature of samsāra is not necessarily a perfecting process. Each incarnation provides an opportunity to work toward release, but it also provides an opportunity to acquire additional karma to be worked off in future lives. The cycle of death and rebirth isn't simply a march toward ultimate release—we can walk backward as well as forward. The horn may be such a question mark—its role is unclear, symbolic of the uncertainty surrounding Roland's unique circumstances. We know Roland has walked this path many, many times before; just as karma and niyati are intertwined, Roland's choices within his cyclical framework are both his chains and means of escape. So will Roland ever be freed? Will he finally experience liberation from his mystical task? Will he finally earn rest after serving as protector, guardian, judge, and father? If he stands. If he is true. And so Roland goes on, because maybe, just maybe, this time will be different. Maybe this time will bring redemption.

So what does this tell us, as modern readers and seekers of role models? Is Roland worth emulating? This is a complex question. On one hand, we see a protector who gives of his own flesh and spirit to protect the universe, worthy of praise and veneration, which we recognize as paralleling any number of heroes from myth, legend, and religion. On the other hand, we see a killer of men, women, and children, willing to sacrifice all in his pursuit of the Dark Tower, a monomania akin to Ahab's pursuit of the white whale, which we recognize as a cautionary tale. It is understandably hard to decide whether we should praise or abhor his actions. We recognize that many of our heroes have flaws, but we still identify with them.

If we choose to emulate Roland, we find ourselves in the unhappy position of Arjuna—asked to do terrible things that would seem to stain our soul. But if we understand the character and text as descriptive of dharma, it is not a call to violence, but rather a call to duty. My role as philosopher and teacher of Hindu philosophy is not one of violence—it would, in fact, be wrong of me to perform actions like those of Roland, Rāma, or Arjuna. Instead, my dharma is to foster, to develop, and to nurture—acting against my role would be just as much adharma as killing or warring upon my neighbors. This same line of reasoning clarifies the duties of the reader—the Dark Tower series is, was, and will be read by people across socioeconomic classes and social roles, all of whom have different dharma. Some *will* be called to perform acts of violence as part of their duties (as these may be necessary to prevent a greater evil, such as the violence endemic to the practice of policing or warfare), while others will be called to govern, to teach, to heal, and so on. Performing one's duties, even when unpleasant, fulfills one's duty and dharma. We need not be perfect like Rāma nor as imperfect as Roland to do our part in protecting the universe—we each stand against disorder and chaos in our own way. To emulate Roland is not to fight and kill, but to stand and be true.

NOTES

1. Eknath Easwaran, *The Upanishads* (Tomales, Calif.: Nilgiri, 2007), 328.
2. Stephen King, *The Dark Tower* (New York: Scribner, 2004), 821.
3. King, *The Dark Tower*, 828.
4. Hinduism has proven to be contentious as a term—the religious traditions native to India have significant variation in terms of deities, sacred texts, etc., so it is difficult to make claims about a generalized Hinduism.
5. Klaus K. Klostermaier, *A Survey of Hinduism* (Albany: SUNY Press, 1989), 105.
6. Klostermaier, *A Survey of Hinduism*, 47.
7. Gavin Flood, *An Introduction to Hinduism* (New York: Cambridge University Press, 1996); Klostermaier, *A Survey of Hinduism*; K. S. Mathur, "Hindu Values of Life: Karma and Dharma," in *Religion in India* (New Delhi: Oxford University Press, 1991); Max Weber, *The Religion of India* (Glencoe, Ill.: Free Press, 1958).
8. Weber, *The Religion of India*, 1958.
9. Jean-Christophe Demariaux, *How to Understand Hinduism*, trans. John Bowden (London: SCM, 1995), 61.
10. Demariaux, *How to Understand Hinduism*, 61.
11. Mathur, "Hindu Values of Life," 69.
12. Rajeshwari Vijay Pandharipande, *The Eternal Self and the Cycle of Samsāra*, 3rd ed. (Needham Heights, Mass.: Simon & Schuster, 1996), 52.
13. Dharma is a complex term and concept—it refers to the underlying order of the universe, the basis for human morality and ethics, the foundation for religion, and the basis for proper action. I will try to keep the contextual distinctions as comprehensible as possible. For further information, see Flood, *An Introduction to Hinduism*; Klostermaier, *A Survey of Hinduism*; and Weber, *The Religion of India*.

14. Mathur, "Hindu Values of Life," 65; Pandharipande, *Eternal Self*, 38.

15. Jake is definitely killed at least twice—Roland allows him to fall to his death in *The Gunslinger* and he is hit and killed instead of Stephen King in *The Dark Tower*. His third death is kind of a Schrödinger's cat situation—he was killed by Mort in *The Gunslinger*, but this death was prevented in *The Drawing of the Three*. Roland has both versions of reality in his head, which produces the paradox and mental duress of *The Waste Lands*, requiring the dead-alive Jake to rejoin the ka-tet and reconcile (?) the paradox. For simplicity's sake, I'll say two and a half deaths, as guilt is the issue, not quantum mechanics.

16. King, *The Dark Tower*, 824.

17. King, *The Dark Tower*, 827.

18. There is a recurring theme in Hindu and Buddhist teaching that personal desire and attachment to material ends are primary sources of karma. Recognizing the impermanence of existence and transcending desire is key to escaping the cycle of death and rebirth.

19. Demariaux, *How to Understand Hinduism*, 44.

6

WHAT'S WRONG WITH ROLAND?

Utilitarianism and the Dark Tower

Greg Littmann

"Please, not again! Have pity! Have mercy!"—Roland Deschain, *The Dark Tower*

Poor Roland! He travels thousands of grueling miles on his quest for the Dark Tower, through territory so inhospitable and dangerous that civilization is dying. He loses years of his life, two of his fingers, and all of his closest friends. But if not for Roland's sacrifice and dedication, every universe would be destroyed. Silvery thinnies in reality would be opening up behind us right now with a screeching warble, and tentacles would be dragging us off screaming into the darkness of todash space. And after all Roland has done for everyone everywhere, what is his reward? He doesn't get so much as a cold drink of water and a tooter-fish popkin at the Tower, just a one-way trip back to the hellish Mohaine Desert to begin his quest again.

There are supernatural rules Roland needs to follow to complete his quest, and until he does, he's going to keep being sent back to the start of *The Gunslinger*.[1] The need to figure out supernatural rules is a common theme in quest fantasy. The Hobbits must learn the dangers of the One Ring in order to get it to Mordor, and Dorothy needs to learn to click her ruby slippers together to get back to Kansas. But what makes Roland's quest particularly interesting is that, as in many versions of the quest for the Holy Grail, the supernatural rules require the hero to change the way he approaches his life before he will be allowed to succeed. When Roland reaches the Tower, he's morally judged and found unworthy. But why? What's wrong with Roland?

The Tower, which is also the creator god Gan, helpfully shows Roland where it thinks he went wrong, just before unhelpfully erasing his memory of the lesson. On each of the Tower's floors, Roland is shown a scene from his life, with particular emphasis on the times he hurt people: "This is a place of death, he thought, and not just here. All these rooms. Every floor. Yes, gunslinger, whispered the Voice of the Tower. But only because your life has made it so."[2]

The Tower begins its report on Roland's moral failings by showing him at fourteen, sacrificing his hawk, David, so that he can defeat Cort, win his guns, and stand up to Marten Broadcloak. Later it shows his one true love, Susan Delgado, burning to death on a Charyou tree fire in Hambry, because he had set off on his quest for the Dark Tower rather than returning to make sure that she would not suffer at the townsfolks' hands for having helped him. We don't get a description of every scene Roland sees, but it becomes clear enough in what way the Tower thinks Roland has made his life "a place of death." He's been sacrificing the lives of others to further his goals.

Lack of concern for other people is the blight of Mid-World. Before the fall of Gilead, the rich of In-World care little for the poor. The salt mine owners of Debaria exploit their workers, keeping them in debt and subjecting them to harsh and dangerous conditions, the landowners of Tree seek to buy land for a pittance from poor farmers who can't pay their taxes, and the powerful Horseman's Association of Hambry take the life and lands of anyone who defies them. Meanwhile, the harriers loot and destroy until they bring Mid-World's civilization to collapse. Even ordinary folks are losing their sense of social responsibility, like Susan Delgado's aunt Cordelia, who plans to sell Susan to be the gilly of Hambry's mayor. Within a few hundred years of the fall of Gilead, individuals who care only for their own pleasure are working to speed the fall of the Tower. The Breakers in Devar-Toi love the "good mind" bliss of breaking and don't care that they are destroying everything. They get simulated sex, excellent meals, and no longer have to put up with a society that mostly rejected them, so why should they care?

But Roland's focus on his own goals is not like this selfishness. After all, Roland's goals involve *protecting* great numbers of people. When he sacrifices David, he does it to allow him to face Marten, whose cruel schemes and affair with the wife of Gilead's leader endanger the entire world. Sure, Roland would like revenge on Marten, too, since the estranged couple in question are his mom and dad, but he's defending society all the same. The stakes are even higher when he sacrifices Susan, since by then he's questing for the Dark Tower, fighting to save every universe from annihilation. Roland hurts other people, but he almost always does it for the greater good. The Tower calls itself a "place of death" because of the deaths Roland has brought about, but if he had failed in his quest by not focusing on it hard enough, there would be nothing but death for everyone. Given which, it is easy to feel that Roland isn't being judged fairly when the Tower finds him morally lacking. We might decide to judge Roland innocent instead. Maybe Roland is just fine and it's the Tower that needs fixing!

A GUNSLINGER'S GOTTA DO
WHAT A GUNSLINGER'S GOTTA DO

Consequentialism is the moral theory that the rightness or wrongness of an action depends entirely on how good or bad the consequences are. The right thing to do is whatever will bring about the best consequences, regardless of the means by which you bring them about. The ends justify the means. The most popular form of consequentialism is utilitarianism, the moral theory that the only thing good in itself is pleasure and the only bad thing bad in itself is suffering. Our actions are morally right if they maximize pleasure and minimize suffering.

That might make it sound as if we should spend our lives trying to have a good time, like the Breakers and weed-eaters, or the drunks in the saloon playing Watch Me and singing "Hey Jude" and "Adelina Says She's Randy-O." On the contrary, since only pleasure and suffering matter in themselves, we must treat everyone's pleasure and suffering as just as important as our own. Only the sum total of pleasure and suffering matter, not who has it. In the words of one of utilitarianism's founders, English philosopher Jeremy Bentham (1748–1832): "It is the greatest happiness of the greatest number that is the measure of right and wrong."[3] This rules out harming people if the benefit we bring about does not outweigh the harm, so we mustn't do things like squeeze the poor for tax, raid towns as a harrier, molest kids like the Gray tribe of Lud, or destroy the world for our own benefit like the Breakers (polluters of earth, I see you very well). More demanding yet, utilitarianism requires us to actively help people whenever we can increase happiness and reduce suffering by doing so, whether we would rather be playing Watch Me or not. Historically, utilitarians have campaigned for welfare for the poor, the abolition of slavery, political equality for women, prison reform, and rights for children and animals, among other humanitarian causes.

Willingness to help others is a rare virtue in Mid-World, in which the growing anarchy increasingly leaves people to fend for themselves. Do-gooders are sneered at. When Roland is passing through Tull, a kid who helps him with directions has his playmates turn on him in disgust, their eyes "ugly and hostile" as they call him a weed-eater and inquire how long he's been "screwin'" his sister. Roland, of course, is different. No hardship is too great for him to endure as he strives to rescue us all. To be fair, he is saving himself as well. If the Dark Tower falls, he'll be a thinny's dinner like the rest of us. Still, given the odds stacked against him, Roland's personal best interests probably lie in doing things he enjoys while reality lasts: dallying with ladies, swapping stories around a fire, and, judging by his enthusiasm in *Wolves of the Calla*, dancing up a storm. The Breakers, who live only for themselves, are "morks," people who don't form close relationships with other people. This explains, in part, why they are content that their own existence is pleasurable and don't worry about the damage they do. Yet even when Roland has his fewest personal ties, as the lone hunter of *The Gunslinger*, he is no less relentless in our service. As the only hope of everyone, he gives everything for the quest. Even before he receives the quest, he dedicates his life to society, risking death for the public good as a young gunslinger facing the supporters of John Farson in Hambry and the shape-changing skin-man in Debaria. To the utilitarian, such selflessness makes Roland a hero.

Utilitarians would likewise approve of other characters in the series who commit themselves to the common good. Steven Deschain, Cuthbert Allgood, Jamie DeCurry, and Alain Johns are as dedicated to their duty as gunslingers as Roland. So, later, are Jake Chambers, and Eddie and Susannah Dean. Susannah (as Odetta) fought for civil rights for African Americans in the fifties and sixties, though this put her in considerable danger and got her arrested at least once. Likewise, Sheriff Hugh Peavy of Debaria bravely tries to hold back the crime and corruption that is destroying his town, the Sisters of Serenity care for the confused Gabrielle Deschain and orphaned Bill Streeter, and Widow Smack of Tree takes it upon herself to educate the village children and to help the ones in need, like Tim Ross. As for Tim, he eventually becomes a gunslinger after he's the only one in Tree brave enough to join a posse some gunslingers are raising. In defiance of the genre conventions of post-apocalyptic literature, the most flourishing society in Mid-World is also the one that cares most about strangers. The people of the Callas, who are welcoming to outsiders like Roland's *ka-tet*, live relatively well-ordered lives without the sorts of brutality seen in towns closer to In-World. They are even served by a charitable order, the Sisters of Oriza, who work as doctors and midwives.

SUSANNAH THROWS HER GUN AWAY

Like Roland, other giving characters often find that serving the public good requires them to make heavy sacrifices. Cuthbert, Jamie, Alain, and all the other gunslingers but Roland die at the Battle of Jericho Hill as they attempt to save civilization. Jake is fatally struck by a Dodge minivan when he shields Stephen King with his body, Eddie is shot in the head by the warden of Devar-Toi during the attack on the prison, and Oy is impaled on a branch where Mordred tossed him. The Widow Smack gets her throat cut by Big Kells for daring to help Tim Ross, while the people of the Callas, and the Sisters of Oriza in particular, have many of their number blown apart by sneetches in their stand against the mechanical Wolves from Thunderclap. The religious head of Calla Bryn Sturgis, Father Callahan, has consistently suffered for the sake of others. In *'Salem's Lot*, he stands up against the vampire Barlow to save twelve-year-old Mark Petrie, only to be forced to drink the vampire's blood and to become a broken man, an exile from his town and his universe. Callahan achieves a rare double martyrdom when he dies twice to avoid capture by vampires, first by throwing himself out the window of a tall building, and later by putting a bullet in his own head in the Dixie Pig diner.

Most people will agree with utilitarians that self-sacrifice is praise-worthy. However, under utilitarianism, self-sacrifice is not just praise-worthy, but *compulsory*. If you can reduce overall suffering by making a sacrifice, then you have a moral duty to do so, no matter how great that sacrifice is. Many philosophers think that these demands are too heavy. They believe that by turning everything that it would be good to do into something that we must do, utilitarianism fails to respect the impor-tance of our individual desires and relationships.

Philosophers consider hypothetical situations, known as "thought ex-periments," to see if they can find cases in which a theory would give the wrong answer, disproving the theory. Any work of fiction is already a series of thought experiments, just waiting to be used. Let's see if we can find cases where utilitarianism seems too demanding.

Under utilitarianism, Susannah had no right to quit the quest for the Dark Tower after Jake and Eddie die. Explicitly choosing life over the good, she leaves, "because Roland's way was the way of the gun. Ro-land's way was death for those who rode or walked beside him. . . . It was all for the good (for what he called the White), she had no doubt of it, but Eddie still lay in his grave in one world and Jake in another."[4] The utilitarian would say that it doesn't matter what she feels, given everything at stake. Regardless of how much it would cause her to suffer to continue with the quest, and how much future pleasure she would miss out on if she dies on the road to the Tower, unless her suffering and loss outweigh all the suffering and loss that would be caused by the end of the universes, she has no moral right to give up. Likewise, under utilitarianism, if any kid can best serve his society by training to be a gunslinger, then that is what he must do, even if in his heart he'd rather be an architect, an artist, or a cowboy. No matter how much Cort shouts at him or punches him in the face, as he punched Cuthbert, he must not quit. Courageous political action, like that taken by Susannah (Odetta), is mandatory wherever it is needed. What's more, when we choose how to act politically, we must not be influenced by which issues affect us personally or which we personally care about most, only where we can do the most good.

Even our personal relationships must be guided by the needs of utility. The utilitarian would say that fourteen-year-old Roland does wrong when he lets his heart guide him in his love affair with Susan Delgado of Hambry. Roland's father is poised to become *dinh* of In-

World and the stability of civilization depends on him. Susan is the daughter of a cattle drover from a provincial town, and someone to whom Roland must explain Gilead manners, like which hand to use when tapping the throat in greeting. Roland does not consider whether Susan will be an asset in court or whether his affections should be directed to the daughters of powerful nobility in order to secure their loyalty. His parents want him to marry Aileen Ritter. How will she feel about Susan? Moreover, by impregnating Susan, Roland may produce a future claimant to Steven's power and a contributor to political instability. To the utilitarian, these concerns should be foremost in Roland's mind, not whether Susan makes him feel hot and cold at the same time. But does utilitarianism go too far in demanding that even true love must yield to the public good?

ROLAND'S REFORMATION: GIVING UP HUMAN SACRIFICE

As if the need for self-sacrifice under utilitarianism is not trouble enough, the theory also demands that we sacrifice *other* people if that will serve the greater good, whether those people want to be sacrificed or not. Many philosophers consider such sacrifices unacceptable, and conclude that utilitarianism must be false. Sacrificing others in just this way is treated by the Tower as Roland's greatest sin. It's certainly a defining characteristic of the gunslinger as a young man. Before he turns fifteen, he's already sacrificed David, his pet, and Susan, his one true love. Not long after, he's sent to Debaria with his friends Cuthbert and Jamie to solve the mystery of the murderous skin-man and decides to risk the life of an eleven-year-old to catch the killer. Bill Streeter is the only living witness but only saw the skin-man's leg. Roland spreads the lie that Streeter knows what the killer looks like, since this will force the skin-man to attempt to kill him, too, allowing Roland to set a trap. Jamie is horrified by the way Roland puts Bill at risk by turning him into bait, though he understands that not setting the trap could risk the lives of many other children and adults, too. Most dramatically, Roland lets his friend Jake fall to his death beneath the Cyclopean Mountains rather than going back to save him, so that he does not lose the man in black after chasing him for twelve years. "Come now gunslinger. Or catch me never!"[5] the man in black promises. Roland hates allowing the boy to die, but with all of Mid-World at stake, he leaves Jake and scrambles on.

Human sacrifice is a traditional sin of Mid-World civilization, one that has sped the breakdown of the universes. The speaking rings, of the sort that Roland visits to receive demonic prophecy and to draw Jake into his world, were the sites of sacrifice by the ancient Druits, which is why reality is thin there. In the days of Arthur Eld, humans were sacrificed on Charyou tree fires to propitiate the gods of Reap and ensure a plentiful harvest. Keeping the tradition alive, the Pubes in the ruined city of Lud perform human sacrifice every day because they believe it will stop the ghosts of the dead rising up to eat the living. Roland tells Sister Jenna of the Little Sisters of Eluria that in the religions of Mid-World "God always drank blood."[6] This presumably also applies to the imported religion of the Man Jesus, since Jesus was a human sacrifice, too.

Over the course of the Dark Tower series, Roland diagnoses his own failings and changes the way he lives. Regretting the degree to which he has sacrificed others in the past, he stops treating the needs of other people as irrelevant in the face of his quest for the Tower, and begins to make them a priority. Whereas in *The Gunslinger*, Roland is so fixated on his quest that he lets Jake fall to his death rather than risk letting the man in black get away, by *The Waste Lands*, he's ready to risk his life, and thus his quest, to save Jake from the violently sadistic, child-raping Grays of Lud. Roland explains to Eddie, "I have already played the betrayer more than once. To my shame. But . . . I think those days are over. We are one, *ka-tet*. If I betray any one of you—even Jake's furry friend, perhaps—I betray myself."[7] Starting with *Wolves of the Calla*, Roland increasingly looks to protect people in general, and not just those close to him. In Calla Bryn Sturgis, he risks his life battling against the Wolves to liberate the Calla towns.

It may be that Roland thinks rescuing Jake and defeating the Wolves gives him his best chance to find the Tower before it falls. After all, he knows that Jake's *ka* is entangled with his own and that the Wolves are speeding the Tower's destruction by supplying children's brain chemicals to the Breakers in Devar-Toi. But saving the Tower as quickly as possible is not his primary motivation. Rather, he saves Jake because he *loves* Jake, not because Jake is an important tool. Likewise, Roland makes it clear that he's defending the Callas for their own sake, not simply because it advances his quest. He explains to Susannah, "We have to help them because it's the Way of Eld . . . and because the way of ka is always the way of duty."[8] Roland has learned not to be so obsessive about the Tower and to care for the people around him.

This relationship-focused morality, based on the sharing of *khef* (the feeling of the bonds of relationship), is a tradition in Mid-World. Mid-Worlders even refer to moral failure as "forgetting the face of your father," turning all moral failings into failings to fulfill responsibilities in personal relationships. Not to act well is to offend against your dad. Appropriately, when Tim Ross acquires three magic objects in Roland's story, he thinks only about how he can use these to rescue his mother. A napkin that protects from weather, a feather that allows flight, and a bottle of drops that cure blindness might do a lot of good in afflicted Mid-World if applied where they are most needed. For instance, those eyedrops might restore the sight of an important gunslinger who has many lives depending on him, or of an honest baron whose people suffer oppression because he can't see what his corrupt counselors are doing. Utilitarians would say that such social considerations should be Tim's primary concern, yet it never occurs to him to do other than save the person he cares most about.

VAMPIRISM, TRUE LOVE, AND OTHER SELFISH VICES

For all that, I think utilitarianism is right and that we can have a moral duty to make such sacrifices. Let's consider some further thought experiments that might make the existence of a duty to sacrifice more plausible. If we can find theoretical cases, however strange, where you say that extreme self-sacrifice is morally required, then you'll have to accept that extreme self-sacrifice can in principle be morally required. Likewise, if we can find cases where you say that the sacrifice of innocents is morally required, you'll have to accept that the sacrifice of innocents can be morally required. Then it only remains to decide where to draw the line.

So could extreme self-sacrifice ever be morally required? You probably think that it is for those monsters who must prey on humans to live. Vampires feed on our blood, the were-insect Dandelo who holds artist Patrick Danville captive feeds painfully on our emotions, and the demonic sex vampires that roam the ruins feed lethally on sex (I assume that sex vampires die if they don't "eat" but maybe they just get moody and irritable). Do you object to being on the vampire menu down at the Dixie Pig? Do you think that the "ancient ones" there, with eyes "as black as blindness" and "the skin of their cheeks and brows—even the backs of their hands—tumorous with wild teeth"[9] do something immoral when they make feasts of the likes of you and me? If so, then you think that they have a duty to give up their "lives" for you and all the other humans who must die if they are to survive.

The extent to which we think people have a duty to be self-sacrificing tends to depend on whom we empathize with. When we put ourselves in the place of the one asked to do the sacrificing, as we tend to when following heroic characters in fiction, we are readier to set limits to what an individual can be asked to give up. As we imagine ourselves as Jake, with the minivan agonizingly crushing our ribs, the idea that the boy has a duty to die like this can seem too brutal. On the other hand, looking at self-sacrifice from the perspective of the ones who need the sacrifice, as we do when we consider ourselves as vampire chow, starts to make utilitarian calculations look more appealing. Of course those monsters should give up their own lives rather than drinking so many of us![10]

Similarly, the idea that we might have a duty to sacrifice relationships that are important to us is more plausible when we consider the perspective of those who would benefit from such sacrifice. Fairy tale and romance have popularized the notion that young nobility like Roland should marry for love rather than politics. The idea is easy to swallow when we place ourselves in the position of one of the starry-eyed young lovers. But those fairy tales never show the price of true love being paid in the blood of strangers. Imagine yourself instead in the position of a poor saddler whose town was burned and family murdered by harriers because fourteen-year-old Roland liked Susan more than Aileen Ritter. Looking at the carnage around you and reflecting on all the other families lying slain in their own blood, you might be more sympathetic to the view that sometimes we should sacrifice our relationships for the good of others. Roland himself takes the right attitude when he declares that choosing his quest over Susan and his unborn child is something he is obliged to do: "I was given a choice: Susan, and my life as her husband and father of the child she now carries . . . or the

Tower. . . . I would choose Susan in an instant, if not for one thing: the Tower is crumbling, and if it falls, everything we know will be swept away. There will be chaos beyond our imagining. We must go. . . . I choose the Tower. I must."[11]

LETTING JAKE DROP INTO THE ABYSS

The utilitarian requirement that we sacrifice innocents in certain cases not only puts unusual moral demands on us, it also requires us to break moral rules that we would normally obey. Under normal circumstances, letting a child fall to his death because you were busy would obviously be morally outrageous. But sometimes we should break the moral rules that we should follow in normal circumstances. It is an important moral rule of thumb that we shouldn't tell lies. But there are times when lying is appropriate. When Steven Deschain sends Roland, Cuthbert, and Alain to Mejis to investigate whether the barony is going over to John Farson, he rightly sends them undercover, posing as Will Dearborn, Arthur Heath, and Richard Stockworth, respectively. Promise breaking can be right, as when Ted Brautigan and other rebel Breakers who had promised to serve loyally in Devar-Toi help Roland's ka-tet attack De-var-Toi instead. Theft can be right, as when Jake and Callahan steal money for taxi fare from a New York City hotel maid. Kidnapping can be right, as when Roland kidnaps Irene Tassenbaum of Manhattan when he needs her car and someone to drive it to Stephen King's house. Even killing can be right, most obviously when it is done in self-defense, as when the armies of the alliance stand against Farson's harriers. In a dangerous place like Mid-World, even the prioress of the Sisters of Serenity must keep a butcher's knife strapped to her calf. Killing can even be rightly done for the protection of others, as when Roland and his ka-tet gun down the dangerous taheen, can-toi, and human guards at Devar-Toi.

Quite likely, you agree that in some extreme circumstances, we should lie, break promises, steal, kidnap, or kill. But you might still not accept that there could *ever* be circumstances where we should sacrifice the innocent. You might say that while there are some general moral rules that have exceptions, there are other moral rules that simply must not be broken, and the rule against sacrificing innocents is one of them.

However, the rule that we must never sacrifice innocents doesn't seem to hold in all cases. For instance, as the people of Mid-World know, it is impossible to use violence without innocents sometimes suffering. When Susan tries to rescue Roland's ka-tet from the Hambry jail, she accidentally shoots "Deputy Dave" Hollis in the heart. At the Battle of Jericho Hill, Roland and Cuthbert accidentally gun down Alain in the sort of "friendly fire" incident that happens in every war. The battle in Calla Bryn Sturgis against the Wolves leaves not only several of the adult townsfolk dead, but also Jake's young friend, Benny Slightman, blown to bits by a sneetch.

In our own world, we condemn innocent people to death whenever we fight a war, even a defensive one. We don't know which of the soldiers who fight in our name are going to die, but we do know that we are sending a number of them to their deaths. Often, enemy soldiers are conscripts who are being forced to fight, and there will always be some civilian casualties, including children. We could refuse to participate in wars by surrendering at once to any aggressor, but the cost would be too great, and so innocents must die. We should hate to condemn innocents to death just as we should hate war itself, but like war, the sacrifice of the innocent can sometimes be our best option. Even in peace, it can't be that we may never permit innocents to die when we could have saved them. We could always spend more tax dollars on foreign aid, public health, and child protective services, just to name three ways of saving innocent lives. Wherever we draw the line on spending, we set a monetary value on life.

We might even have a duty to sacrifice an innocent we have a personal relationship with. Consider Ben Slightman senior of Calla Bryn Sturgis. Slightman sells out his community to save his only son, Benny. He secretly informs on his town to Andy the robot in return for Andy ensuring that Benny will not be selected by Wolves to be taken and "roont" by having chemicals removed from his brain. Slightman protects his own son, but at the cost of sabotaging any resistance his town might take against the Wolves, and thus condemning many other children to being roont. In this case, we empathize with all the kids and parents in the town and can see that it would be better to sacrifice (or at least endanger) the innocent Benny to serve the greater good.

Roland and Susannah themselves do their best to kill their son, the spidery Mordred, for the greater good. Susannah fires at him, though she only succeeds in shooting off one of his legs. Roland is more successful, dispatching his baby with one bullet to the face and three to the belly. Yet since Mordred is newly born, we can't hold him to blame for anything. It's true, by the time Susannah tries to kill him, he's already killed his other mother, Mia, and sucked her corpse dry down to a big dust bunny, but this doesn't show that he knew what he was doing. Babies put everything in their mouths. Even when he's a few hours older with a bit more murder under his belt, he's had no guidance and no experience of people and the world. As the Tower points out, the child never knew love and was excluded from the bonds of friendly *tet*.

This is hard on Mordred, but would you want Susannah and Roland to act differently, given the terrible danger Mordred poses? The Crimson King plans to use Mordred to bring the apocalypse, and according to prophecy, Mordred is going to kill Roland, topple the Tower, and destroy every universe. We can't know how the lonely boy might have reformed if Roland or Susannah had welcomed him instead, throwing open their arms with a traditional Mid-World cry of "Penny, posy, Jack's a-nosy! Do ya say so? Yes I do-so! He's my sneaky, peeky, darling bah-bo!" Yet the risk to everyone of sparing Mordred's life is too great, since sparing Mordred seems likely to result in the quest's failure. Even if Mordred is savable, Roland doesn't have time to connect with his baby son and try to raise him right. By the time Mordred is born, four of the six beams holding the universes together have already collapsed, and if Roland stops to try to play "This Sma' Piggie" with Mordred's spider feet, he can expect the final beams to disintegrate in the meantime. His need to get to the Tower means that instead of an embrace, he must greet his son with bullets. Mordred must be sacrificed for the greater good.

But maybe you don't accept that Mordred is innocent. Perhaps you regard him as naturally blameworthy in virtue of being naturally malicious, or think that the choices he made in his short life eliminate the innocence that he might have claimed at birth. If so, I have one last thought experiment to offer to convince you that sacrificing the innocent can be our moral duty. If this won't do it, I'll cry off and let you be.

Let's return to Jake hanging over the abyss, his fingers clutching a railroad trestle that is slowly bending under his weight. "Help me," he begs Roland as the trestle descends ever farther toward the chasm, the metal "screaming" from the strain. Now let's add a twist. Let's say that for Roland to rescue Jake doesn't merely risk the quest, but like sparing Mordred, makes it *very likely* that the Tower will fall. Should Roland sacrifice the child and sprint after the man in black, or should he stop to help Jake at the likely cost of everything?

Still not sure? Let's dial this up to nineteen. Let's say that rescuing Jake would make it *certain* that the Tower would fall and all universes would die. Let's say . . . oh, that the man in black has a North Central Positronics transmitter in his hand, set up to send a signal that detonates dynamite packed around the base of the Tower, blowing it to todash space. To keep the Western feel, let's give the transmitter a T-shaped plunger to press, like the one bandits use to blow up railroads in movies. Now let's say that the man in black is getting ready to depress the plunger and destroy the universes, laughing maniacally all the while. "Come now, gunslinger. Or catch me never!" he sneers. Let's also allow that once the Tower is gone, the universes will move on slowly enough for Jake to live out his natural life if Roland helps him, so saving the boy really is in Roland's power . . . if he'll just condemn reality to certain doom.

Consider how badly everyone in every universe would prefer to continue existing rather than suffering a horrible death as all the universes move on. Now add to that the loss of all those people who would have been born if the universes had not disintegrated, along with every relationship they would have had and everything they would have achieved. We are only seriously considering everyone involved if we keep our sense of the enormous scale of the loss we are weighing against Jake's life. We can't think of it in the way we would think of a relatively measly loss like the death of everyone in New York City or the end of all life on earth. This is every universe gone forever!

If you will grant as little as this—that Roland should let Jake die if the alternative is the certain end of everything—then you have given up the principle that we must never sacrifice the innocent for the greater good. All that remains to determine is where to draw the line. How high do the stakes have to be before Roland should let Jake drop? As a utilitarian, I say that Roland should do his best to determine whether stopping to save Jake will give him a better or worse chance of reaching the Dark Tower. If saving Jake is most likely to help, he should save him; if stopping to save Jake makes it more likely that the quest will fail, he should let him die.

ROLAND DESCHAIN IS INNOCENT!

That's why I find Roland innocent. As a utilitarian, I think that the Dark Tower is in error when it judges Roland to be morally lacking for the sacrifices he has made. Instead of rejecting him and sending him back to try again, it should register his success, lighting up and vomiting coins like a slot machine, or whatever it does when Roland finally gets it right. This is not to criticize Stephen King, whose job is to take us on a gripping adventure, not to describe ideal magic machinery. On the other hand, North Central Positronics is way overdue for a lawsuit and I think Roland has excellent grounds.

But what does any of this have to do with our own lives—we who never get to go on quests or make life-and-death decisions while standing on the brink of an abyss? The moral certainly isn't that we should sacrifice more innocents. Utilitarians say that sacrificing innocents should almost never be done, though there are some circumstances where there are no better options. Rather, the important moral is that we must not assume that just because we are doing the right thing, we can't be hurting anyone innocent. For many people, once they become convinced that a course of action is right, they become unable to see any innocent people who are being harmed by it. To their minds, admitting that innocents are harmed would be admitting that the action is wrong. Since they can't see these innocent people, they feel no sympathy for them. But the world is not so black and white. Crying your pardon, but if you can't think of any ways innocents would be harmed by your preferred political policies, whatever those policies are, then you haven't fully thought the consequences through. I set my watch and warrant on it.

NOTES

1. For a discussion of Hindu philosophy, karma, and Roland, see chapter 5 in this volume.

2. Stephen King, *The Dark Tower* (New York: Pocket Books, 2006), 1026.

3. Jeremy Bentham, *A Fragment on Government* (Cambridge: Cambridge University Press, 1988), 3.

4. King, *The Dark Tower*, 929.

5. Stephen King, *The Gunslinger* (New York: Pocket Books, 2003), 210.

6. Stephen King, "The Little Sisters of Eluria," in *Everything's Eventual: 14 Dark Tales* (New York: Scribner, 2002), 147.

7. Stephen King, *Wizard and Glass* (New York: Pocket Books, 2003), 106.

8. Stephen King, *Wolves of the Calla* (New York: Pocket Books, 2006), 235.

9. King, *The Dark Tower*, 13.

10. Note how in *Cycle of the Werewolf* Marty sends Reverend Lowe a note asking, "Why don't you kill yourself?" Again, the point seems to be that it is the duty of the luckless lycanthropic to kill himself lest any more townspeople go missing on nights with full moons. (Even if it's not his fault that he is a werewolf.)

11. King, *Wizard and Glass*, 605.

7

STEPHEN KING AND ARISTOTELIAN FRIENDSHIP

An Analysis of *The Body* and *Rita Hayworth and the Shawshank Redemption*

Bertha Alvarez Manninen

People are often surprised to hear that Stephen King penned the two novellas that inspired the films *Stand by Me* (1986) and *The Shawshank Redemption* (1994). It's clear that King has been typecast, primarily, as a writer of horror. Yet, from my perspective, *The Body* and *Rita Hayworth and the Shawshank Redemption*, both found in the book *Different Seasons*, are some of his best work. In both stories, King explores intimate, nonsexual friendships among males (whether that be young boys in *The Body* or grown men in a prison setting in *Rita Hayworth and the Shawshank Redemption*). Consequently, both of King's stories serve as a window through which to explore two of the most important philosophical pieces ever written on the nature of friendship: Aristotle's *Nicomachean Ethics* and *Eudemian Ethics*. In addition to helping us understand Aristotle in this capacity, King's stories illustrate both instances of laudable and desirable friendships, as well as dysfunctional ones that we should strive to avoid.

DIFFERENT FRIENDSHIPS, DIFFERENT SEASONS:
THREE TYPES OF ARISTOTELIAN FRIENDSHIP

In *The Body*, four adolescent boys (Gordie Lachance [the narrator], Chris Chambers, Teddy Duchamp, and Vern Tessio) embark on a weekend trek to locate the dead body of another boy their age who had disappeared days prior. Throughout the story, they encounter many obstacles, such as fighting with the neighborhood bullies (who include Ace Merrill, and Vern's and Chris's older brothers) and coming to terms with their individual psychological demons, mostly involving their own abusive childhoods. While King portrays all the boys as close friends, Gordie and Chris share a particularly intimate bond. This kind of friendship is also present in *Rita Hayworth and the Shawshank Redemption* between Andy and Red, who, while members of a larger group of friends who band together to survive prison life, share a unique relationship with each other.

In his *Nicomachean Ethics*, Aristotle argues that having friends is an essential component to living a good life: "For no one would choose to live without friends even if he had all the other goods . . . in poverty, also, and in the other misfortunes, people think friends are the only refuge."[1] This relates back to Aristotle's view, as expressed in *The Politics*, that humans are essentially social beings who desire to live in a community, the polis, by their very nature. In *Eudemian Ethics*, Aristotle emphasizes the difficulty in coming to a single definition of friendship, for there is no essential trait that can "do justice to all the different perceptions people have [of friendship] . . . a single definition does not fit all."[2] Yet it remains true that not even the richest man can live well without relationships and social contact; "friendlessness and solitude [are] quite terrible."[3]

At first, when Andy Dufresne gets sent to Shawshank State Prison for the murder of his wife and her lover, he is reticent to have any friends and prefers to keep to himself (this is probably not an unexpected reaction when one has to deal with being falsely imprisoned). Red, the story's narrator, tells us that "Andy had no cellmate, and I'd heard that was just the way he wanted it . . . he had a reputation for being a snob and a cold fish."[4] Yet even Andy couldn't remain in solitude forever, and he eventually approaches Red, becoming friends with him and his group of prison inmates. Although he initially sought solitude as a way of dealing with his despair, eventually Andy seeks refuge in other people.

Even though any kind of friendship is vital for living a flourishing life, according to Aristotle, not all friendships are equal. He writes that there are three types of friendships, and we can find examples of all of them in King's two stories.

Like Busboys in a Restaurant:
Friendships of Utility and Pleasure

First, there are friendships among people who "love each other for utility . . . [in these kinds of friendships people] love the other not in himself, but insofar as they gain some good for themselves from him."[5] Individuals who are friends in this capacity do not form the relationship because they care to know the other individual personally, but rather because he provides services that the other finds useful. Friendships of utility are casual—the kind that you would have with your mailperson, or a store merchant whom you see on a regular basis. Often, these relationships will exist between those with opposite traits, such as "of poor to rich or ignorant to knowledgeable; for we aim at whatever we find we lack, and give something else in return."[6] Friendships of utility are easily dissolvable, insofar as they only exist so long as the mutual utility exists; once the instrumental reason behind the friendship disappears, there is nothing keeping the relationship going: "What is useful does not remain the same, but is different at different times. Hence, when the cause of their being friends is removed, the friendship is dissolved too."[7] Aristotle reminds us (in what I take to be a rather sad, albeit truthful, admission) that "most people's friendships are based on utility."[8]

Andy and Red's friendship starts as a relationship of this sort—what drove Andy to finally introduce himself to Red was his desire for certain items from the "outside": a rock hammer, rock blankets, and the coveted Rita Hayworth poster. However, their friendship successfully evolves past this stage because they become "fond of each other's characters from being accustomed to them."[9] Yet, this isn't the case with many friendships of utility. The clearest example of this can be seen between Andy and the prison guards. When Byron Hadley, the head guard, complains about the taxes he has to pay on a $35,000 inheritance, Andy, who had been a banker on the outside, offers to fill out the necessary paperwork rendering Hadley's inheritance tax-free. In return, Andy asks that Hadley compensate him by providing beers for his friends, who are hard at work tarring one of the prison's roofs. Andy's financial knowledge wins him even more esteem among the guards when he begins doing their annual income tax returns free of charge, as well as setting up trust funds for their children. Andy even uses his abilities to launder money for the prison warden, Samuel Norton. In exchange for his services, Hadley and the rest of the guards protect Andy from a group of prison rapists, who had, up until that point, repeatedly assaulted him. Moreover, Andy is given a job in the Shawshank library, and is allowed to expand the operation to help inmates receive an education. Andy's friendship with the guards and with Norton is purely utilitarian—while they each get what they want, they remain on friendly terms.

But these friendships were never based on any desire to know Andy as a person, or to ensure his welfare for his own sake; rather, any special treatment Andy received was always to ensure a benefit for his superiors. As Red notes, "There was a need for Andy's services. They took him out of the laundry and installed him in the library, but if you wanted to look at it another way, they never took him out of the laundry at all. They just set him to work washing dirty money instead of dirty sheets."[10] When Tommy Williams arrives at Shawshank prison, he comes with knowledge of the real culprit behind Andy's wife's murder. When Andy tries to share this news with the warden, Norton dismisses him, mainly because he doesn't want to lose Andy and his laundering abilities. When Andy attempts to assure Norton that he would never reveal his illegal activity if he were released, Norton turns on him: "Don't you mention money to me again . . . not in this office, not anywhere. Not unless you want to see that library turned back into a storage room and paintlocker again. Do you understand?"[11] Norton transfers Tommy to a minimum-security prison so long as he never reveals his knowledge of Andy's wife's killer (in the film, Tommy's fate is much bleaker, as Norton has Hadley kill him), and with him goes any prospect of Andy's freedom. This underscores Aristotle's points that friendships of utility do not exist out of an interest for the involved parties' welfare—they exist solely to extract some benefit. When Norton can no longer extract this benefit from Andy willfully (due to Andy's anger at losing Tommy's potential testimony), he threatens Andy with renewed sexual assault from the prison rapists in order to force him to comply.

Aristotle considers whether a friendship of this kind, especially between a good person like Andy and a clearly bad person like Norton, should rightly be called a friendship at all. This is an aspect of his view of friendship that is unclear. In *Nicomachean Ethics*, he says: "It is necessary that friends bear good will to each other and wish good things for each other."[12] By this definition, Norton and Andy wouldn't meet any definition of friendship, not even one based purely on utility, since it is unlikely that Norton has any goodwill toward Andy. Yet, in *Eudemian Ethics*, he writes as if goodwill is only part of friendships of virtue (which will be discussed below): "When friendship is divided into three kinds, goodwill is not found either in the friendship of utility or the friendship of pleasure. If you will good to another because it is useful to you to do so, it is your interest, not his, that is the motive of your wish."[13] By this definition, Norton's lack of goodwill toward Andy would be no impediment to calling their relationship a friendship of utility, since all friendships of utility lack goodwill. Moreover, Aristotle says in *Eudemian Ethics* that "it is also possible for a good man and a bad man to be friends if one is useful to the other for a particular purpose."[14] It is unclear, then, exactly how Aristotle would regard the kind of relationship shared between Andy and Norton.

The second type of friendship is referred to by Aristotle as a friendship of pleasure. Here, people become friends because they genuinely enjoy and take pleasure in each other's company: "Those who love for pleasure . . . love a witty person not because of his character, but because he is pleasant to themselves."[15] This is the kind of friendship often found among colleagues, or with peers in groups to which one belongs. These friendships are better than friendships based solely on utility, insofar as they approximate more closely friendships of virtue, because typically, the persons in these friendships do genuinely enjoy each other's company and care for each other: "These people wish to spend their days together and to live together; for this is how they gain [the good things] corresponding to their friendship."[16]

This kind of friendship is most prevalent among the young, since "their lives are guided by their feelings, and they pursue above all what is pleasant for themselves and what is near at hand."[17] Like friendships based on utility, these kinds of friendships, also, are easily dissolvable once the parties involved no longer find that they take pleasure in each other's company. Because the kinds of things one takes pleasure in are changeable, friendships of this sort, also, are ephemeral because it is based on what one takes pleasure in at the time. This is why the friendships that are formed in youth often do not last a lifetime (unless they evolve into friendships of virtue): "As [the young] grow up [what they find pleasant] changes too. Hence, they are quick to become friends, and quick to stop; for their friendship shifts with [what they find] pleasant, and the change in such pleasure is quick."[18]

This is the kind of friendship shared by the boys in *The Body*, particularly between Gordie and Chris in relation to Teddy and Vern. The boys really do genuinely enjoy being together in their tree house, where they play cards, smoke cigarettes, and look at pornographic magazines (such are the activities that twelve- and thirteen-year-old boys find pleasant). Gordie, being a creative writer, shares his stories with his interested friends. They talk about the same television shows, enjoy camping together, playfully tease each other, and band together against a common enemy when forced to confront the town bullies (however, in the end, Vern and Teddy succumb to fear and leave Chris and Gordie alone to face them). In his narrative, Gordie remembers them fondly, writing, "I never had any friends later on like the ones I had when I was twelve."[19] Clearly, there is a level of care and intimacy among the boys that is not present in friendships based solely on mutual utility.

As is revealed at the end of the story, however, Gordie and Chris break off from Vern and Teddy because a disparity eventually exists between their interests and level of maturity. After getting beat up by the neighborhood bullies, and banding together one last time because of this common experience, Gordie writes:

> When the casts came off and the bruises healed, Vern and Teddy just drifted away. They had discovered a whole new group of contemporaries that they could lord over. . . . Chris and I began to drop by [the tree house] less and less frequently, and after a while the place was theirs by default. . . . Teddy and Vern slowly became just two more faces in the halls or in three-thirty detention. We nodded and said hi. That was all. It happens. Friends come in and out of your life like busboys in a restaurant, did you ever notice that?[20]

As Aristotle notes, the young are quick to cease being friends because "their characters change as they grow up, [and] so do their pleasures."[21] Gordie and Chris go on to take college-level courses and become interested in their future education, while Teddy and Vern do not share in these ambitions (and as a result of their failure to mature, they both die young: Vern in a house fire at a party and Teddy in a car accident due to his reckless driving while under the influence of drugs and alcohol). Whatever glue kept them together when they were twelve dissolved with time and age. Friendships based on utility and pleasure fail to endure because the persons themselves, their innermost characters, are incidental to the friendship. This is what primarily distinguishes these two kinds of friendships from the most excellent kind: it is in friendships of virtue where the parties appreciate each other for their intrinsic worth and good character.

No Good Thing Ever Dies: Friendships of Virtue

After Andy escapes from prison, he leaves Red with directions and the monetary means to find him in Zihuatanejo, Mexico—the small fishing village where Andy takes up residence. In his letter to Red, Andy writes, "Remember that hope is a good thing, Red, maybe the best of things, and no good thing ever dies."[22] Aristotle argues that this is one of the defining features of the third, most complete, kind of friendship—friendships of virtue: they endure. They are an example of a good thing that never dies.

For Aristotle, friendships based on virtue are the most complete kind of friendship. Here, the parties involved in the relationship are friends not solely because they extract some sort of mutual service from the other (whether that be pleasure, or some other end), but because they appreciate and care for each other as a person—their admiration and love of each other's character is the glue that keeps them together. According to Aristotle, what cements these friendships is mutual goodness—the parties involved must be good people and share similar values (a saintly person couldn't be intimate friends with an unrepentant murderer because they would not be "similar in virtue"). Moreover, they take interest in each other's welfare, and prize what is good for the other, rather than simply what is good for the self:

> But complete friendship is the friendship of good people similar in
> virtue; for they wish goods in the same way to each other in so far as
> they are good, and they are good in themselves. [Hence they wish
> goods to each other for each other's own sake.] Now those who wish
> goods to their friend for the friend's own sake are friends most of all;
> for they have this attitude because of the friend himself, not coinci-
> dentally. Hence these people's friendships last as long as they are
> good; and virtue is enduring.[23]

Like friendships of pleasure and utility, friends of this sort derive
benefit from each other's presence (at the very minimum, they find it
pleasurable to be together), but that benefit is not the primary reason
they are friends—the pleasurable aspects could dissipate and the
friendship would remain because the person remains, and it is the person himself who is the object of love and care. As much as I enjoy
performing activities with my best friend (watching films, reading together, painting), the friendship would not go away if she became unable to do those activities.

Aristotle also notes that these friendships tend to be the most rare,
take the most time to develop, and require a level of care and intimacy
that cannot be found among a large group (thus he cautions against
having too many "close" friends). Trust is also much stronger in this
kind of a relationship, and so these friends are likely to confide in each
other more, and to not believe, when told by a third party, that their
friend has slandered them:

> Moreover, it is only the friendship of good people that is immune to
> slander. For it is hard to trust anyone speaking against someone
> whom we ourselves have found reliable for a long time; and among
> good people there is also trust, the belief that he would never do an
> injustice [to a friend], and all the other things expected in a true
> friendship. But in the other types of friendship [distrust] may easily
> arise.[24]

In addition to caring for the welfare of the friend above any self-
serving desires, parties in a friendship of virtue help each other become
better human beings: "Good people's life together allows the cultivation
of virtue."[25] Friends of this kind also like to spend much time together
not just in enjoyment of common activities, like in friendships of pleas-

ure, but also to experience more intimate activities, such as "shared conversation and thought."[26]

What separates Andy and Red's friendship from that of the other inmates, and what separates Chris and Gordie's friendship from that with Teddy and Vern, is that these two sets of friends come the closest to Aristotle's account of friendships of virtue. Andy and Red are the only two inmates (that we see in the story) whose friendship endures; it spans several decades, and lasts beyond their time in prison. Their shared conversations, especially when alone together, consist of more intimate issues, such as Red's guilt over the crime he had committed that brought him to Shawshank, the lament of their lost years due to their respective sentences, and Andy's dreams of living in Zihuatanejo if he were to ever leave prison (later the reader discovers that this was Andy's way of letting Red know how to find him). Andy confides in Red, and only him, about the ways he has successfully laundered Norton's money (through creating the alias "Paul Stevens," whose identity Andy later assumes upon his escape in order to retrieve the laundered money). It is clear that the kinds of "shared conversations and thought" in which they engage is of a qualitatively different kind than the casual and pleasant conversations they share with their other friends.

Aristotle emphasizes that in friendships of virtue the participants deeply and genuinely care for the welfare of the other. It would have been easy for Andy to have forgotten about Red after his escape from prison—instead, he went to great lengths to provide Red the opportunity to join him in Zihuatanejo. Andy goes as far as leaving behind $1,000 for Red to find, even though he could never be sure Red would indeed discover the money and, if he did, whether he would use it to come to Zihuatanejo. Andy's actions illustrate not only an incredible depth of trust between them, but a genuine concern for Red's welfare (since Red had previously expressed doubts about his ability to survive outside of prison), and a desire to spend their remaining years together (indeed, Aristotle writes that when it comes to friendships based on virtue, "nothing is as proper to friends as living together").[27]

When Andy escapes, Red deeply mourns his loss, but consoles himself by remembering that Andy never belonged in prison in the first place, and that his freedom was the best thing for him:

> Some birds are not meant to be caged, that's all. Their feathers are
> too bright, their songs too sweet and wild. So you let them go, or
> when you open the cage to feed them they somehow fly out past you.
> And the part of you that knows it was wrong to imprison them in the
> first place rejoices, but still, the place where you live is that much
> more drab and empty for their departure.[28]

Someone who takes so much pleasure and comfort in the good fortune
of his friend, even when that fortune entails suffering for himself, is
undoubtedly the kind of friend who does "wish good to their friend for
the friend's own sake."[29]

Despite Aristotle's contention that the young mainly concern themselves with friendships of pleasure, Gordie and Chris's relationship mirrors that of Red and Andy's in many relevant respects. They share
personal conversations and confidences that they do not share with the
others. Chris, for example, reveals to Gordie that, after he stole the
class's milk money and returned it to the teacher, the teacher turned
around and kept the money herself, allowing Chris to take the blame.
As he tells this story, Chris is on the verge of crying, something a "tough
guy" like him would never do in front of the other boys. Believing that
he is doomed to repeat the same mistakes of his alcoholic father and
hoodlum brother, and also believing that Gordie's talent for writing is
his key to getting out of Castle Rock and attaining a successful life,
Chris encourages Gordie to break off the friendship with the three of
them:

> Those stories you tell, they're no good to anybody but you, Gordie. If
> you go along with us just because you don't want the gang to break
> up, you'll wind up just another grunt, making C's to get on the teams.
> You'll get to High and take the same fuckin shop courses and throw
> erasers and pull your meat along with the rest of the grunts. Get
> detentions. Fuckin *suspensions*. And after a while all you'll care
> about is getting a car so you can take some skag to the hops or down
> to the fuckin Twin Bridges Tavern. Then you'll knock her up and
> spend the rest of your life in the mill or some fuckin shoe shop in
> Auburn or maybe even up to Hillcrest pluckin chickens. And that pie
> story will never get written down. *Nothin'*ll get written down. Cause
> you'll just be another wise guy with shit for brains.[30]

Here, Chris pushes Gordie away in the hopes that his friend's life would be far better than his own. Like Red, Chris puts aside his own happiness in order to do what he perceives is best for his friend.

The difference in intimacy between Gordie and Chris's friendship when compared to Teddy and Vern is clearly seen when, in the midst of confronting Ace and his gang, Teddy and Vern abandon Chris, who is holding the bullies off with a gun. But Gordie stays right with him, even after Ace specifically targets him for violence: "Vern gave in first, with a wailing scream. He fled up the embankment in huge, gangling strides. Teddy held out a minute longer, then ran after Vern, his hands held up over his head. . . . 'Stick with me, Gordie,' Chris said in a low, shaky voice. 'Stick with me, man.' 'I'm right here.'"[31]

In the film *Stand by Me*, this difference is humorously highlighted when Chris and Gordie's personal conversation is contrasted with Teddy and Vern's. While the former two discuss their future lives and prospects, how they are perceived by society, and how they deal with their abusive home lives, the latter two are enthralled in a conversation concerning who would win a fight between Superman and Mighty Mouse.

Aristotle's claim that friends of this sort help in the cultivation of each other's virtue is clearly illustrated when Gordie spends years tutoring Chris in an effort to help him improve his education and inch closer to college—something no one in their neighborhood, including Chris himself, thought he was capable of doing. Throughout those years, Gordie emphasizes how much they relied on each other for continued strength and mutual support, and how devastated he was when Chris died:

> Chris enrolled in the college courses in his second year of junior high. . . . Everyone jawed him about it: his parents, who thought he was putting on airs, his friends, most of whom dismissed him as a pussy, the guidance counsellor, who didn't believe he could do the work, and most of all the teachers, who didn't approve of this duck-tailed, leather-jacketed, engineer-booted apparition who had materialized without warning in their classrooms. . . . We studied together almost every night, sometimes for as long as six hours at a stretch. . . . We both dated through high school, but no girl ever came between us . . . it was our only survival. We were clinging to each other in deep water. I've explained about Chris, I think; my reasons for cling-

ing to him were less definable. His desire to get away from Castle
Rock and out of the mill's shadow seemed to me to be my best part,
and I could not just leave him to sink or swim on his own. If he had
drowned, that part of me would have drowned with him. . . . When I
read the news [that he had died], I told my wife I was going out for a
milkshake. I drove out of town, parked, and cried for him.[32]

Gordie was so invested in Chris's success and well-being that he
would have suffered had Chris not made it out of Castle Rock (which he
did—by becoming a lawyer). Clearly, this is a relationship where each
party is deeply invested in the other's welfare, where they "rejoice for
no other reason than his partner is rejoicing."[33] By Gordie referring to
Chris's dreams and hopes as the "best part" of himself, this illustrates a
friendship where their identities were deeply intertwined. Red talks
about Andy in this way, too, describing him as "the part of me they
could never lock up, the part of me that will rejoice when the gates
finally open for me and I walk out."[34] In this sense, these two sets of
friends mirror Aristotle's famous quote that "true friends share a single
soul."[35]

One of the reasons Aristotle maintains that the young are not capable of friendships of virtue, in addition to having transient desires and
interests, is that friendships of this sort need time to develop: "You
cannot make a friend without trial or in a single day; you need time."[36]
While this is a piece of conventional wisdom that likely rings true for
many, we shouldn't be quick to dismiss the kind of emotional attach-
ments young people are capable of forming. While no doubt Chris and
Gordie's friendship grew deeper with time, it is clear that their relationship approximated a friendship of virtue even when they were boys. But
while King's two novellas can provide a valuable opportunity to study
the different kinds of Aristotelian friendships, there are also examples
in the books that present challenges to Aristotle's account.

IMPORTANT THINGS ARE THE HARDEST TO SAY: SOME
DIFFICULTIES WITH ARISTOTLE'S VIEW ON FRIENDSHIP

Aristotle maintains that friendships of virtue are only possible among
good men. In *Nicomachean Ethics* he writes that "clearly, however, only
good people can be friends to each other because of the other person

himself; for bad people find no enjoyment in one another if they get no benefit."[37] In *Eudemian Ethics*, he calls friendships of virtue "primary friendships" and reiterates again that it is "the friendship of good people . . . bad people may be friends with each other for the sake of utility or pleasure. However, some say that they are not really friends because the primary friendship is absent: a bad man will wrong another bad man, and those who are wronged by each other do not love each other."[38] This may make some sense at first—I doubt anyone would trust Norton, Hadley, or Ace to be loyal and caring friends. But Aristotle's view becomes far more complicated when taken in conjunction with the rest of his moral writings, given that his definition of what it means to be a "good" person is very specific. According to Aristotle, a good anything, whether a person or an object, performs its function well. For example, the function of a butter knife is to spread butter without cutting the bread, so a good butter knife is one that is dull and performs that function well. The function of a human being, his distinctive purpose or activity, is to reason. Reasoning well, according to Aristotle, involves avoiding excesses and finding the mean between extremes—the virtues. The virtue of honesty, for example, is not about always telling the truth in every single situation. No one would consider it a detriment to someone's status as an honest person if they lied to a murderer about the whereabouts of a potential victim. Rather, honesty is about knowing when it is appropriate to tell the truth—it is the mean between the extremes of being a liar and being too blunt. And it is not enough to just be good once in a while—a truly good and virtuous person can be counted upon to consistently act according to the mean. A good person, a virtuous person, is one who habitually follows his reason and performs the action that illustrates the (situationally specific) mean between extremes.

Given this precise definition, very few people meet the criteria of goodness from an Aristotelian standpoint, and therefore very few people are capable of friendships of virtue. Andy and Red certainly wouldn't meet Aristotle's standards. Red deliberately murdered his wife in an attempt to collect insurance money by cutting the wires in her car, and accidentally took the life of their neighbor and infant son who were in the vehicle when she crashed. He consistently makes his living in prison by breaking the rules and selling contraband items. Andy, while he didn't kill his wife, is still in possession of flawed character traits. He abused alcohol before his life in prison, had a jealous streak when it came to his wife, helps Norton launder thousands of dollars (though this may be justified from a utilitarian standpoint, given that he was allowed to expand the library and educate many of the inmates in return), and flawlessly executes an escape from prison. (Although most wouldn't probably describe this action as immoral, Socrates, as is evident from the *Crito*, may have taken issue with Andy's escape.) Despite these flaws, however, we probably wouldn't describe them as bad people, and they were certainly capable of a friendship that, as above mentioned, seems like a clear example of a friendship of virtue.

The upshot here is that either Aristotle's account of goodness, or his contention that one has to be morally virtuous in order to partake in perfect friendships (or both), is dubious. Human psychology is much more complex than Aristotle acknowledges, and certainly there seems to be gradations in virtue and vice. While neither Andy nor Red approximate the Aristotelian virtuous person, they seem to be far better human beings than Norton or Hadley. Just as Chris and Gordie contradict Aristotle's claim that youths are mostly only capable of friendships of pleasure, Red and Andy illustrate that even the morally flawed are capable of intimate and deep friendships. Indeed, if Aristotle is right, not many of us would ever be capable of friendships of virtue, given that very few people consistently practice the mean between extremes in all of life's situations.

In addition, Aristotle states that his three classifications of friendship only apply to friendships between "equals" (defined only as men with comparable levels of virtue). Friendships between "unequals," such as relationships between parents and their children, rulers and the ruled, and (according to Aristotle) husbands and their wives, are subject to a wholly different analysis. Here I will focus on what Aristotle has to say of the friendship between parents and children, since it is most relevant for the purposes of this chapter. He argues that the love between parents and children comes from their genetic connection: "A parent loves his children as [he loves] himself. For what has come from him is a sort of other himself . . . children love a parent because they regard themselves as having come from them."[39] Their relationship is akin to that of "the friendship of human beings to a god . . . [because] the parent conferred the greatest benefits, since he is the cause of their being and nurture and their education once they are born."[40] As a result, a child would always be in debt to his parents, and it is a debt that he can never discharge. A child is, consequently, never allowed to "disavow his father, but a father is free to disavow his son. For debtor should return what he owes, and since no matter what a son has done he has not made a worthy return for what his father has done for him, he is always the debtor."[41] A child who has no desire to repay his parents, his father in particular, for the debt he has incurred for being given life is described by Aristotle as vicious.

Needless to say, Aristotle's view of the parent-child relationship is problematic. Earlier in *Nicomachean Ethics*, he regards children as akin to property, and therefore concludes that they cannot be treated unjustly by their parents because "there is no unconditional injustice in relation to what is one's own; one's own possession, or one's child" (his view of the relationships between husbands and wives is equally problematic).[42] Still, he continues, he doubts whether any parent really would treat his or her child badly, since a child is "part of oneself, and no one decides to harm himself."[43] Yet clearly in *The Body* there are examples of relationships between fathers and sons that call Aristotle's analysis into serious question; for here, it seems clear that the fathers are acting in ways that are vicious toward their children, and one could hardly fault the kids for reacting with animosity.

Gordie is all but ignored by his father, especially after the death of his older brother Dennis, whom his parents clearly preferred. While he is never beaten, being ignored can often leave equally deep scars (it can serve as a type of solitary living Aristotle says impedes human flourishing). Gordie compares his role in his family to that of the main character in Ralph Ellison's *The Invisible Man*; he is never seen by either of his parents, who were always too busy revering his brother and later mourning him. Consequently, Gordie believes that they would have much rather that he had died instead. Chris is routinely beaten by his father, and accordingly, "we all knew that he hated him like poison. Chris was marked up every two weeks or so, bruises on his cheek and neck or one eye swelled up and as colorful as a sunset, and once he came into school with a big clumsy bandage on the back of his head."[44] Teddy's father, clearly suffering from posttraumatic stress disorder from his days in World War II, "took Teddy over to the big woodstove at the back of the kitchen and shoved the side of Teddy's head down against one of the cast-iron burner plates. He held it down there for about ten seconds. Then he yanked Teddy up by the hair and did the other side."[45]

Normative ethical theories based on virtue typically hold filial piety in high regard; in addition to Aristotle, for example, Confucius's *Analects* are full of passages where he endorses an almost categorical reverence toward parents by their children. When I teach these passages to my students, inevitably the issue of child abuse comes up, and whether this affects whatever moral obligations children are said to have toward their parents. Would Aristotle still contend, when considering these cases, that the boys are irrevocably in debt to fathers who abuse them? What kind of friendship could exist between these "unequals"? If Gordie, Chris, or Teddy decided to cut ties to their fathers given the abuse they endured, would Aristotle be so keen to call them vicious?

To be fair, none of these issues pose such a threat to Aristotle's account of friendship that it renders the whole analysis void. However, human ethical behavior and psychology does confess to being more complex than Aristotle's taxonomy would have us believe. This just points to how philosophically rich the issue of friendship can be, and how right Aristotle was to devote so much analysis to it (even if the analysis is lacking in some points). Sometimes we are simply unable to fully capture all the dimensions and facets of the most important aspects of human existence—"the most important things are the hardest things to say."[46]

HOPE SPRINGS ETERNAL: CONCLUDING THOUGHTS

Studying Aristotle in conjunction with King's works accomplishes many things. Philosophy, sadly, gets a bad rap—portrayed by many as useless, navel-gazing, purely academic work with no relevance to the real world. For those who regard philosophy thusly, studying Aristotle's writings may seem like a waste of time. However, once we note how much works of popular fiction are infused with philosophical concepts and ideas, we begin to see that philosophy is everywhere, and that having an understanding of certain philosophical ideas and concepts can add depth, and enjoyment, to our reading of literature (this goes not only for the topics covered in this chapter, but for all the other chapters in this book as well). Another important aspect to highlight is how King's stories humanize Aristotle's concepts. By seeing Andy reach out to Red in the depths of his loneliness and despair, we can understand why Aristotle is so adamant about the importance of friendship in living a flourishing life. By comparing the depth of Chris and Gordie's relationship to that of Teddy and Vern's, we can see that there are, indeed, relevant differences in the kinds of friendships that we have, and how we should strive to cultivate friendships of virtue over those of utility and pleasure.

In the process of reviewing Aristotle's theories of friendship, and watching it played out by King's characters, I thought of my own friends, and the very few I have who count as friendships of virtue (you know who you are). And I felt so deeply grateful for them. And I hope that for the rest of my life I can keep them and appreciate them the way Aristotle emphasizes I should. I hope that I can look back on my childhood and youth with them with the innocence and purity Gordie feels when he looks back on his friends. I hope I can grow old with them as Aristotle recommends I do, and as Red and Andy grow old together. I hope that others can see the profound affects philosophy and literature can have on our everyday lives, and how it adds beauty and depth to our everyday experiences.

I hope.

NOTES

1. Aristotle, *Nicomachean Ethics* (Indianapolis, Ind.: Hackett, 1985), 1155a–13.
2. Aristotle, *Eudemian Ethics* (New York: Oxford University Press, 2011), 1236a25–26.
3. Aristotle, *Eudemian Ethics*, 1234b33.
4. Stephen King, *Rita Hayworth and the Shawshank Redemption*, in *Different Seasons* (New York: Signet, 1982), 27.
5. Aristotle, *Nicomachean Ethics*, 1156a10–12.
6. Aristotle, *Nicomachean Ethics*, 1159b12–14.
7. Aristotle, *Nicomachean Ethics*, 1156a20.
8. Aristotle, *Eudemian Ethics*, 1236a33.
9. Aristotle, *Nicomachean Ethics*, 1156b3012–13.
10. King, *Rita Hayworth and the Shawshank Redemption*, 52.
11. King, *Rita Hayworth and the Shawshank Redemption*, 69.

12. Aristotle, *Nicomachean Ethics*, 1156a4.
13. Aristotle, *Eudemian Ethics*, 1241a3–5.
14. Aristotle, *Eudemian Ethics*, 1238b–15.
15. Aristotle, *Nicomachean Ethics*, 1156a11–12.
16. Aristotle, *Nicomachean Ethics*, 1156b5–7.
17. Aristotle, *Nicomachean Ethics*, 1156a31–35.
18. Aristotle, *Nicomachean Ethics*, 1156a34–37.
19. Stephen King, *The Body*, in *Different Seasons* (New York: Signet, 1982), 337.
20. King, *The Body*, 429.
21. Aristotle, *Eudemian Ethics*, 1236b.
22. King, *Rita Hayworth and the Shawshank Redemption*, 105.
23. Aristotle, *Nicomachean Ethics*, 1156b7–14.
24. Aristotle, *Nicomachean Ethics*, 1157a21–25.
25. Aristotle, *Nicomachean Ethics*, 1170a12.
26. Aristotle, *Nicomachean Ethics*, 1170b12.
27. Aristotle, *Nicomachean Ethics*, 1157b20.
28. King, *Rita Hayworth and the Shawshank Redemption*, 100.
29. Aristotle, *Nicomachean Ethics*, 1166a5.
30. King, *The Body*, 378.
31. King, *The Body*, 412.
32. King, *The Body*, 431–32.
33. Aristotle, *Eudemian Ethics*, 1240b.
34. King, *Rita Hayworth and the Shawshank Redemption*, 99.
35. Aristotle, *Eudemian Ethics*, 1240b2.
36. Aristotle, *Eudemian Ethics*, 1238a.
37. Aristotle, *Nicomachean Ethics*, 1157a20.
38. Aristotle, *Eudemian Ethics*, 1236b3–13.
39. Aristotle, *Nicomachean Ethics*, 1161b25.
40. Aristotle, *Nicomachean Ethics*, 1162a4–10.
41. Aristotle, *Nicomachean Ethics*, 1163b18–23.
42. Aristotle, *Nicomachean Ethics*, 1134b10–13.
43. Aristotle, *Nicomachean Ethics*, 1134b13.
44. King, *The Body*, 302.
45. King, *The Body*, 292.
46. King, *The Body*, 289.

8

PROPAGANDA AND PEDAGOGY FOR APT PUPILS

Michael K. Potter and Cam Cobb

In 1982, Stephen King published a collection of novellas titled *Different Seasons*. One of the stories in this collection, *Apt Pupil*, explores the dynamics of a student-teacher relationship in horrific circumstances. As the story unfolds, Todd Bowen arrives at the home of an elderly man going by the name of Arthur Denker in his Santo Domingo, California, neighborhood. Only, Arthur Denker is really Kurt Dussander, a fugitive Nazi war criminal. And Todd—an "all-American kid"[1] —is interested not in turning Dussander in, but rather in hearing the old man recall his experiences as a torturer and killer. As Todd listens to these stories, he transforms into a different person—and Dussander regresses into the monster he was in the past.

Todd Bowen and Kurt Dussander vacillate between the roles of teacher and student as they wrestle to outwit one another and control their shared situation, hating and fearing each other as they come face-to-face with their own sadism, hatred, and violence. What Todd experiences, through Dussander, drives him first to sleeplessness and nightmares, then to violent thoughts, and eventually to sexual violence and murder. And as we see Todd's life spiral out of control in this horrific narrative, we are reminded that in educational relationships, power and persuasion come with risks.

"P" IS FOR PERSUASION, PROPAGANDA, AND POWER

Successful teachers sell ideas—convince the young to taste them, try them on, and give them a spin. Stripped of ideologies and agendas, this is what learning is. Teaching is a set of activities intended to bring about learning. What does that imply? If nothing else, it means that, to be successful, teachers must go further than mere appeals to reason, for reason alone rarely leads to persuasion, acceptance, and internalization. They must, in other words, transcend the limitations of *logos* (appeals to reason) through the skillful use of *ethos* (appeals to credibility) and *pathos* (appeals to emotion).[2]

Successful teachers are, necessarily, propagandists. Most English-speaking people bring negative associations to the term "propaganda," because it is typically used to deride communications from people other than ourselves, to make those whose messages we dislike appear dishonest and ourselves, by contrast, trustworthy. Many, if not most, definitions of propaganda in the English-speaking world are moralistic; that is, rather than trying to describe the phenomenon, they pass judgment on it, usually in favor of oneself and one's in-group and against others that one wishes condemned.[3] Examples abound, but perhaps one will help us see why this practice is problematic. Leonard Doob, in *Public Opinion and Propaganda*, offers this definition: "Propaganda can be called the attempt to affect the personalities and control the behaviour of individuals toward ends considered unscientific or of doubtful value in a society at a given time."[4] The first part of the definition is fine, if a little strong: propaganda is intended to persuade, which may be interpreted reasonably as an attempt to control others. Yet the second part of the definition creates unnecessary problems, as it depends not on features of the phenomenon itself for its identity, but on assumptions about whether its ends are "desirable."

As Pratkanis and Aronson write, echoing our cautions against moralistic definition, "In many ways, it is dangerous to apply the labels 'education' and 'propaganda' to a communication merely on the basis of whether it agrees or disagrees with one's values."[5] It is more honest and less problematic to use descriptive definitions, looking for common properties shared by examples of the phenomena whatever judgments have been passed on them.

So we need a neutral, descriptive definition that doesn't rely on an ideology or morality. We do this by focusing on shared characteristics found in all or most definitions of the word, then stripping away any moral, political, ideological, or otherwise judgmental assumptions. The key is in the more appropriate, and neutral, use of the term in Latin American countries, where it is a synonym for "advertising."[6] *Propaganda is persuasive communication through nonrational means.* The point of propaganda is to persuade people to believe something, do something, accept something—or to *not* believe, do, or accept something. As a form of communication, propaganda doesn't try to merely convey information, and its point is not to convey truth. That doesn't mean that all propaganda is dishonest, just that conveying truth isn't the point. The point is to persuade, and if you can do that while being honest, great—it's still propaganda if you accomplished persuasion through nonrational means. But if you attempt to persuade by being dishonest, that's also propaganda—if you accomplished the goal of persuasion through nonrational means. You can even attempt to persuade by bullshitting, in the technical sense, which means that your communication is indifferent to the truth or falsity of what you're saying.[7] The truth or falsity of what you're communicating, and your attitude toward it, is irrelevant to the question of whether that communication is propaganda.

Why does propaganda use nonrational means? It does so *because* its purpose is persuasion. Although people like to believe they are convinced by evidence and logic, that their beliefs and (what they call) knowledge are rational, research from philosophy, social psychology, advertising, sociology, and other disciplines converges on one conclusion: logos—logic and evidence—are usually irrelevant to what persuades us, and what we believe.[8] The acknowledgment of this is crucial to the success of all forms of propaganda—including teaching. This is why logical fallacies and cognitive biases drive so much of our decision making, and why advertisers don't simply present us with a list of product specifications in the hope that we'll purchase their wares. Successful propagandists use nonrational means to persuade their audiences, including the classical rhetorical principles of ethos (credibility) and pathos (emotion). Rational means may still be included in propaganda—indeed, the *honest* propagandist will always use logic and evidence in some form—but they are secondary to what works.

Must teachers be propagandists? No. Only *engaging* teachers need to be propagandists, if we think of effective teachers as those who are able to bring about learning in their students (whatever sort of learning we might have in mind). Think about the difference. A teacher who refuses to be a propagandist recites facts, shows slides of statistics, assigns textbook readings, and does many of the other things we associate with traditional education. These approaches, on their own, don't work for the same reasons reliance on logos outside of the educational context doesn't work. Teacher-propagandists, on the other hand, establish credibility and authority so students listen and take them seriously, help students make emotional connections to ideas through metaphorical and analogical associations and experiences, frame issues in a way that students can create meaning from and understand, and otherwise lead students to see their learning as relevant, and develop and retain information. Put this way, it doesn't seem very offensive, does it? Yet it's propaganda. Successful teaching is a form of persuasion—at bare minimum, teachers must persuade students to accept and internalize ideas, which is what we call learning—and all of the more pedagogically useful strategies we've just described are nonrational means of accomplishing that persuasive goal.

"C" IS FOR CONTROL

Central to the success of propaganda and teaching are the twin concepts of power and control. Indeed, one cannot have control without power. Bertrand Russell (1872–1970) wrote that power is "the production of intended effects"[9]—and he was speaking primarily of social power, power over other people. Power is a foundational—and indeed fundamental—dimension of the ever-shifting and complex teaching-learning relationship between Todd Bowen and Kurt Dussander.

Todd's initial confrontation with Denker—an aggressive list of memorized facts about who he used to be—is a blatant assertion of power, and Denker's reaction, though he tries to hide it, is one of fear: "But the toothless mouth was quivering in an infirm, panicking way."[10] On the other hand, Todd's behavior during this encounter is eerie: a constantly smiling faux friendliness. This encounter leads to a further show of power that mocks the authority we expect an old man to have over a young boy when, like a vampire, Todd forces Denker to "invite" him into his home.

Todd wastes no time informing Denker that he knows his true identity and threatens to call the police—"You will [tell me about it], though. If you don't, I'll tell everyone who you are."[11] His threat has the intended effect. Todd has the power to force Dussander to cooperate, successfully blackmailing Dussander into teaching him about horrors of World War II and the Holocaust—particularly Dussander's lived experiences as a torturer and killer. Eventually Dussander counters back, threatening Todd: "I will drag you down, boy. I promise you that. If anything comes out, *everything* will come out. That is my promise to you."[12] He makes good on his promise.

The young "all-American kid" wields more power when he informs Dussander that he has given one of his friends a letter revealing the man's true identity as a fugitive Nazi. Toward the end of the novella, as the teacher-student dynamic between them becomes more complicated, Dussander uses his own blackmail bluff—the threat of having a revealing letter tucked away in a safety-deposit box at a bank—which mimics Todd's approach of using student threats to manipulate the teacher's behaviors and actions. Power, and the struggle to hold it, is at the center of Todd and Dussander's relationship. Dussander, essentially, manages to invert the power dynamic by becoming Todd, behaviorally.

For both Todd and Dussander, this approach of threats, blackmail, and manipulation works—to a degree. Yes, they successfully manipulate one another. Yet their approach locks both into a power binary where in any given moment, one holds power and the other wants to take it. It is a dynamic where the two are perpetually vying to outwit one another and take control of their teacher-student relationship and curriculum. And while Todd and Dussander enter into a duel of sorts, their sparring for power goes beyond a binary relationship. It is, on a larger level, a competitive system that is shaped by their actions, or as Michel Foucault (1926–1984) would say, their "strategies" and "mechanisms."[13] In Foucault's words, "Power in its exercise . . . passes through much finer channels, and is much more ambiguous, since each individual has at his disposal a certain power, and for that very reason can also act as a vehicle for transmitting a wider power."[14]

Although this sort of pedagogy appears, and may be, harmful, it only seems unique and shocking because the artifice of traditional teacher-student relationships has been stripped away. Teachers and students are ultimately in an unbalanced power relationship, or system. As teachers are in a position of institutional authority, they are responsible for interpreting institutional policy and implementing (or overseeing) a justice system in the classroom, and expected to persuade students. Students, we typically assume, have less power because they're usually younger, dependent on teachers for guidance (in the form of feedback, instruction, and facilitation) and approval (in the form of grades), and forced to comply with teachers' expectations and rules. They are expected to be the passive objects of persuasion. Yet the situation is much more complicated than this, as students may—in varying circumstances—have substantial power over teachers. Teachers have long been vulnerable, for instance, to student complaints. And the results of student evaluations of teachers have been used, though infrequently, to punish teachers—or, to use the prevailing euphemism, "to make personnel decisions."[15] In an academic world increasingly dominated by contract instructors, teachers are especially vulnerable. A complaint or a poor evaluation can easily lead to loss of employment, especially in educational environments that increasingly rely on adjunct and casually employed teachers.

"A" IS FOR APPEARANCES

Stephen King plays with our expectations regarding the student-teacher power dynamic. He takes great care in establishing Todd as pure and innocent, the picture of ideal white American boyhood. He's handsome, intelligent, enterprising, hardworking, positively Aryan in appearance, an early riser—and prudent enough to know that he needs to moderate how intelligent he appears to others if he's to maintain a "normal" social life. He's also an optimist: "He had not pictured it happening quite like this. But it would work out. Things would come into focus. Of course they would. Things always did."[16]

Dussander, on the other hand, is presented as Todd's opposite, impure and corrupt. He's foul and old. King's descriptions emphasize his age and ugliness, his unkemptness, and even his laziness (at 10:00 a.m., for instance, we're drawn to the fact that he's neither dressed nor showered). "The eyes looking out at Todd were watchful but deeply sunken, laced with snaps of red."[17] Todd compares him, mentally, to winos that lurk in railway yards, comparing this vision of him to the false face he wears in public; this ugly and unkempt man is who he is "with his street face put away—hanging in the closet, you might say, along with his umbrella and his trilby."[18] In fact, Dussander's appearance becomes worse the longer he knows Todd. After six months, his face is "haggard and yellowed," his hair receding and "lusterless and brittle," his body "gaunt."[19]

With these descriptions well established, we're led to expect the pure and innocent boy to be abused and manipulated by the dirty old man—only to have our expectations frustrated when Todd begins manipulating Dussander as soon as they meet. To be sure, at the beginning of their relationship there are moments where Todd is frightened that he might lose control. He reacts to his fear of losing power by dropping the pretense of friendliness—"Todd said coldly: 'You better not do that.'"[20]

Who is really influencing whom in Dussander and Todd's informal teacher-student relationship? Todd gradually falls under Dussander's influence, which seems, superficially, to lead to his corruption as he becomes increasingly malevolent. Also, on the surface, Dussander's role as a teacher is presented as openly propagandistic in the common, moralistic, sense—manipulative and malicious. Yet, scratch the surface and their teacher-student relationship is, again, more complicated than it first appears, as is the analogous relationship between victimizer and victim; each teaches, learns from, and is corrupted by the other. Todd, as student, also serves as a teacher-propagandist, complicit in his own moral degradation, manipulating his teacher into manipulating him. His use of power is strictly teleological, even principled in a way: he wants to use it to learn. As he explains to Dussander, "I want to hear about it. That's all. That's all I want. Really."[21]

The teacher-student relationship between Dussander and Todd is complicated, in part, because Todd is an unusually self-motivated and self-directed learner. In this way he represents the ideal for many contemporary educators and administrators. His credentials as a particularly gifted student—an "apt pupil"—are established early in the story, and reinforced throughout. His abilities as a student are tied to his social skills and attention to detail. He knows, for instance, that he has to adopt a tone of horror when writing about the Holocaust, even though he doesn't feel it, because not meeting that expectation would arouse alarm.[22] Intellectually, he is perfectly capable of writing a great essay about the Holocaust no matter what tone he takes. Yet, by faking the expected affect, he meets a demand of the hidden curriculum his teachers may not recognize consciously. Long before Todd asserts control over his relationship with Dussander, King also ensures we know how intelligent and observant he is, "into deductions" and hoping "to become a private detective when he grew up."[23] He's overattentive to small details, obsessive, and persistent.

"E" IS FOR EXPERIMENTAL LEARNING

Central to Todd's control of Dussander is the difficulty he seems to have, initially, in seeing Dussander as a real person. Todd repeatedly dehumanizes the older man and either rebuffs or ignores Dussander's attempts to humanize himself, as with a desperate reference to his wife.[24] Yet, Dussander's humanity is what makes him vulnerable to Todd's manipulation. Dussander is clearly haunted and full of regret. His power is limited by the emotional pain his memories cause him, and his desire to retreat from it. Yet Todd, after listening to Dussander's story and how hard he's tried to put his past behind him, refuses to let him move on. "If you don't, I'll tell everyone who you are."[25]

It doesn't take long before Todd becomes dissatisfied with storytelling. He yearns for a more experiential learning experience, and as this desire grows, he starts to control Dussander in other ways—"He was really going to have to do something about the way Dussander dressed when he was at home. It spoiled some of the fun."[26] For Christmas, he gives Dussander an SS uniform, "complete with jackboots."[27] Dussander is horrified and refuses to put it on until Todd reminds him what happened to Eichmann. Enraged, Dussander raises his fist to strike Todd, who responds coldly—"'Yeah,' he said softly. 'Go ahead and touch me. You just touch me *once*'"[28]—using the power created by social expectations: a boy attacked by an old man is automatically considered a victim, and victimhood carries with it tremendous social power.[29]

Despite Dussander's begging, Todd forces him to wear the uniform, and thus he finally begins to resemble Todd's idealized vision of him. "For the first time Dussander looked to Todd as Todd believed he should look."[30] Todd immediately begins barking orders at the newly costumed Dussander, and Dussander finds himself, unthinkingly, obeying like an automaton. Again, this reaction is not what Todd was expecting, so he becomes anxious about losing control: "Todd was scared—really scared. He felt like the sorcerer's apprentice, who had brought the brooms to life but who had not possessed enough skill to stop them once they got started. The old man living on his pension was gone. Dussander was here. Then his fear was replaced by a tingling sense of power."[31] Todd's power over Dussander now seems complete. "As for Dussander, he felt disgust, discomfort . . . and a mild, sneaking sense of relief. He partly despised this latter emotion, recognizing it as the truest indicator yet of the psychological domination the boy had established over him. He was the boy's prisoner, and every time he found he could live through yet another indignity, every time he felt that mild relief, the boy's power grew."[32]

It is only when Todd has complete psychological power over Dussander, making him march around the kitchen in uniform, that he begins to fully appreciate the horror of who Dussander was, and the horror of the Holocaust itself. This realization finally frightens him, and he forces Dussander to stop. But now that momentum has been built, it takes the old man a while to stop. "Todd let out a silent breath of relief and for a moment he was furious with himself. *Who's in charge here, anyway?* Then his self-confidence flooded back in. *I am, that's who. And he better not forget it.*"[33] He reasserts his power by critiquing Dussander's performance and giving him permission to remove the uniform. The power that Todd wields in this teacher-student relationship does not, of course, end at that artificial conceptual border. Todd uses his control over Dussander to make himself feel better over the things in life that seem to be out of his control, like his grades, his new penchant for talking to himself, and his dreams.[34]

We often suppose that power relationships are pleasant for those who wield the most power, not those over whom power is wielded. As Friedrich Nietzsche (1844–1900) explained at length, this is not so—entire moralities, religions, and cultures are prefaced on the pleasant experience of subordination.[35] Dussander finds some solace in his subordination to the boy, as it at least alleviates his loneliness and improves his memory: "He supposed he talked to the boy as all old men talk, but he guessed he was luckier than most old men, who had impatience, uninterest, or outright rudeness for an audience. *His* audience was endlessly fascinated."[36] He also takes solace in seeing the influence he is having over Todd, his growing power: "He and the boy were loathsome, he supposed, feeding off each other . . . eating each other. If his own belly was sometimes sour with the dark but rich food they partook of in his afternoon kitchen, what was the boy's like? Did he sleep well? Perhaps not. Lately Dussander thought the boy looked rather pale, and thinner than when he had first come into Dussander's life."[37] After this, recognizing that his subordination is perhaps not permanent, he puts on the uniform, and sleeps well. This change in Dussander marks the turning point in the teacher-student relationship.

"C" IS FOR CURRICULUM

The true topic of Todd's curriculum, the theme that ties all of his questions and preoccupations together, is human suffering. He is particularly fascinated by concentration camps and the torture of women, but his interests include suffering more generally. By the time Todd first knocks on Kurt Dussander's front door, the young boy already has a learning plan in mind. Poring over photographs of World War II— particularly of the death camps and the trials of Nazi war criminals— and otherwise indulging his obsession leads Todd to suspect that Arthur Denker, this unremarkable old man in his neighborhood, is truly Nazi torturer and killer Dussander, who fled to South America after the war. By the time they meet, Todd has been researching, stalking, and spying on Dussander for at least two months.

True to his youth and innocence, Todd is guileless in admitting his obsession once he begins coercing Dussander: "I get off on it. I'm interested."[38] Dussander sees him for what he is, but offers a more neutral term: "An aficionado . . . is one who grooves. One who . . . gets off on something."[39] Yet later, when Todd reveals that he wants to use his power to learn, by forcing Dussander to wallow in, and share, his memories of the Holocaust, the elderly man is less neutral: "Dussander stared at him with a certain amazed detachment, the way a veterinarian might stare at a cat who was giving birth to a succession of two-headed kittens. 'You are a monster,' he said softly."[40]

Todd's interest was initially piqued by a fourth-grade Career Day lesson about finding "YOUR GREAT INTEREST"[41]—which was described to him in highly romantic terms, like "falling in love for the first time."[42] A connection was forged between this object of romance and the Nazi atrocities by the fortuitous discovery of a box of old magazines in a friend's garage, which ignited the romantic feelings he'd been led to expect; "his head began to ache with a mixture of revulsion and excitement."[43]

Todd is strongly affected by the contrary messages he receives. Although the stories in the magazines say the Holocaust was bad, they're surrounded by advertisements for Nazi memorabilia and photographs that revel in exquisite gory details. Repeatedly, we are told that Todd experiences this as "falling in love," combined with detailed, romanticized, sensory memories of the scene surrounding his discovery of the magazines. He is in love, and with this love comes an awakening: "He remembered thinking: *I want to know everything that happened in these places. Everything. And I want to know which is more true—the words, or the ads they put beside the words.*"[44] He doesn't want the context, the rationales, the politics, the ideology—any of the information that would help him understand—all he wants are the details of the atrocities.

So Todd has set a curriculum. In terms of method, Todd aims to complete this curriculum through conversation, listening to Dussander's stories, asking questions, and relating the new details to what he has already learned from books and magazines. The boy's learning program, or curriculum, draws from lived experiences shared through narrative conversations. It is a curriculum narrowly focused on a particular history, details of the death camps that were shuttered nearly four decades earlier. And, perhaps most important, it is a curriculum that is entirely student driven. Todd, a tremendously driven self-directed learner, chooses and controls every detail of the curriculum and the methodology by which it is taught and learned—at least, at the beginning. And the boy's curriculum contributes to unpleasant consequences later in the narrative.

The horrific content of Todd and Dussander's curriculum soon drives the boy to the point of nightmares and sleeplessness. It is an oppressive curriculum both in terms of method *and* content. Reflecting on oppression, Paulo Freire (1926–1997) notes that "one of the basic elements of the relationship between oppressor and oppressed is *prescription*. Every prescription represents the imposition of one individual's choice upon another, transforming the consciousness of the person prescribed to into one that conforms with the prescriber's consciousness."[45] Freire, himself an able and influential propagandist, is condemning the sort of propaganda people usually associate with the term. In teacher-student relationships, oppressive conditions arise when the voice of one (teacher or student) is silenced—which can be caused by the nature of their interactions (a matter of method) or the subject matter of the learning (a matter of curricular content).

Although Todd prescribes his own curriculum—in seeking out Dussander and pressuring the old man to share his ghastly stories—the content of this curriculum at once mesmerizes, horrifies, and alters the young boy's mind. While listening, eagerly, to Dussander's vicious stories, the young boy revels in details of such horrors as gas ovens, and the effects of various experimental gases on human beings.[46] Thus, rather than grounding themselves in such values as care and compassion, Dussander and Todd coconstruct a curriculum rooted in hate and sadism— a "prescriptive" system of oppression. Todd and Dussander revel in the horrific content of their curriculum as they play power games with one another. Initially, Todd is troubled by his nightmares. Yet he continues to meet with the fugitive Nazi. Overwhelmed by violent thoughts and images, the boy's nightmares persist—and over time, his impulses take over, leading to sadism, animal cruelty, and multiple murders. Todd Bowen loses his own identity as he transforms into a serial killer. "Were a few bad dreams too high a price to pay?" Stephen King asks.[47] The answer to this question is vividly illustrated as Todd's personality and life spiral out of control and ultimately end in violence.

"L" IS FOR LESSONS LEARNED

Apt Pupil raises interesting questions about the nature of the pedagogical relationship between teacher and student. It complicates our notion of power, which is all too often seen (and treated) as existing in a binary relationship—between teacher and student, one who holds power and one who is bereft. Yet power is not *within* people, and—rather than being an object of possession—it is nuanced and fluid. Describing its ecological nature, Foucault notes that there is an "order of power."[48] Stephen King captures this complicated nature of power, as well as its ties to pedagogy, in *Apt Pupil*. As the story unfolds, Todd and Dussander establish a power system, or "order," that is rooted in deception, manipulation, and oppression. And what unfolds is a terrifying tale about the purposes of education versus the purposes of propaganda, of the moral evaluation of a teacher's work and curriculum itself, and about the inescapability and ubiquity of power and manipulation in formal and informal educational contexts.

The power system established between Todd and Dussander resembles the power system of education in its everyday and banal forms. Edward Bernays, playing on the sorts of moralistic definitions we cautioned against earlier, writes, "The only difference between 'propaganda' and 'education,' really, is the point of view. The advocacy of what we believe in is education. The advocacy of what we do not believe is propaganda."[49] This is not hyperbole. As Noam Chomsky reports, in the United States the Trilateral Commission traced the "crisis of democracy" it perceived to the failure of the education system (from early childhood to university) to properly indoctrinate citizens, recognizing that its purpose had been propaganda from the beginning.[50] Education has long been, perhaps has always been, about persuasion, power, and control over the minds of students. "Far from creating independent thinkers, schools have always, throughout history, played an institutional role in systems of control and coercion. And once you're educated, you have already been socialized in ways that support the power structure, which, in turn, rewards you immensely," he writes.[51] Todd and Dussander, in other words, are merely creating their own model of what we take for granted and do not see all around us, but that exists in educational systems the world over.

Yet the role of educational systems as institutional vehicles for propaganda and the role of educators as propagandists are separable. You could conceivably teach within a propagandistic system without being a propagandist (by, for instance, being an unsuccessful teacher), and an educator could be a propagandist even when not teaching within a propagandistic system. You could even have propagandistic educational systems that contained successful propagandist teachers whose persuasive goals were contrary to those of the system in which they work. In fact, the latter possibility may be what we see at work in *Apt Pupil*.

Although Stephen King presents us with an extreme case, it has more pedestrian analogues in even the most common educational situations, so the questions it poses are worth grappling with, the answers worth seeking—so that we can avoid particularly toxic uses of power and persuasion even as we accept ourselves as educational propagandists. The teacher-student relationship between Dussander and Todd is, arguably, successful. Todd becomes a better student at school as a result of Dussander's tutelage, even as he becomes a worse human being. The young boy has achieved his intended outcome—and more. Yet, for Todd, this achievement involves violence and deception. Ultimately, Todd Bowen's learning—and his interlocking descent—leads to the suffering and deaths of others as well as his own demise. When this misguided "apt pupil" faces capture and punishment, the "all-American kid" goes on a shooting spree. In the end, "it was five hours later and almost dark before they took him down."[52]

NOTES

1. Stephen King, *Apt Pupil*, in *Different Seasons* (New York: Signet, 1983), 111.

2. Aristotle, *Rhetoric*, trans. W. Rhys Roberts (http://classics.mit.edu/Aristotle/rhetoric.html).

3. Charles Stevenson calls these "persuasive definitions." See Charles Stevenson, *Ethics and Language* (New Haven, Conn.: Yale University Press, 1944), 210.

4. Leonard Doob, *Public Opinion and Propaganda*, 2nd ed. (Hamden, Conn.: Archon, 1948), 240.

5. Anthony Pratkanis and Elliot Aronson, *Age of Propaganda: The Everyday Use and Abuse of Persuasion* (New York: Freeman, 2001), 265.

6. Randal Marlin, *Propaganda and the Ethics of Persuasion* (Peterborough, ON: Broadview, 2002), 16.

7. Harry G. Frankfurt, *On Bullshit* (Princeton, N.J.: Princeton University Press, 2005).

8. For specific studies, see, for instance: Ellen Langer, Arthur Blank, and Benzion Chanowitz, "The Mindlessness of Ostensibly Thoughtful Action: The Role of 'Placebic' Information in Interpersonal Interaction," *Journal of Person-*

ality and Social Psychology, 36 (1978): 635–42; and Carl I. Hovland and Walter Weiss, "The Influence of Source Credibility on Communication Effectiveness," *Public Opinion Quarterly* 15 (1951): 635–50. For a useful compilation and discussion of these studies and more, see Pratkanis and Aronson, *Age of Propaganda*.

9. Bertrand Russell, *Power: A New Social Analysis* (London: Routledge, 1992), 25.

10. King, *Apt Pupil*, 115.

11. King, *Apt Pupil*, 133.

12. King, *Apt Pupil*, 165.

13. Michel Foucault, *Power/Knowledge: Selected Interviews and Other Writings, 1972–1977*, ed. Colin Gordon, trans. Colin Gordon, Leo Marshall, John Mepham, Kate Soper (New York: Pantheon, 1980), 51.

14. Foucault, *Power/Knowledge*, 72.

15. Pamela Gravestock and Emily Gregor-Greenleaf, *Student Course Evaluations: Research, Models and Trends* (Toronto, ON: Higher Education Quality Council of Ontario, 2008) (see http://www.heqco.ca/SiteCollectionDocuments/Student%20Course%20Evaluations.pdf).

16. King, *Apt Pupil*, 116.

17. King, *Apt Pupil*, 113.

18. King, *Apt Pupil*, 114.

19. King, *Apt Pupil*, 140.

20. King, *Apt Pupil*, 118.

21. King, *Apt Pupil*, 129.

22. King, *Apt Pupil*, 122.

23. King, *Apt Pupil*, 124.

24. King, *Apt Pupil*, 117.

25. King, *Apt Pupil*, 133.

26. King, *Apt Pupil*, 133.

27. King, *Apt Pupil*, 141.

28. King, *Apt Pupil*, 142.

29. Diane Enns, *The Violence of Victimhood* (University Park: Penn State University Press, 2012).

30. King, *Apt Pupil*, 142.

31. King, *Apt Pupil*, 143.

32. King, *Apt Pupil*, 142.

33. King, *Apt Pupil*, 144.

34. King, *Apt Pupil*, 145.

35. Friedrich Nietzsche, *On the Genealogy of Morals*, trans. Walter Kaufmann and R. J. Hollingdale (New York: Vintage, 1887).

36. King, *Apt Pupil*, 149.

37. King, *Apt Pupil*, 150.
38. King, *Apt Pupil*, 119.
39. King, *Apt Pupil*, 123.
40. King, *Apt Pupil*, 129.
41. King, *Apt Pupil*, 119.
42. King, *Apt Pupil*, 119.
43. King, *Apt Pupil*, 120.
44. King, *Apt Pupil*, 120.
45. Paulo Freire, *Pedagogy of the Oppressed*, trans. Myra Bergman Ramos (New York: Continuum International, 2000), 46-47.
46. King, *Apt Pupil*, 133, 139.
47. King, *Apt Pupil*, 149.
48. Foucault, *Power/Knowledge*, 71.
49. Edward Bernays, *Crystallizing Public Opinion* (New York: Boni and Liveright, 1923), 212.
50. Noam Chomsky, *Language and Politics*, ed. C. P. Otero (New York: Black Rose Books, 1988), 671.
51. Noam Chomsky, "Beyond a Domesticating Education: A Dialogue," in *Chomsky on MisEducation*, ed. Donaldo Macedo (Lanham, Md.: Rowman & Littlefield, 2004), 16.
52. King, *Apt Pupil*, 290.

9

THE SHINING'S OVERLOOK HOTEL AS HETEROTOPIA

Elizabeth Hornbeck

As the setting for the disturbing events of Stephen King's 1977 novel *The Shining*, as well as Stanley Kubrick's 1980 film adaptation, the Overlook Hotel represents architecture as a force to be reckoned with. Space, for King, is not neutral. His great spatial creation, the Overlook Hotel, provides a paradigm case of space that is charged with subversive power and meaning. The argument of this chapter is based on Michel Foucault's (1926–1984) theory of the heterotopia. Foucault suggests that space itself plays a role in social intercourse, and he attempts to explain the nature of that role through the relationship between heterotopias and the more normative spaces of daily life. The types of spaces that he calls heterotopias are those in which "all the other real arrangements that can be found within society are at one and the same time represented, challenged, and overturned: a sort of place that lies outside all places and yet is actually localizable."[1] Foucault's concept is premised on an understanding of architectural space as social space, that is, of its being defined socially through its use. A heterotopia is created not by the architectural form of a building but by the social interactions that take place within it. In this chapter I will examine King's Overlook Hotel as a heterotopia, and suggest that Foucault's theory of the heterotopia is a potentially powerful tool for analyzing space as it is constructed in the narrative media of novels and films.

Foucault saw our age as one concerned mainly with space, in contrast to the concern with time (in the form of history) that dominated the nineteenth century. In his 1967 lecture *"Des espaces autres: Utopies et heterotopies"* ("Of Other Spaces: Utopias and Heterotopias"), unpublished during his lifetime, Foucault offers the idea of heterotopias as spaces that subvert social norms. Despite his neutral language, Foucault's text implies that transgressing social norms is a desirable activity, at times, and that providing social spaces for those transgressions is necessary; the heterotopia encourages but also limits transgression, protecting all other social spaces from its threats.

While some transgressions are liberatory (though how many and which ones is subjective), it is equally true that some are horrific. *The Shining*—both novel and film—presents transgressions of family life and relationships that not only subvert social norms, they are horrific indeed. Jack Torrance is the husband/father turned into a monster, a perversion of his expected role as nurturer, protector, and provider. Here King's self-acknowledged role as "an agent of the status quo" or "an agent of the norm" is apparent; his Overlook Hotel is a character in the story, the main villain that undermines the nuclear family and hence the entire social order. This is the chief difference between King's heterotopia and Foucault's heterotopia; while Foucault works to unmask power and to question the status quo, King finds transgression and subversion deeply threatening. In *Danse Macabre*, King observes that the entire horror genre is, in fact, conservative, because vanquishing the monster is a metaphor for restoring the status quo.[2]

The most unsettling aspect of *The Shining* is the disintegration of the Torrance family (Wendy, Jack, and Danny) due to the husband/father's psychological unraveling. Bob Fear suggests that the family unit is inextricably bound to the house in virtually any successful horror film, based on his assertion that "the greatest horror stories are those that subvert the familiar." Horror films, he says, exploit our fear of "losing our basic security and comfort."[3] Fear is correct in his observation, but his essay doesn't go far enough in theorizing just *how* domestic architecture in the horror genre subverts the familiar. Foucault's theory of the heterotopia explains more effectively the phenomenon observed by Fear. By subverting the familiar, those horror movie homes affirm their own status as heterotopias. According to Foucault, "home" is not supposed to be a heterotopia. Home is one of the normative social spaces against which the heterotopia is defined. Neither crisis nor deviance belongs in the safety of the "home," in an ideal world; but when the family has run amok, even that safe space of the home may become a heterotopia.

To expand on Fear's argument, I believe that domestic architecture in film is *always* used to represent the family, regardless of genre— think of *The Grapes of Wrath* (John Ford, 1940), *A Raisin in the Sun* (Daniel Petrie, 1961, based on Lorraine Hansberry's 1959 stage play), *Sweet Land* (Ali Selim, 2005), *Gosford Park* (Robert Altman, 2001), and even the comedy *Mr. Blandings Builds His Dream House* (H. C. Potter, 1948)—but we see it most clearly in horror films, from the rural house in *The Amityville Horror* (Stuart Rosenberg, 1979) and the suburban houses in *The Stepford Wives* (Bryan Forbes, 1975) and *Poltergeist* (Tobe Hooper, 1982) to the urban house in *Panic Room* (David Fincher, 2001) and the apartment building in *Rosemary's Baby* (Roman Polanski, 1968, based on Ira Levin's 1967 novel). The home structures social relationships and reflects family dynamics and power relationships, including those based on gender, race, class, age, and other social signifiers. But it is only in horror films and novels where the home may function as a heterotopia, as does the Overlook Hotel, which serves as the Torrance family's temporary home, and which provides none of the familiar comforts and reassurances of the idealized normative home. The Overlook Hotel traps the Torrance family in a malicious perversion of home, a heterotopia in which not even Foucault would want to live.

FOUCAULT'S HETEROTOPIAS

Foucault first put forth the term "heterotopia" in his 1966 book *Les Mots et les Choses* (*The Order of Things*, 1970), in which the term refers not to physical or social space but to language, taxonomy, and our culturally specific ways of ordering and hence understanding the world. In his preface to *The Order of Things*, Foucault explains how language as an ordering tool is not neutral, but instead creates a figurative place (i.e., a nonplace) where relationships among words and the things they stand for are mapped out. In *The Order of Things* Foucault identifies "utopia" and "heterotopia" as linguistic tropes, the former associated with the category of the "Same," and the latter with the "Other." For example, Foucault explains that "the history of madness would be the history of the Other—of that which, for a given culture, is at once interior and foreign, therefore to be excluded (so as to exorcise the interior danger) but by being shut away (in order to reduce its otherness)."[4] Here is where heterotopia as a linguistic trope dovetails with heterotopia as a spatial trope: individuals occupying heterotopian spaces are "Others" to individuals who conform to social norms, just as, for Foucault, "madness" is a social category that denotes alterity. But it's not the people who are "Other," it's the institutions and spaces they occupy that designate them as "Other." He is suggesting that by moving from one type of place to another, an individual may either be normative or its opposite.

In *The Order of Things*, Foucault writes that "heterotopias [of language] are disturbing" because they resist efforts at categorization and classification. A year later, Foucault adapted the heterotopia to his discussion of space. In both cases, linguistic and spatial, Foucault's heterotopia is fundamentally an instrument of political and social critique.[5] Foucault describes three categories of space: utopias, heterotopias, and all other spaces. Both utopias and heterotopias "are endowed with the curious property of being in relation to all the other[space]s, but in such a way as to suspend, neutralize or invert the set of relationships designed, reflected or mirrored by themselves." Correlating them to utopias, which by definition are not real, Foucault claims that heterotopias really exist. They are, in Foucault's terms, "effectively realized utopia[s]."[6]

Foucault describes numerous examples of heterotopias, all of which demonstrate these six basic principles: first, the heterotopia "is a constant feature of all human groups"; second, a heterotopia may function in different ways at different times in a given society; third, "the heterotopia has the power of juxtaposing in a single real place different spaces and locations that are incompatible with each other"; fourth, they are linked to bits and pieces of time; fifth, "heterotopias always presuppose a system of opening and closing that isolates them and makes them penetrable at one and the same time"; and sixth, "they have, in relation to the rest of space, a function that takes place between two opposite poles."[7] Through these six principles, Foucault analyzes how heterotopias exercise their power to "represent, challenge, and overturn" the normative spaces of society. Thus heterotopias have the potential to liberate subjects from the social norms that most social spaces police and reinforce. The family home, for example—not usually a heterotopia—constrains the parent-child relationship, the spousal relationship, intergenerational relationships, and so forth, all according to socially defined roles. Breaking away from those norms is facilitated by leaving the normative space of "home" and entering the subversive space of a heterotopia.

Foucault identifies two different categories of heterotopias: heterotopias of crisis and heterotopias of deviance. He writes that heterotopias of crisis are "privileged, sacred or forbidden places that are reserved for the individual who finds himself in a state of crisis with respect to the society or environment in which he lives: adolescents, women during the menstrual period or in labour, the old, etc.," and they belong chiefly to "so-called primitive societies." These, Foucault said in 1967, are steadily disappearing from our society. He identifies sexual initiation as one form of crisis, and the spaces designed to accommodate it as heterotopias: the boarding school or military service for young men, and the tradition of the honeymoon for young women, so that sexual initiation could take place away from the home and the family.[8]

In contrast, heterotopias of deviance are reserved for individuals whose behavior deviates from the norm, such as rest homes, psychiatric clinics, and prisons, each of which confines deviant individuals and isolates them from the rest of society. These heterotopias both protect "normal" spaces from nonnormative activity and they provide a space in which nonnormative activities can take place safely—that is, without risk to the rest of society. Foucault's examples of heterotopias of deviance include old-people's homes (which are also heterotopias of crisis), cemeteries, theaters, cinemas, gardens, museums, libraries, fairs, holiday villages, hammams and saunas, motel rooms, brothels, colonies, and ships.

Foucault describes motel rooms as heterotopias "where illicit sex is totally protected and totally concealed at one and the same time, set apart and yet not under an open sky." They conform especially to Foucault's fifth principle by being both isolated and penetrable spaces, requiring special permission for entry.[9] Hotels also fit this definition. While Foucault does not mention hotels in his essay, they satisfy his description of the heterotopia of deviance because of the unique kind of social space they offer. Hotels bring together individuals whose paths might not normally cross, and they create relationships and social hierarchies new to those individuals—relationships and hierarchies that do not always correspond to the individuals' "normal" relationships outside of the hotel. In subverting the status quo they are fundamentally political spaces in the broadest sense. While, according to Foucault, heterotopias exist in all societies, they are not determined by a building's formal characteristics; they are not even really created by architects, but by society as a whole.[10]

THE OVERLOOK HOTEL AND ITS GHOSTS

King's horror in *The Shining* is based on a Freudian understanding of psychological trauma and repression. King has said that "monsters are real, ghosts are real too. They live inside us and sometimes they win."[11] In *The Shining*, Jack Torrance's monsters and ghosts are the traces of childhood physical abuse at the hands of his father; violence perpetrated on his mother; and the hereditary alcoholism that beleaguered both his father and himself. In the "normal" spaces of everyday life, these monsters and ghosts are kept somewhat in check; but at the Overlook Hotel, they make him all the more vulnerable to the controlling influence of the heterotopian, "haunted" space.

The Shining's Overlook Hotel is full of ghosts. As heterotopias, buildings can be "haunted" by the traces of the past; this is what is meant by a "socially determined" space. The Overlook Hotel is a heterotopia as a consequence of the kinds of illicit behaviors that have taken place there over many decades, including a long history of sexual transgressions. It is the social use of the hotel over a long duration that defines the nature of events that take place in the novel/film's diegetic present, and these are the kinds of social uses to which hotel spaces are universally put. Early in King's novel we learn about Mrs. Massey, a sixty-year-old woman who came to the hotel with her much younger lover, and then committed suicide when he deserted her. Later Mrs. Massey appears as the decaying corpse in room 217 in the novel (room 237 in the film), whose presence is more than just an apparition; Danny and Jack both encounter it as a physical danger. Another example of sexual transgression at the Overlook Hotel appears to Wendy near the end of Kubrick's film: a man in a dog suit performing oral sex on a man in a tuxedo. Many such details are not explained in the film, but are explained in King's novel. Readers of the novel can identify the man in the tuxedo as Harry Derwent, a onetime owner of the Overlook Hotel, and the man in the animal costume (in the novel it is a silvery, spangled dog costume) as his lover, Roger. In the novel the two men carry on a sadomasochistic flirtation at the masked ball, which Jack attends in the Colorado Lounge. Later the dogman confronts Danny, with his mouth, chin, and cheeks smeared with blood. [12]

Besides illicit sexual activities, the Overlook Hotel has been the scene of worse transgressions. The Overlook Hotel's unsavory past is one that its financiers would like to forget; but in King's novel the maintenance man, Watson, tells Jack, "I figure there's maybe forty-five people died in this hotel since my grandfather opened it for business in 1910." [13] The long list of the dead includes three members of the hotel founder's family, including his young son, who died as early as 1908 or 1909 during the hotel's construction; a later president of the ownership corporation, who killed himself in 1957 after being indicted in a scandal; a writing student who crashed through a third-floor window in 1961; the triple shotgun slaying in 1966 of a gang overlord and two bodyguards in the hotel's presidential suite; and a senator who died of a heart attack in 1968, during a period when Jack believes the Overlook was being used as a brothel (another variety of heterotopia according to Foucault). And a woman checking out of the hotel on the day that the Torrances arrive mentions that her husband died on the roque court from a stroke in 1955 (which hasn't prevented her from continuing to come to the Overlook every year since).

The most significant deaths at the Overlook, in terms of foreshadowing the Torrances' experience, are Delbert Grady's murder of his wife and two daughters, just a few years prior to the Torrances' stay at the Overlook. Like Jack, Grady had once been hired as the hotel's winter caretaker. According to Stuart Ullman, Grady had killed his two daughters with a hatchet, then killed his wife and himself with a shotgun. The family had inhabited the same living quarters within the Overlook Hotel that the Torrances were preparing to occupy. In Kubrick's film the ghosts of the two girls appear to Danny multiple times, inviting him to play with them "forever and ever."

In *The Shining* we can see how space and time converge at the Overlook Hotel to create what Foucault calls a "chronic heterotopia" or a heterotopia of time, "which accumulates [time] *ad infinitum*." In heterotopias of time, "time does not cease to accumulate, perching, so

to speak, on its own summit." Foucault gives as examples museums and
libraries, which assemble moments from all different times into the
same place, but a place that is itself outside time:

> The idea of accumulating everything . . . or creating a sort of univer-
> sal archive, the desire to enclose all times, all eras, forms and styles
> within a single place, the concept of making all times into one place,
> and yet a place that is outside time, inaccessible to the wear and tear
> of the years, according to a plan of almost perpetual and unlimited
> accumulation within an irremovable place, all this belongs entirely to
> our modern outlook.[14]

The heterotopia of time, or chronic heterotopia, foregrounds the
intersection of what Foucault sees as a nineteenth-century obsession,
time/history, with space, an obsession with which he sees as the source
of modern anxiety. History, that "great and obsessive dread," looms
over the Overlook, generating the ghosts that terrorize the Torrance
family and claim Jack Torrance for eternity.

In King's novel, Jack Torrance discovers a scrapbook in which all of
the hotel's history, including its darkest moments, is documented. The
supposed ghosts of the hotel are traces from those times; the past is
alive here. Kubrick's film ends on an image that reinforces that collapsing of time: a photograph from a July 4 party that took place in 1921,
with Jack himself at its center. While Wendy and Danny have escaped
from this living death, Jack has become immortalized in the very place
where he has died. Thus the Overlook is like a cemetery, for Foucault
"a highly heterotopian place," which "begins with that strange heteroch-
ronism that is, for a human being, the loss of life and of that quasi-
eternity in which, however, he does not cease to dissolve and be
erased."[15] Jack Torrance will not be erased entirely, though, unless the
entire hotel is destroyed, as it is in King's novel by a massive fire
brought on by the explosion of the antiquated boiler.

The history of murders recounted in King's novel does more than
simply foreshadow Jack's murderous spree, and it does more than account for the ghosts that inhabit the hotel. The hotel's sinister history
defines the building as a space of transgression, a heterotopia in which
"normal" social behavior can be distorted, inverted, or perverted. In
The Shining, this allows Jack Torrance, a husband and father, to go
berserk and try to kill his own wife and son, away from the normative

space of "home," which might have kept his behavior in check (or at least would have given Wendy access to police, medical, and legal intervention). Read on a supernatural level, the Overlook Hotel is haunted, and its ghosts make Jack try to kill his family. Read at the level of the heterotopia, we see that social norms are discarded in a space that exists in order to provide a space free of those norms. The Overlook Hotel derives both its unsavory ghosts and its disruptive power from its status as a heterotopia.

Not all individuals will choose to discard, subvert, or transgress the social norms, even within a heterotopia. While Jack Torrance discards those social norms, Wendy and Danny Torrance struggle to maintain the norms of the nuclear family in their temporary home, but theirs is a losing struggle. Jack had never upheld those norms; through his alcoholism and his physical abuse of Danny, he had already undermined his paternal role. In the heterotopian space of the Overlook Hotel, though, he wins that struggle against Wendy and Danny. His own ghosts emerge, tipping the scale in favor of this horrific transgression.

Secluded and even inaccessible during the winter, the Overlook Hotel traps the Torrance family so that they have no access to their normal social interactions, routines, and obligations, or even help from outside the family. As a heterotopia of deviance it contains Jack as he grows increasingly insane and violent, separating him from society, as Foucault's best-known heterotopias—the prison and the insane asylum—are meant to do. At the same time, though, it traps his wife and son there with him in a heterotopia of crisis. Normal family relations, based on love and protection, are inverted and subverted as this non-normative domestic space wields its influence on the troubled patriarch.

Foucault's concept of the heterotopia helps us to understand how architecture in film can function like a character in a narrative. Architectural space in film is essentially a representation of social relations. Thus, in the context of film, architecture does not simply serve as a backdrop or stage for the narrative to take place. Architecture conveys meaning in its own right, reinforcing emotional or psychological aspects of characters and themes. It "acts" on the other characters in the narrative, it helps drive the plot, and so it can be said to be a character. In *The Shining*, the Overlook Hotel makes possible Jack Torrance as the perversion of a good father.

THE HOTEL FILM

The theory of the heterotopia is to my mind most useful as a tool for both literary and film analysis. While literary texts may describe a heterotopian space in all of its power, the film narrative allows us to visualize the space as an actor. It is worth pointing out in this context Alfred Hitchcock's frequent use of luxury hotels as settings for his suspense films. In *Rebecca* (1940), a wealthy English aristocrat falls in love with a young orphaned American woman in the lobby of a hotel. (Could it happen anywhere else?) In *To Catch a Thief* (1955), a retired jewel thief passes himself off as a midwestern American businessman in order to investigate a jewel theft, and it is in the hotel's lobby and restaurant spaces that he perpetrates his deception of a rich American widow and her socialite daughter. In *North by Northwest* (1959), a businessman sitting in a hotel bar is mistaken for a known spy, creating the mistaken identity that sets the entire narrative in motion. A similar heterotopian space, the motel, is used compellingly in *Psycho* (1960), closely following Orson Welles's sinister use of a motel setting in *A Touch of Evil* (1958).

It is interesting to examine all of these films in the context of what Geoffrey Cocks describes as the "hotel mode" in literature and cinema, a significant theme that, he argues, began with Stephen Crane's 1898 story "The Blue Hotel." In his monograph on Stanley Kubrick, Cocks situates *The Shining* within this literary and cinematic discourse on hotels. He claims that "between 1898 and 2001, there were made in the world no fewer than 289 films just on hotels per se," and he identifies *Grand Hotel* (Edmund Goulding, 1932) as an important early example.[16] At the Grand Hotel people often are not what they seem: the baron is a hotel thief; Preysig, the upstanding businessman and family man, decides in desperation to lie to potential investors and to embark on an extramarital affair; the glamorous ballerina Gruschinskaya turns out to be lonely, insecure, and unsure of her popularity and her talent.

The hotel in *Grand Hotel* constitutes a heterotopia for a variety of reasons. In the film we witness social relationships being turned on their heads. For example, General Preysig, a wealthy capitalist, and Otto Kringelein, the lowly bookkeeper who until recently worked in Preysig's factory, exchange social identities over the course of the film. In the heterotopia of the hotel, Preysig's public persona is revealed as a sham. In this spatial context, he breaks the rules of his normal bourgeois life, lying to his business associates in order to forge a new partnership, attempting to initiate a sexual liaison with a young stenographer, and ultimately committing murder. He is led away from the hotel in hand-cuffs, disgraced and ruined, with the implication that this situation has allowed his true persona finally to emerge. At the same time, his former employee Kringelein experiences a rags-to-riches transformation, and leaves the hotel with the beautiful stenographer on his arm. Goulding's Depression-era fantasy optimistically metes out justice in a reassuring manner, but nonetheless is premised on the ethereal ability of the hotel to reveal the characters' essential qualities.

A comparison between the Grand Hotel and the Overlook Hotel illustrates the difference between Foucault's two main spatial tropes, the heterotopia and the panopticon. Foucault discussed the panopticon in *Discipline and Punish* (1977). The panopticon, a building type used in prisons and other institutions of social control, uses visuality to exert power and maintain authority. In the panopticon penitentiary, originally designed in 1791 by Jeremy Bentham (1748–1832), architectural design provides maximum visual surveillance. Thus, design both induces and coerces individuals to internalize the ever-present (or at least ever-threatening) gaze of the authority. Heterotopias, on the other hand, do not rely on design; they may take any architectural form. A brothel, for example, is a heterotopia because the social relations that prevail there are so different from those that prevail outside its walls; it does not require any specific spatial design (like Claude-Nicolas Ledoux's 1780 plan for a brothel in the shape of an erect phallus!) in order to be a heterotopia.

The Grand Hotel (a set designed by MGM set designer Cedric Gibbons) is designed as a panopticon, with a circular floor plan at each level and an open atrium in the center. Each hall is monitored visually by a clerk, and trying to evade detection is a challenge for the hotel thief. Heterotopias, on the other hand, need not adopt any specific architectural form. In contrast to the high level of visibility of the Grand Hotel, the Overlook Hotel is a mazelike space with an intricate network of corridors. The perception of secret, hidden knowledge, symbolically housed in the rooms of the hotel, is fundamental to both King's and Kubrick's creation of suspense. As the camera follows Danny riding his Big Wheel through its halls, we expect to find horror around every corner. The hotels in these two films could not be more different, yet both function as heterotopias.

This hotel "genre," or "hotel mode" (Cocks uses both terms), which he says evolved rapidly in the 1970s, variously presented the hotel as a place of intrigue, mystery, and danger; as a "location and symbol of public danger and state power"; as a dangerous and even delirious microcosm of the surrounding society; and, metaphorically, as a place for individuals "to lose to the forces of worldly power and universal indifference." Cocks specifically describes the Overlook Hotel in *The Shining* as "a symbol of great human evil."[17] The Overlook Hotel fits into the model of the heterotopia because it is a site for all sorts of behaviors that would not take place so easily in more "normative" spaces, such as the home.

Without invoking Foucault, Cocks comes closest to describing the heterotopia when he states that "the literary or cinematic hotel—and, ever since *Psycho*, motel—is a home that is not home, a place of privacy but also of vulnerability, of collectivity but also of isolation." His "home that is not home" resonates with the Foucauldian definition of heterotopias as spaces that "stand in relation to all other spaces, but invert" normal social relationships. However, Cocks immediately follows this statement with a quote from Siegfried Kracauer, who describes the hotel lobby as "a space that does not refer beyond itself,"[18] which is entirely opposite to the heterotopia. For Foucault, the heterotopia is by definition connected with all the other spaces in a society. Heterotopias and their counterparts, normative spaces, stand in relationship to each other through "unrelenting opposites" such as sacred and profane, urban and rural, protected and open, which are holdovers from medieval thought. Space is not empty and homogenous, but "saturated with qualities" that derive their value from being juxtaposed with spaces that have different qualities.[19]

CONCLUSION

While it is quite useful for analyzing narrative media, the theory of the heterotopia is, in my opinion, not helpful for analyzing real architecture; it describes social spaces, not built spaces. Henry Urbach surveys various ways in which, during the 1970s, architectural theorists (including

Demetri Porphyrios, Manfredo Tafuri, and Georges Teyssot) attempted to translate Foucault's theory into architectural design, reducing it to formal characteristics and a stable essence. However, as Urbach argues, such attempts ignore the importance of Foucault's theory, in which the heterotopia is a powerful political tool that "dissolves, destabilizes and interrupts power."[20] Heterotopias undermine our sense of ordering, defining, and understanding, and hence to some extent *controlling*, the spaces we occupy. Unlike their counterparts, normative spaces, heterotopias are spaces where the transgressive can take place without censure. They are not created by architects; they are made by the users of architecture.

Stephen King's Overlook Hotel stands as a paradigm case of the heterotopian space in narrative media—both novel and film—seen as a threat to social norms. Architecture in the form of the Overlook Hotel is not neutral or inert; it is a character in the drama, an actor that influences human behavior and emotions. It doubles as home and hotel for the Torrance family—"home" signifying a normative social space, and "hotel" signifying the "Other" space that subverts it, undermining the reassuring normalcy of the nuclear family. Within its walls Jack is free to let his darkest urges run wild; within those same walls, Wendy and Danny are terrorized almost to death. Anything can happen in the absence of social control; its absence may be liberatory, but it may also be horrific. The ghosts may manifest themselves, and they may win.

For Foucault the heterotopia "represented, challenged, and overturned" all the other "real arrangements that can be found within society." Making explicit what Foucault only implies, Urbach sees the heterotopia's effects as salutary because they expose "the apparent normality of other spaces as fictitious and restrictive."[21] But *The Shining* suggests that we need to be wary of what we unleash, because the threats of transgressive behaviors are very real. Sometimes the monsters unleashed in these "other spaces" can win. In King's novel, Jack knows all too well that the hotel is using him to destroy his family; in order to escape from the hotel's sinister heterotopia and evil intentions, the father must sacrifice his own life, a final gesture that restores the father to his role as protector of his family and upholder of social norms. In the conservative horror genre, heterotopias are never salutary, which may be the biggest difference between Stephen King and Michel Foucault.

NOTES

1. Michel Foucault, "Of Other Spaces: Utopias and Heterotopias," n.d., reprinted in *Rethinking Architecture: A Reader in Cultural Theory*, ed. Neil Leach (London: Routledge, 1997), 352.

2. Stephen King, *Danse Macabre* (New York: Everest House, 1981), 81, 85.

3. Bob Fear, "Evil Residence: The House and the Horror Film," in *Architecture and Film II* (London: Wiley-Academy, 2000), 37.

4. Foucault, preface to *The Order of Things* (*Les Mots et les Choses*) (Paris: Editions Gallimard, 1966; New York: Random House,1970), xxiv.

5. As discussed in Henry Urbach, "Writing Architectural Heterotopia," *Journal of Architecture* 3 (Winter 1998): 347–48.

6. Foucault, "Of Other Spaces," 352.

7. Foucault, "Of Other Spaces," 353–56.

8. Foucault, "Of Other Spaces," 353.

9. Foucault, "Of Other Spaces," 355–56.

10. Urbach criticizes the appropriation of the term "heterotopia" by architects who see it as a category of design methodology, and who use it "to identify and praise certain works, projects and places" ("Writing Architectural Heterotopia," 349). Such appropriation trivializes the idea of the heterotopia, undermining its political import and its theoretical potential.

11. Stephen King, introduction to *The Shining* (New York: Pocket Books, 2001), xvii.

12. King, *The Shining*, 506–9, 526–42. Steven Bruhm reads Danny's vision of the dogman with bloody mouth as a threat of castration. Steven Bruhm, "On Stephen King's Phallus; or, The Postmodern Gothic," in *American Gothic: New Interventions in a National Narrative*, ed. Robert K. Martin and Eric Savoy (Iowa City: University of Iowa Press, 1998), 77, 87.

13. Stephen King, *The Shining* (1977; repr., New York: Pocket Books, 2001), 34.

14. Foucault, "Of Other Spaces," 355.

15. Foucault, "Of Other Spaces," 354.

16. Geoffrey Cocks, *The Wolf at the Door: Stanley Kubrick, History, & the Holocaust* (New York: Peter Lang, 2004), 184.

17. Cocks, *Wolf at the Door*, 177.

18. Cocks, *Wolf at the Door*, 182.

19. Foucault, "Of Other Spaces," 351.

20. Urbach, "Writing Architectural Heterotopia," 349.

21. Urbach, "Writing Architectural Heterotopia," 351.

10

BROADCAST DYSTOPIA

Power and Violence in *The Running Man*
and *The Long Walk*

Joseph J. Foy and Timothy M. Dale

*It is true that storytelling reveals meaning without committing the
error of defining it.*—Hannah Arendt[1]

Stephen King is known as the "crown prince of horror." His terrifying
novels have frightened generations of readers who drive more quickly
past cornfields, look skeptically at clowns, and learned to look for the
devil behind their desires for "needful things." When writing under the
pseudonym of Richard Bachman, however, King becomes a horror
writer of a different kind. The dystopian realities of the worlds he
creates aren't dominated by creatures in the mist, zombie pets, or psychotic automobiles with their own animus. They are infested with monsters of a different stripe, human beings who use structural and physical
violence as a means of political control.[2]

From this particular philosophical standpoint, the ideas expressed
within two of the Bachman books, *The Long Walk* (1979) and *The
Running Man* (1982), reflect ideas articulated within the social and
political philosophy of Hannah Arendt (1906–1975), a German-born,
Jewish political theorist who escaped the Holocaust and became an
American citizen. Like *The Long Walk* and *The Running Man*, Arendt's
political philosophy focuses on politics, authority, and power. Through
the lens of her work, readers of the dystopian works composed by King

under the Bachman pseudonym can gain a richer appreciation for the context and framework in which King is operating in these novels. Concomitantly, by weaving these nightmarish narratives with Arendt's political theories on power and violence, we can cast a light on our places within our own violent world and the impact of the voyeuristic consumption of violence and entertainment as a means of escape.

LET THE GAMES BEGIN

Both *The Long Walk* and *The Running Man* are based in a fictive version of the near-future United States, each representing a different dystopian look at the concentration and application of power and violence. In *The Long Walk*, the concentration of power and application of power is centered within a militaristically structured government, which has transitioned into a type of police state. In *The Running Man*, the state continues but the real power seems to be vested within a large corporate entertainment industry known as the Games Network. Both novels present gladiatorial types of competition in an effort to provide both spectacle and serve as a reminder of the control of the ruling authority over the masses.

The Long Walk centers on an annual, governmentally sponsored competition where one hundred teenage boys are selected for a grueling test of endurance where they must continue walking without end at a pace of no less than four miles per hour without assistance from anyone but the soldiers monitoring the walk. If a walker fails to maintain an average speed of four miles per hour, he is given a warning. After three warnings a walker is said to have "bought a ticket"—a euphemism for execution. To lose means death. The winner of the competition is given the ultimate prize: whatever he wants for the rest of his life. The winners of the competition do not live carefree lives, however. They suffer many ailments, both physical and mental, from their torturous involvement in the Walk.

The Running Man also focuses on a life-or-death competition. In this novel, the Games Network is the predominant entity of control. The ubiquitous Free-Vee provides constant broadcasts of its brutal lineup that is half sport and half reality television. Some of the more basic programs have individuals with physical disabilities competing for cash with escalating challenges that ultimately result in most of them dying on live television. The most popular, and barbaric, of all of the competitions is *The Running Man*. This show selects individuals of high intelligence and physical capabilities and sets them free into the United States to run from "Hunters" and the police. They are given money for every Hunter or police officer they kill, and earn cash rewards the longer they stay alive. Anyone who survives thirty days is given a grand prize of $1 billion. Prior to the entry of the novel's protagonist, Ben Richards, no one had ever survived longer than 197 hours.[3]

THAT FREE-VEE SHIT IS FOR EMPTY HEADS

The "gladiatorial competition as spectacle" motif is one that we find in a number of popular dystopian narratives, ranging from *The Hunger Games* to *Battle Royale* and *The Maze Runner* to *Rollerball*. King's dystopian writing often includes a story in which the state uses violence and the consumption of its spectacle as a form of control. This is what we find in *The Long Walk* and *The Running Man*, each containing exaggerated forms of violence that take over all parts of life. In these stories violence becomes the norm, and is so pervasive that it makes it difficult to have any relationship with others outside of the experience of violence. In each case, the state uses violence as a means for trying to maintain political control and domination, and the spectacle serves both as a means of pacifying the masses through image-based entertainment as well as an inherent threat to those who might challenge its authority.

In her "Reflections on Violence," Hannah Arendt describes the way in which violence—not power or force or strength—has, through technological development and historical evolution, become a means confused with its end.[4] Rather than violence being the way in which regimes pursue goals that they deem necessary, violence itself becomes one of the purposes of society. The existence of war in this context becomes a pervasive condition of society instead of a limited activity of necessity. The people who live in such a society must accept that human life is expendable, and willingly accept that violence is to be preferred over connection to others. As a result, image-based societies will rely heavily on creating a spectacle of violence as a means of creating a disposability of the individual to sever affective ties. Like the Network in *The Running Man* framing and editing its "competitors" as violent criminals to work the crowds of spectators into a violent frenzy with chants of "TURN HIM IN" and "KILL HIM," Arendt argues that these spectacles of violence limit the possibility of revolutionary sentiments that might challenge state authority or action. An effective tool for a strategy of divide and conquer summed up by Killian: "You keep forgetting that you're an anachronism, Mr. Richards. People won't be in the bars and hotels or gathering in the cold in front of appliance stores rooting for you to get away. Goodness! no. They want to see you wiped out, and they'll even help if they can. The more messy the better."[5]

Though power and violence are often considered closely linked, Arendt argues that violence and power are on the opposite ends of a spectrum. In Arendt's terms, power requires coordination while violence requires coercion, and as one becomes more present the other is diminished. In examining the technological advancements of the twentieth century, particularly in the militaristic realm of the state, Arendt articulates a difference between power, which arises from a group or groups acting collectively toward a common end, and violence, which uses implements to force action or agreement. Violence is an artificial means of achieving the same goals as the application of power, but its intent is to force capitulation and compliance. In *On Violence*, Arendt explains that this relationship between violence and power leads to one of the ironic consequences of the modern state; in it, people who hold power resort to violence, thereby losing power over time.[6] This happens because political elites often confuse violence and the control it brings with actual power. This creates a cycle of power decline, however, because the more violence that is exercised, the more people question the power of the state. The application of violence, therefore, corresponds with the declining loss of power by the state. The result is a revolutionary fervor that begins to amass in those subjugated to the abuses of violence, which will explode in a revolutionary outburst that ultimately results in a total loss of power by those who once possessed it.

Arendt's perspectives on power and violence are woven throughout King's dystopian works. For example, in *The Running Man* the United States of the future lacks the capacity or the collective will to provide adequate resources and protections for its people. Instead, it employs the Free-Vee and the Games Network to pacify the masses through extreme violence. Death of those competing in the games is not an anomaly or unintended consequence, it is a regularity that keeps individuals tuned in. The Walk and the Games Network broadcasts, therefore, become artificial displays of power by those holding positions of privilege in order to try and maintain perceptions of authority and control. By using competitors as examples of the "power" that the state and its various apparatuses holds over life and death through the use of extreme violence, the spectacle becomes a means of maintaining control and preserving order.

The violence gets more and more extreme and pervasive, as does the structural violence within the system designed to maintain the extreme gaps between the wealthiest and the poor. As is postulated by Arendt when describing the divergence of power and violence, the more violence that is applied, the more resources and efforts the state must dedicate to that violence, further diminishing its ability to meet the needs of governance. In turn, this erodes feelings of support or trust for the state and its agencies, which is a further dilution of power that requires even more violence to maintain control. Thus, not unlike the change over time of the Walkers' attitudes toward the Major moving from admiration before the walk begins to ridicule as the competition wears on ("Everyone wants to piss on the Major"),[7] the more the state applies violence as a means of control the more it will be met with resistance and frustration from its citizenry.

REAL MEN DON'T RUN FOR PRESIDENT

When considering Arendt's perspectives on violence, it might be easy for one to dismiss all uses of violence as necessarily unwarranted or illogical. This is not the case. According to Arendt, as long as violence does not become a goal in itself, it may be used as a rational means for achieving short-term, immediate goals. Richards is presented with a life that is defined by the structural violence of pervasive poverty born out of extreme class division. His family does not have access to adequate nutrition (pellets), nor do they have the means to purchase needed medicine for his dying daughter, Cathy. Sheila is forced to sell her body just to try and purchase essentials, but the medicine available to impoverished families through the pharmacies is, according to Richards, "shit." The black market, promulgated by individuals like Mrs. Jenner, has essential goods but is too expensive. Prior to being blacklisted from his trade for his attitude, Richards could seek employment, but the type of jobs he could secure were inhumane. Radiation leaks and lack of appropriate worker safety are just a couple of the common examples of what is out there for him or workers like him. The systemic violence of poor working conditions for the laboring classes—as well as the resulting, poverty, hunger, and sickness—leaves Richards no choice but to enter the violent games, and in doing so may rationally employ violence in response to his oppressive circumstances.

Occasionally violence might appear to be an acceptable tactic, but the short-term goal it achieves may also lead to unpredictable long-term consequences. Arendt argues that "the means used to achieve political goals are more often than not of greater relevance to the future world than the intended goals."[8] Under the impression that the state gains legitimacy through fear, the violent acts become more important than the objectives they sought to obtain. Subsequently, and contrary to the goal of legitimacy, the more violence is applied by the state and the institutions that support it, the more resistance builds up among those who are threatened by this violence. Soon, the apparatuses that support state action become reviled, and the state must exercise more violence to attempt to regain control. As Stacey tells Richards, "I hate them [cops] worse than anyone. Even the devil."[9] The resentment and resistance that builds up as a response to violence instills a revolutionary fervor that will lead to mass resistance. As Bradley notes when talking with Richards before helping him, "People is mad. They've been mad at the honkies for thirty years. All they need is a reason. A reason . . . one reason . . ."[10]

WALKING TOWARD THE BANALITY OF EVIL

If Bradley is correct, one may ask why the individuals within King's novels don't organize and resist the violent acts of the state. The answer, at least for these novels, is that King does not like telling those kinds of stories. King instead focuses on the grueling struggles of Garraty and Richards as they compete for the promise of their own "ultimate prizes." In these stories those who live subject to violence are complicit in it because of the lure of competition that is promised within the system. For King, the competitive violence that exists in society causes people to be content with exercises of violence, and develop a willingness to become part of it. In this way, King intends to cast a light back on the dark shadows of our own natures.

Of course, there are several reasons the people of these dystopian Americas may not engage in revolutionary acts. First, an individual sense of fear often manifests in collective nonaction. In both *The Long Walk* and *The Running Man*, it is clear that the state has nothing holding it back from offering capital consequences for what may seem like minor infractions. Soldiers in *The Long Walk* will openly execute someone who receives four warnings during the competition, and the entire purpose of the *Running Man* show is to broadcast the live killing of people who are running for their lives. Such active or permissive brutality by the state instills fear in the populace, and so suppresses open resistance.

Similarly, feelings of disempowerment often exist in violent contexts. The fictive worlds King presents offer a look into societies in which there is a tremendous gap between the haves and have-nots. In *The Running Man*, there are numerous examples of individuals suffering under the weight of poverty and a lack of resources. One example is given of a five-year-old girl named Cassie who has lung cancer from pollution and waste pouring into the air and the streets of impoverished neighborhoods (nose filters that cost upwards of $200 don't provide protection and the ones that do can only be afforded by the very wealthy). Her story is not uncommon. Richards's wife, Sheila, has to turn tricks to try and buy the basic necessities for her husband and their young daughter, Cathy, who is herself suffering from extreme illness. *The Long Walk* begins by introducing us to Garraty's beleaguered and suffering mother, who has lost her husband and risks now losing her son because he saw no other option in life than to try and succeed in the walk. So intent are these individuals on mere survival, without any additional complication that might come from calling attention to an unforgiving state, that the possibility of revolution is suppressed. As Sheila starts to tell Richards when he indicates he is going to sign up for the Games, "Ben, this is what they want—for people like you, for people like us,"[11] indicating that the Games Network feeds off people who do not see any other choice but the Games in their lives.

According to Hannah Arendt, however, the reasons people do not resist violence can run deeper than fear or disempowerment. Arendt makes such an argument in one of her more controversial works, *Eichmann in Jerusalem: A Report on the Banality of Evil*. While covering the trial of the Nazi war criminal Adolf Eichmann, Arendt describes how evil has a seductive way of drawing everyday, average people into committing horrible acts because they are simply "following orders" or uncritically conforming to popular sentiments and opinions. The soldiers who put bullets into the Walkers after their fourth warning, the Hunters chasing the Runners, and even the police regulating society with brutal authority and the common citizen cheering for the deaths of competitors or reporting Runners even though they know it will mean the death of another person—these are examples of individuals just "doing their jobs" and getting swept into the uncritical acceptance of the dominant paradigm.

Falling within the dystopian or apocalyptic literary genre, the worlds created by King are fantastical and extreme but the roots of what is present in both are not unfamiliar to us in our current realities. The fascination with gladiatorial-type combat spectacles can be seen in the growing popularity of mixed martial arts (MMA) and ultimate fighting, as well as the violence of the National Football League. The continued popularity of so-called reality television also reveals a voyeuristic strain of a desire to see "regular people" competing in staged games or scenarios. Though not used as a means of state control in the same way identified by King in his works, the use of such violence and voyeurism as spectacle provides a market-based form of escapism that enables individuals to disconnect from the social and political realities of the world around them, and primes a social perspective that wears away at the affective bonds that unite us within a common sense of humanity. Certainly, one does not have to stretch the imagination far to be able to envision a reality like the one King provides. Though we may make excuses for cheering brutal hits on the football field despite the mounting evidence that the competitors will suffer long-term mental and physical debilitation and even possibly shorter lives, how not unlike Killian or the Major are we when rationalizing that the high levels of compensation more than make up for the harm done to the athlete? If we stop seeing the competitors as human—if the affective ties that bind are diminished or severed—does it not become all the easier to feel some rush or thrill when they are leveled by one of our champions for our entertainment?

It is the final question that brings Arendt's political philosophy full circle. If the state is able, through the use of normalized violence and other dehumanizing means, to wear away at the affective bonds of humanity, then what might otherwise seem an impossible leap—for people to imagine crowds of spectators cheering the deaths of competitors—becomes a real possibility. Perhaps one of the most frightening prospects Stephen King ever introduced to the world through the persona of Bachman was the reminder of what Arendt argues in *The Life of the Mind*: "Evil, we have learned, is something demonic; its incarnation is Satan, a 'lightning fall from heaven.' . . . However, what I was confronted with was utterly different and still undeniably factual. I was struck by a manifest shallowness in the doer that made it impossible to trace the incontestable evil of his deed to any deeper level of roots or motives. The deeds were monstrous, but the doer . . . was quite ordinary, commonplace, and neither demonic nor monstrous."[12]

. . . MINUS 001 AND COUNTING . . .

The Running Man concludes with Richards mortally wounded, flying a hijacked Lockheed aircraft into the Games Building, where it "rained fire twenty blocks away."[13] His act, the last desperate and revolutionary act of a man who had everything taken from him by a brutal, authoritarian state. For Garraty, such an act does not seem possible. Instead, faced with even the promise of the ultimate prize, when a dark hand reaches out to touch his shoulder (the Major declaring his victory?) he finds within himself the strength only to run. Both are personal acts of resistance, but the revolutionary change that would cast off the brutality of state oppression never comes. Though the stories end for Garraty and Richards, we are left with an Orwellian sense of defeat, the image of a boot forever stomping on a human face. Nothing changes. Nothing improves. The dark shadow reaches for our shoulder and the nightmarish visions of a not-too-distant future persist.

The purpose of dystopian literature, however, is to protect us from this fate by inviting readers to reflect on themselves and the world in which they live. That is the power of King's writing. If Arendt is correct, violence and evil are at their most dangerous when individuals never stop to think about what they are doing. People in society must exercise conscious judgment about the structures in which they live, and consider the appropriate responses to violence and evil. Philosophically speaking, through the Bachman books Stephen King provides us an opportunity to stop and think. We are invited to enter a world none of us would wish to live in, knowing that when we return to our own we might be better prepared to make conscious choices. We might walk away from violence, and run to the safety of real power formed through the affective bonds of our common humanity.

NOTES

All references to the Bachman books in this chapter are cited from the First Plume (Omnibus) printing of *The Bachman Books: Four Early Novels by Stephen King* (New York: Plume, 1985).

1. Hannah Arendt, *Men in Dark Times* (New York: Harcourt, Brace, 1983), 147.

2. The other two Bachman books are *Rage* (1977), a novel about a school shooting that is available only through the omnibus collection *The Bachman Books* after King let it fall out of print following actual school shootings in the 1980s and 1990s, and *Roadwork* (1981), about a deeply suffering protagonist who is driven to extreme ends after he finds out his home and livelihood are slated to be destroyed due to the extension of an interstate highway. Though both focus on many aspects of the human condition as it relates to society and community, neither presents a comprehensive perspective on political philosophy similar to that of *The Long Walk* and *The Running Man*.

3. In 1987 *The Running Man* was released as a full-length action film starring Arnold Schwarzenegger. Though the film is the entry point for many to the story of *The Running Man*, and there are common elements between the two related to state- and entertainment-promulgated violence, there are also many dramatic differences between the film and the novel, so much so that King left his (and the Bachman) name off the film credits. This chapter focuses on the novel only.

4. Hannah Arendt, "A Special Supplement: Reflections on Violence," *New York Review of Books*, February 27, 1969, accessed September 10, 2015, http://www.nybooks.com/articles/archives/1969/feb/27/a-special-supplement-reflections-on-violence/ .

5. Stephen King, *The Running Man*, in *The Bachman Books: Four Early Novels by Stephen King* (New York: Plume, 1985), 558.

6. Hannah Arendt, *On Violence* (Orlando, Fla.: Harcourt, 1970).

7. Stephen King, *The Long Walk*, in *The Bachman Books: Four Early Novels by Stephen King* (New York: Plume, 1985), 238.

8. Arendt, *On Violence*, 4.

9. King, *The Running Man*, 592.

10. King, *The Running Man*, 599.

11. King, *The Running Man*, 534.

12. Hannah Arendt, *The Life of the Mind: "Thinking"* (San Diego, Calif.: Harcourt, 1978), 3–4.

13. King, *The Running Man*, 692.

11

STEPHEN KING AND
THE ART OF HORROR

Greg Littmann

I love the part in *The Shining* when Wendy Torrance is running in terror through the corridors of the Overlook Hotel, fleeing her murderous, mallet-wielding husband, and the masked ghost of a dead guest pops out of his room at her, screaming "Great party, isn't it?" in her face, and pulling the string on a party favor. I love the part in *It* when Pennywise the Clown appears to Ben Hanscom in the Derry Public Library, glaring at him out of empty sockets and then transforming into Dracula with bloody steel razor-blade teeth. I love the part in *Pet Sematary* when the dead cat Church comes home from the burying ground, his movements clumsy and the smell of death on him. What kind of a sick bastard am I?

I've loved horror fiction for as long as I can remember, and I find that a bit embarrassing. There's something not quite socially acceptable about it in many circles. A passion like mine is seen as both unhealthily morbid, what with all the violence and death; and absurdly childish, what with the magic and monsters.

Strangely, philosophers of art have devoted relatively little attention to horror art.[1] As Stephen King noted in his *Entertainment Weekly* column: "Artsy/intellectual discussions have little to do with how I felt when I saw Rob Zombie's The Devil's Rejects . . . . I'll never forget some exuberant (and possibly drunk) moviegoer in the front row shouting: 'This movie KICKS ASS!' I felt the same way. Because it did."[2] But intellectual discussions about art can't just ignore the joy people get from art like *The Devil's Rejects* (2005). It may be that many theorists find some or all horror distasteful, but for art theorists to ignore forms of art because they find them distasteful would be like biologists refusing to study the digestive system because it's gross. Even if we think that some or all horror fiction is harmful, that's no more reason to ignore it than biologists have to ignore harmful parasites and dangerous diseases.

In fact, much traditional philosophy of art is applicable to horror fiction. This shouldn't surprise us, since the debate over what sorts of fiction people should enjoy is at least as old as philosophy, and many of the issues horror fiction raises are just as ancient. In fact, traditional philosophy of art can offer us a framework for the *appreciation* of horror fiction and for the recognition of its value as literature—stinky dead cats and all. Let's begin, though, with the case for the prosecution, by noting that the earliest known philosopher of art would surely condemn the horror art of Stephen King and the entire horror genre.

LIES AND BLASPHEMIES: PLATO EXPELS CARRIE WHITE

The ancient Greek Plato (427–347 BCE) is one of the most influential thinkers in history, having written groundbreaking works on morality, politics, and metaphysics. Plato was deeply suspicious of fiction. He saw philosophy and fiction as being essentially at odds, since philosophy strives to tell the truth and fiction tells lies. When Plato described his ideal society in *Republic*, he reserved the right to lie to the government and banned fiction, declaring that "hymns to the gods and praises of famous men are the only poetry which ought to be admitted into our State."[3] King, like Plato, believes that good fiction tells the truth. In *On Writing*, he says, "The job of fiction is to find the truth inside the story's web of lies"[4] and in *Danse Macabre*, "The primary duty of literature [is] . . . to tell us the truth about ourselves by telling us lies about people who never existed."[5] But to Plato, some truth just isn't enough.

Plato was particularly troubled by the way that authors of fiction describe things they know nothing about. He criticizes Homer, the most respected of the Greek poets, for mentioning naval and medical techniques in his tales of heroic adventure. Homer has no expertise in such matters and so should keep his trap shut. King believes that as long as an author tells key truths, they should write about "anything you damn well want. Anything at all . . ."6 Plato, however, would criticize King for writing about topics he's no authority on, like medicine (*The Dead Zone, Pet Sematary, Doctor Sleep*, etc.), police work (*The Dark Half, Needful Things, From a Buick 8*, etc.), and mental illness (*Carrie, The Shining, Misery*, etc.).

Worst of all, in Plato's view, is when ignorant storytellers speak about the supernatural. Plato would be disgusted by the way King, who is no expert on the real supernatural world, writes about ghosts, psychic phenomena, and possessed machinery, potentially spreading harmful ideas. He would be just as appalled at the entire supernatural horror tradition, from moaning, translucent specters, through cursed family estates, aristocratic vampires, nameless things from beyond, and burned dead janitors who slay teenagers in their dreams.

The very worst way to misrepresent the supernatural, in Plato's view, is to misrepresent the gods. He dismissed traditional tales of the gods, like those of Homer, as the inventions of people who knew nothing about the divine realm. In his ideal city, he banned tales of "gods warring, fighting, or plotting against one another, for they aren't true."7 He would be aghast at the way that so much horror fiction has supported the false religion of Christianity, with crosses repelling vampires and Christian priests able to exorcise demons. Even worse would be horror fiction that invents gods who are imperfect, or worse, malicious. H. P. Lovecraft (1890–1937), the writer who got King hooked on horror literature, famously turned traditional religion on its head, inventing a universe governed by gods who are sadistic, nuts, or mindless. Where Plato saw divinity as reasonable, Lovecraft gave us a universe governed by "the blind idiot god Azathoth, Lord of All Things."8 Where Plato saw the divine as good and a force for order, Lovecraft gave us gods plotting for the day when "with laws and morals thrown aside and all men shouting and killing and reveling in joy . . . all the earth would flame with a holocaust of ecstasy and freedom."9

Plato would be almost as horrified at King's gods. Unlike Lovecraft's pantheon, King's default pantheon of Gan, Turtle, the White, and the Outer Dark skew to good rather than to evil. All the same, they are far too defective to fill Plato's notion of divine perfection. Gan is morally ambivalent, creating the world, but then rolling it away into the abyss, while the Turtle is kind but mostly powerless to help. The nebulous

White might make an acceptable representation of goodness and order, and the Outer Dark of evil and chaos, but Plato could not countenance the relationship between the two. In King, the White needs the help of good people in order to win out. To Plato, the divine is strong enough not to need help from anyone. Moreover, the divine is eternal and so could never be defeated by evil and chaos. Sometimes, of course, King paints even worse gods than these, or simply borrows Lovecraft's.

Plato likewise believed that it's important not to misrepresent the afterlife. People must not be presented with stories that make death seem frightening or unattractive, since this would make them feeble in war. Rather, stories should show that death holds no horrors for those who have lived well. This is obviously at odds with a great deal of horror fiction, in which the dead can be cursed to walk the earth as moaning specters or ravenous zombies, or sent on to painful afterlives. In King's stories, innocent souls may linger on as tormented prisoners, like the murdered twin daughters of caretaker Delbert Grady who roam the Overlook Hotel in *The Shining*, and the children killed by *It* who "all float down here" in the sewer. Worst of all, we learn in *Revival* that after death, all human souls are persecuted by the sadistic Mother and her army of vicious ant-demons.

Though few people today would want to defend Plato's conception of the gods, the fear that horror fiction will cause dangerous misunderstandings of the supernatural remains common. Supernatural fiction has often been called "satanic" and accused of leading young people away from God. Carrie White's religious mother never comments directly on the genre, but it's a fair bet that Carrie isn't allowed to have any horror fiction for just this reason.

SICK STORIES AND MORAL DEGENERATION

Like so many media critics since, Plato was worried that entertainment could corrupt the public by setting them a bad example. If characters, especially sympathetic or heroic ones, did bad things in stories, people might act similarly in real life. He would be appalled by the way that horror cinema has turned murderers and sadists into protagonists and stars with franchises based on slasher films like *The Texas Chainsaw Massacre* (1974), *Halloween* (1978), and *A Nightmare on Elm Street*

(1984), and worse, on "torture porn" films like *Saw* (2004), *Hostel* (2005), and *The Human Centipede* (2010).

Plato was particularly worried about the breakdown of authority, especially paternal authority. He condemns as "the greatest of all lies" the myth in which the king of the gods Uranus is castrated and overthrown by his son Kronos, who is then overthrown by his own son Zeus.[10] He writes, "Nor should a young person hear it said that in committing the worst crimes he's doing nothing out of the ordinary, or that if he inflicts every kind of punishment on an unjust father, he's only doing the same as the first and greatest of the gods."[11]

Plato would find it unacceptable that children in Stephen King novels so often know better than their parents and elders. In *Carrie*, Carrie's deranged mother is such a bad source of guidance that she tells her daughter that both her period and her breasts were caused by sexual sin. In *'Salem's Lot*, it's twelve-year-old Mark Petrie, not Father Callahan, who understands how to use faith against the vampire Kurt Barlow. In *It*, if the seven members of the "Loser's Club" had been obedient to their parents, they would have ended up floating facedown in the sewer. Instead, they had to disobey to conquer a threat that their elders did not understand. Fathers are particularly liable to be dangerously violent, like Jack Torrance in *The Shining*, who stalks the halls of the Overlook Hotel looking to give his wife and son their "medicine" with a polo mallet. *It* even has two paranoid, violently abusive dads, one for heroine Beverly Marsh and one for school bully Henry Bowers.[12]

Plato hated the way that fiction of his day excited the emotions rather than encouraging self-control: "And in the case of sex, anger, and all the desires, pleasures, and pains that we say accompany all our actions, poetic imitation . . . nurtures and waters them and establishes them as rulers in us when they ought to wither and be ruled."[13] For this reason, he didn't want stories to depict good people being in the grip of intense emotion. He writes, "We must accept what has happened as we would the fall of the dice, and then arrange our affairs in whatever way reason determines to be best. We mustn't hug the hurt part and spend our time weeping and wailing like children when they trip."[14]

A ban on the expression of powerful emotion is incompatible with a genre whose signature is the scream of terror. It is almost essential that protagonists of good horror stories feel awful fear that threatens to overpower them. If they don't, the reader feels no fear for them, and the story doesn't engage. For example, as if deliberately flouting Plato's words, King writes in 'Salem's Lot, "Barlow reached from the darkness and plucked the cross from his fingers. Callahan cried out miserably, the cry that had vibrated in the soul—but never the throat—of that long-ago child who had been left alone each night."[15] The terror of the protagonist of a good horror story can easily leave them hysterical, or even on the verge of madness. From *Misery*: "He had no idea what was going to come out or if anything really was . . . until it came. 'AFRICA!' Paul screamed. Now his trembling hands flew up like startled birds and clapped against the sides of his head, as if to hold in his exploding brains. 'Africa! Help me! Help me! Africa!'"[16]

Our moral concerns today might not be the same as Plato's, but his fear for public morality is echoed in modern objections to horror. Every time a slasher flick pushes a new boundary or does big box office, there will be people arguing that the film encourages violence. Most of the official efforts to keep horror out of the hands of kids has been motivated by the worry that they will pick up evil ideas. For instance, when King's beloved childhood horror comics suffered a devastating crackdown by the introduction of the Comics Code Authority in 1954, the intention was to protect youthful morals. King himself has allowed his novel *Rage* to go out of print for fear of inspiring school shootings like the one in the book.

The complete lack of evidence that horror fiction leads to crime might make us lose our fear for public safety. Yet we might still be concerned about the messages horror fiction sends. In *Danse Macabre*, King observes that horror stories tend to follow moral rules: "Within the framework of most horror tales we find a moral code so strong it would make a Puritan smile."[17] This can be a good thing: the horror story's "strict moralities make it also a reaffirmation of life and good will and simple imagination."[18] But horror can be morally simplistic, too. As King notes, "The mythic, 'fairy-tale' horror film intends to take away the shades of gray . . . it urges us to put away our more civilized and adult penchant for analysis and to become children again, seeing things in pure blacks and pure whites."[19] This black-and-white morality leads easily to harsh treatment of wrongdoers. King writes, "In the old E.C. comics, adulterers inevitably came to bad ends and murderers suffered fates that would make the rack and the boot look like kiddy rides at the carnival."[20] Likewise, in film, "We have the comforting knowledge when the lights go down in the theater or when we open the book that the evildoers will almost certainly be punished, and measure will be returned for measure."[21] But this is not a lesson in healthy morality and goodwill, but a celebration of the joy of bloodletting, with the criminality of the victim used to anesthetize our compassion. Sadism toward imaginary people hurts nobody in itself, so need not be a wicked pleasure, but if it conveys any moral lessons at all, they aren't good ones.

What's more, according to King, horror by its nature inclines us against social change. He writes, "When we discuss monstrosity, we are expressing our faith and belief in the norm and watching for the mutant. The writer of horror fiction is neither more nor less than an agent of the status quo."[22] Plato was no fan of individuality, but he was disgusted with the status quo and wanted to see dramatic social change. He accused his fellow citizens of caring only for wealth and glory, when they should be worried about living virtuously. He wanted to abolish democracy, luxury, and for government employees, even marriage and family. We, too, might wish to see certain social changes, which is inconvenient if we are in love with an art form that serves the status quo.

VAMPIRE NEIGHBORS AND MAGIC CLOWNS: IT'S ALL A BIT SILLY, ISN'T IT?

Had enough of the attack on horror? Ready for the defense? Well, tough Tommyknockers. The earliest philosophy of art has more trouble for us yet. Aristotle (384–322 BCE) was Plato's pupil and one of the few thinkers who can rival him for historical influence. Like Plato, he investigated morality, politics, and metaphysics, while his interest in the natural world made him one of the founders of science to boot.

Aristotle stressed that serious stories must make sense rather than being a series of improbable events. He writes in *Poetics* that "the unraveling of the plot, no less than the complication, must arise out of the plot itself."[23] In other words, once the premise of the story has been set in place, things must unfold reasonably given what has gone before. This does not in itself rule out supernatural fiction. While Aristotle believed that it's a virtue for a story to be plausible, he also accepted that sometimes, it is all right to include improbable elements if they give the story more impact. He writes, "Any impossibilities there are in his descriptions of things are faults. But from another point of view they are justifiable, if they serve the end of poetry—if . . . they make the effect of . . . the work . . . more astounding."[24] Thus, the artist can invent stories about gods, prophecies, monsters, and the other wonders found in Greek literature. However, even these stories must unfold believably: "There should be nothing improbable among the actual incidents."[25]

Yet horror often relies for its effect on *not* making sense. As King explains in *Entertainment Weekly*, "Nightmares exist outside of logic, and there's little fun to be had in explanations; they're antithetical to the poetry of fear."[26] H. P. Lovecraft writes that in a really good horror story, there must be "a malign and particular suspension or defeat of those fixed laws of Nature which are our only safeguard against the assaults of chaos and the daemons of unplumbed space."[27] The Overlook Hotel is a scary place to stay because things happen there that shouldn't be able to happen, like bloated corpses appearing in the bathtub out of nowhere. A horror story needs to make *some* kind of sense, of course. The name of a town can't change between chapters and magic rules that are arbitrary when they are laid down have to be followed later. If faith can repel vampires in chapter 1, then faith must be able to repel vampires in chapter 30. Some questions, however, are better left as mysteries. How did that big clown get down that little drain? It's the fact that it's inexplicable that makes it disturbing.

Strikingly, the most influential horror literature of the nineteenth and early twentieth centuries almost uniformly makes use of the most implausible plots, even if we ignore supernatural elements. Whatever makes the likes of Mary Shelley (1797–1851), Edgar Allan Poe (1809–1849), Bram Stoker (1847–1912), and Lovecraft continue to fascinate readers, it isn't how neatly their stories make sense. King's own plots don't always make enormous sense, and his endings can arrive from nowhere. In *The Stand*, for instance, the heroes are being led by their own dreams and the visions of Mother Abigail, and so form their plans without always being able to give a rational reason for what they are doing. Their antagonist Randall Flagg is finally defeated by divine intervention, his magic suddenly canceled and a nuclear device detonated in his presence by holy power.

The demand that stories remain plausible is particularly problematic for world builders like Lovecraft and King who link their stories together to become part of a single mythology. Their versions of earth grow increasingly bizarre as fresh stories add fresh horrors and improbability piles on improbability. In King's Maine, the town of Castle Rock is home to an author's pseudonym come to murderous life (*The Dark Half*), a shopkeeping wizard who can sell you anything you desire (*Needful Things*), and a brain-injured psychic who alone can save humanity from nuclear war (*The Dead Zone*), not to mention a vengeful truck ("Uncle Otto's Truck"), a magic camera that is a portal between worlds (*The Sun Dog*) and a woman who can drive between worlds in a two-seater Mercedes ("Mrs. Todd's Shortcut"). Nearby, the town of Derry plays host to a serial child-murdering ghost on a revenge spree (*Bag of Bones*), a serial child-murdering spider-clown from space (*It*), a wizard who can add extra years to your life for the right price ("Fair Extension"), a time-traveling schoolteacher on a mission to save JFK from assassination (*11/22/63*), an invasion force of telepathic aliens who specialize in biological warfare (*Dreamcatcher*), and a retired widower whose insomnia-driven hallucinations make him the only one who can save not just this universe, but all of them (*Insomnia*). And all this is just a short drive from the vampire-infested town of Jerusalem's Lot ('*Salem's Lot*), the psychic-teenager-trashed town of Chamberlain (*Carrie*), the psychic-spaceship-dominated town of Haven (*The Tommyknockers*), and the little town of Ludlow, where the dead periodically come back to life (*Pet Sematary*). A touch of realism is added to the mythology in *Firestarter* by the introduction of "The Shop," an arm of the U.S. government tasked with investigating paranormal phenomena. At least it isn't going unnoticed that people living in small-town Maine are never more than thirty feet from a monster.

Aristotle believed that just as the plot must make sense, so the characters must be believable and consistent: "The right thing . . . is in the characters just as in the incidents of the play to seek after the necessary or the probable; so that whenever such-and-such a personage says or does such-and-such a thing, it shall be the necessary or probable outcome of his character."[28] King's depth and consistency of characterization are signatures of his style. Whatever fantastic events occur, his characters always speak and act according to their established personality and background. In *On Writing*, he states that the job of building characters in fiction "boils down to two things: paying attention to how the real people around you behave and then telling the truth about what you see."[29] That said, King recognizes that thin characterization may be appropriate in horror. In *Entertainment Weekly*, he describes the characterization in the film *The Strangers* (2008): "'Why are you doing this to us?' she whispers. To which the woman in the doll-face mask responds, in a dead and affectless voice: 'Because you were home.' In the end, that's all the explanation a good horror film needs."[30] If horror characterization need not be deep, this is good news for many of the seminal works of horror fiction. The protagonists of *Frankenstein* and *Dracula* are paper thin, while the protagonist of a tale by Poe or Lovecraft is almost always just a barely disguised version of the author himself. Not one of the four authors captured the way real people speak, nor showed much interest in trying.

Encouragingly for the horror fan, Aristotle recognized that pleasure gained from art is important in itself. In *Politics*, he judges it appropriate to listen to music as a form of recreation, writing that "the end is not desirable for the sake of any future good, nor do the pleasures which we have described exist for the sake of any future good but of the past, that is to say, they are the alleviation of past toils and pains. And we may infer this to be the reason why men seek happiness from these pleasures."[31] However, Aristotle only defends intellectual pleasures: "It is clear . . . that there are branches of learning and education which we must study merely with a view to leisure spent in intellectual activity, and these are to be valued for their own sake."[32]

But how intellectual is the pleasure of reading or watching horror fiction? In principle, a work of horror fiction could provide any level of intellectual engagement that any realistic story could, since a realistic story could be made part of a work of horror fiction. But how intellectual is horror in reality? King doesn't class his own work as intellectual fare, stating in *On Writing* that "a writer would have to be a lot crazier than I am to think of *Carrie* as anyone's intellectual treat."[33]

But then, King rejects the idea that a pleasure has to be intellectual to be worthwhile. In *Entertainment Weekly* he writes, "Guilty pleasures aren't even overrated; the idea is meaningless, an elitist concept invented by smarmy intellectuals with nothing better to do."[34] Indeed, King thinks it's good for people to gain pleasure from what he calls "junk art." He warns in *Danse Macabre* that "the fan loses his taste for junkfood at his or her own peril"[35] because "once you've seen enough horror films, you begin to get a taste for really shitty movies."[36] What goes for films presumably goes for literature.

Certainly, there's nothing intellectual about plenty of relaxations that seem perfectly appropriate. There's nothing intellectual about going for a run, admiring the leaves in fall, or petting a kitten. If such activities are all right, I see no reason why a piece of literature must be intellectually demanding in order for it to be appropriate to enjoy it. I've had a lot of fun reading and watching "junk" horror when nothing better is at hand. There's nothing particularly impressive about the miniseries *The Langoliers* (1995), or the films *Thinner* (1996) or *Carrie* (2013), but they are all good fun and not to be missed by the horror fan. Not any old junk will do, of course. The film *The Lawnmower Man* (1992), theoretically based on King's short story of the same name, is just painful, as are the sequels to *Children of the Corn* (1984).

Yet King's attitude to "junk" is not entirely indulgent. He thinks that it's all right to enjoy bad films, but not to treasure them: "Bad films may sometimes be amusing . . . but their only real usefulness is to form that basis of comparison: to define positive values in terms of their own negative charm. . . . After that has been determined, it becomes, I think, actively dangerous to hold on to these bad films . . . and they must be discarded."[37] King is perhaps more sympathetic to treasuring crude literature. He praises the timeless urban legend of "The Hook": "The story of The Hook is a simple, brutal classic of horror. It offers no characterization, no theme, no particular artifice; it does not aspire to symbolic beauty or try to summarize the times, the mind, or the human spirit."[38]

LEARNING TO LOVE HORRORS: ARISTOTLE CLIMBS INTO THE SEWER

Not all of what Aristotle had to say is so unsupportive of horror fiction. Let the case for the defense begin, Judge Flagg presiding! Aristotle believed that it's an important function of art to help us think about humanity and the universe, by presenting us with hypothetical situations to consider. In *Poetics*, Aristotle claims that the difference between history and poetry is that "the one describes the thing that has been, and the other a kind of thing that might be. Hence poetry is something more philosophical and of graver import than history."[39]

King believes that horror art can help us to better understand ourselves. He writes in *Danse Macabre*, "A good horror story is one that functions on a symbolic level, using fictional (and sometimes supernatural) events to help us understand our own deepest real fears."[40] But this only scratches the surface of the way a work of horror fiction might help us to think about the world. *Carrie*, for instance, might lead us to consider the position of bullied and ostracized kids. King writes of the novel, "If it had any thesis to offer, this deliberate updating of *High School Confidential*, it was that high school is a place of almost bottomless conservatism and bigotry, a place where the adolescents who attend are no more allowed to rise 'above their station' than a Hindu would be allowed to rise above his or her caste."[41] In *On Writing*, King lists his recurring themes:

> How difficult it is—perhaps impossible!—to close Pandora's techno-box once it's open (*The Stand, The Tommyknockers, Firestarter*); the question of why, if there is a God, such terrible things happen (*The Stand, Desperation, The Green Mile*); the thin line between reality and fantasy (*The Dark Half, Bag of Bones, The Drawing of the Three*); and most of all, the terrible attraction violence sometimes has for fundamentally good people (*The Shining, The Dark Half*). I've also written again and again about the fundamental differences between children and adults, and about the healing power of the human imagination.[42]

Analyzing the work of other horror authors in *Danse Macabre*, he notes, "Shirley Jackson uses the conventions of the new American gothic to examine characters under extreme psychological—or perhaps occult—pressure; Peter Straub uses them to examine the effects of an evil past upon the present; Anne Rivers Siddons uses them to examine social codes and social pressures."[43]

Using literature to think about the world requires more than just accepting the authors' opinions or adopting their worldview. Even when authors seem wise to us, it can only be because of how right we think they are about the world, which is to say, the degree to which they share our own preexisting opinions. Rather, it's when we use horror fiction as a tool to help us think critically and question our own beliefs, rather than being passive recipients of other people's messages, that horror fiction serves the truth. Far from horror fiction automatically supporting the status quo, our use of it can be as subversive as it needs to be. Likewise, though King classes his work as not "intellectual," our use of his work can be as intellectual as we like.

Appropriately, King has no desire to preach to us through fiction. In *On Writing*, he advises aspiring writers to "take all those messages and those morals and stick em where the sun don't shine, all right?"[44] On the other hand, he's happy for us to think through the issues he raises for ourselves: "There is no *moral* to *The Stand*, no 'We'd *better* learn or we'll probably destroy the whole damned planet next time'—but if the theme stands out clearly enough, those discussing it may offer their own morals and conclusions."[45]

Supernatural fiction can be a particularly useful tool for thinking about society and the universe, precisely because of all the bizarre situations that occur. Stories about vampires raise moral questions about what we are justified in doing in order to survive, stories about malicious hotels and angry cars raise questions in cognitive science and the philosophy of personal identity, stories about time travel raise questions about the metaphysics of space-time, and so on. This very book you hold is an attempt to use the writings of Stephen King as a tool to examine important philosophical issues.

Works of fiction are useful tools for analysis even when analysis is not in the spirit of the work. King writes in *Danse Macabre*, "The horror movie asks you if you want to take a good close look at the dead cat . . . but not as an adult would look at it. Never mind the philosophical implications of death or the religious possibilities inherent in the idea of survival."[46] Yet nothing stops us from reveling in a story about a dead cat, enjoying it on its own terms, and *then* using it to help us consider the philosophical implications of death. In fact, our time spent philosophizing may be all the more pleasant because we get to spend it thinking about the maggoty moggy we enjoyed so much in the story.

ON NOT BLOWING YOUR BOILER: ARISTOTLE CHECKS
IN TO THE OVERLOOK HOTEL

So far so good, but we still haven't defended the use of horror in literature per se—just the potential literary value of works that happen to be
horrifying. *It* could still function as a sociological study and even a wild
tale of the supernatural without Pennywise feeling the need to chomp
down on his own mouth with his razor-blade teeth: "'KEEE-RUNCH!'
it screamed, and its jaws snapped closed. Blood gouted from its mouth
in a red-black flood. Chunks of its severed lips fell to the glowing white
silk of its formal shirt and slid down its front, leaving snail-trails of blood
behind."[47] One justification for horror in art is simply that horrible
things happen in the real world and so thinking about horrors is an
important part of thinking about the world. But Aristotle also thought
that confronting horrors in fiction is an important tool for becoming a
more virtuous person.

Like his teacher Plato, Aristotle thought that good serious literature
improves us morally and that the protagonists should set us an example
of righteous behavior. However, Aristotle recognized that among the
moral lessons we need to learn is that a fundamentally good person can
still be brought to disaster by his or her flaws. Unlike Plato, Aristotle
was a fan of Greek tragic theater, in which people sometimes did awful
things and frequently had awful things happen to them. Like horror
stories, tragedies wallow in dark themes and human suffering. For instance, in Aristotle's favorite tragedy, Sophocles's *Oedipus the King*,
Oedipus accidentally kills his father, marries his mother, and has four
kids with her. Upon realizing what he's done, he tears his own eyes out
in remorse and goes off to live as a homeless wanderer.

Aristotle thought that horror in art is an important means of cleans-
ing our soul of negative emotions. Through feeling pity and fear for the
protagonists of a tragedy, we purge those feelings from our own system,
a process he called catharsis. By suffering along with someone like
Oedipus, we become more stable and gain greater control over our
emotions. King takes a similar attitude to horror. In *Danse Macabre*, he
explains, "We make up horrors to help us cope with the real ones. The
term *catharsis* is as old as Greek drama. . . . The dream of horror is in
itself an out-letting and a lancing."[48] The catharsis of horror is particularly likely to be required by the imaginative: "For us [imaginative peo-

ple] horror movies are a safety valve . . . we're able to let off the pressure that might otherwise build up until it blows us sky-high. . . . We take refuge in make-believe terrors so the real ones don't overwhelm us."[49] What's more, King thinks that only supernatural horror provides situations bad enough for maximum catharsis. He writes in the foreword to *Night Shift*, "Only the writer of horror and the supernatural gives the reader such an opportunity for total identification and catharsis."[50]

In fact, the word "catharsis" is a lot older and more primal than Greek drama. It refers to any kind of purging, including the act of throwing up. It was Aristotle, as far as we know, who first suggested that watching a good tragedy is like a good vomit for the soul. Aristotle would surely appreciate King's masterful ability to make us feel pity and fear on behalf of imaginary people. Will little Danny Torrance of *The Shining* get his head mashed? Will Paul Sheldon of *Misery* escape from his insane captor Annie Wilkes? How will Dr. Louis Creed of *Pet Sematary* cope with the loss of his three-year-old son, Gage? How will he cope when his three-year-old son comes *back*? From bullied schoolkids to wretched apocalypse survivors to the victims of a clown attack, King engages our sympathies for people in trouble.

King suggests that horror catharsis might also purge us of cruelty. He writes in *Danse Macabre*, "But anticivilization emotions don't go away, and they demand periodic exercise. . . . The mythic horror movie, like the sick joke, has a dirty job to do. It deliberately appeals to all that is worst in us. It is morbidity unchained, our most base instincts let free, our nastiest fantasies realized."[51] He compares our most vicious emotions to hungry alligators, with good horror being meat we throw to them to keep them placid.

Still, the catharsis model of horror has serious problems. If horror fiction purges us of negative feelings, why do we enjoy the horror fiction itself rather than just feeling relieved when we're finished? There is no pleasure in the act of tossing one's cookies. The benefit comes afterward, when one no longer feels so sick. Yet I *like* reading a scary story, and the better I like the story, the sorrier I feel when it ends (why the hell isn't *The Mist* a full-length novel, anyway?).

Besides, horror fiction can easily leave us with more fear rather than less. As a child, creeping upstairs after watching *The Evil* (1978) on latenight television, I was scared as hell, and every shadow held a potential monster. I thought it was about the best movie I'd ever seen. A film that gives you the creeps like that provides the sort of thrill that horror junkies can spend their life chasing. I'm sure you've had similar experiences of reading or watching something so good that you didn't want to turn the light out when you were done. If horror purges our fears through catharsis, shouldn't we have been fearless instead of hiding under the covers? It seems that if we want to explain the pleasure of horror fiction, and so assure ourselves that it's nothing wicked or unhealthy (what we might call the "sick bastard theory" of horror art), we'll need to look beyond catharsis.

PAIN INTO PLEASURE: DAVID HUME LETS THE VAMPIRES BITE HIM

Scottish philosopher David Hume (1711–1776) made important contributions to the philosophy of mind, metaphysics, morality, and religion. Influential among scientists as well as philosophers, Hume's work was acknowledged by Charles Darwin as inspirational for the theory of evolution. Like Aristotle, Hume was fascinated by the puzzle of tragic art. He writes in *Of Tragedy*, "It seems an unaccountable pleasure which the spectators of a well-written tragedy receive from sorrow, terror, anxiety, and other passions, that are in themselves disagreeable and uneasy."[52] In *Danse Macabre*, King ponders the attraction of horror in the same way, asking, "Why are people willing to pay good money to be made extremely uncomfortable?"[53]

For some reason, we can love to witness things in fiction that we would hate to witness in real life. Hume writes, "It is certain that the same object of distress which pleases in a tragedy, were it really set before us, would give the most unfeigned uneasiness."[54] When I read about Paul Sheldon's fictional car crash in *Misery*, I enjoyed it. Yet when I read a semifictional account of Stephen King being hit by a Dodge minivan in *The Dark Tower*, I found the scene unpleasant, precisely because I knew it was to some degree a description of a real, horrible event. What's more, if I ever saw somebody hit by a speeding minivan in real life, I would be traumatized. In the foreword to *Night Shift*, King describes horror fiction as good "for people who like to slow down and look at car accidents."[55] Yet strangely, horror fiction is also beloved by people like me who don't want to see real blood.

Hume's explanation for our love of the horrible in tragedy is that the tragedian harnesses the power of our negative emotions and redirects them into pleasure at the excellence of the art. If we did not have such strong negative emotions, then there would be less for the tragedian to convert into pleasure, and so we would enjoy ourselves less. Not only aren't tragedy fans morbid or cruel, it's the very fact that they aren't morbid or cruel that inspires their horror, and hence their delight at the artist's skill. The application to horror fiction is straightforward: we like horrors in our fiction because it stirs strong emotions in us that can then be channeled into pleasure by appreciation of art.

One problem with the Humean model is that when engrossed in a story, we can easily forget about how skillfully it's being told. Even though it's the artist's skill that leads us to enter the world of the story, once we are in that world, that's the world that has our attention. If we've placed ourselves in the Derry Public Library, watching Ben Hanscom as Pennywise grins at him with a mouth full of razor-blade teeth, our concern is for Ben's safety, not literary evaluation, and the more we are sucked into the story like a child down a sewer, the less literary evaluation is likely to enter our head.

A potentially more serious problem for this model is that horror can so often be enjoyable even if it isn't skillfully made. As King observed, the connoisseur can get a taste for really shitty art. What's more, even when dealing with superior horror art like King's, much of our pleasure *doesn't* seem to be a direct product of the artist's skill. For a start, the mere fact that a book is horror fiction makes it more likely to appeal to people like me who have a soft spot for stories about fearsome apparitions and things that go bump in the night. More arbitrary yet, we are all scared by different things, so our response to a work of horror art will depend on what particular horrors it involves. If you've always been scared of clowns, *It* will be a more disturbing novel; if dead things freak you out, *Pet Sematary* will freak you out, too; and if you are terrified of dogs, *Cujo* will bite particularly hard. As King writes in *Danse Macabre*, good horror art searches for your "phobic pressure points. The good horror tale will . . . find the secret door to the room you believed no one but you knew of."[56] Yet regardless of how skillfully that searching is done, it's the nature of our phobic pressure points that is doing a lot of the work in scaring us.

Sheer love of the traditions of the genre can likewise increase the fan's pleasure. As King notes, "You begin to see and appreciate patterns in horror movies, and to love them."[57] Love of traditions can be as powerful in literature. For instance, it gives me a thrill of fannish pleasure when King overtly includes ideas from Lovecraft, as he does in "Jerusalem's Lot" and *Revival*, and the short stories "I Know What You Need," "Crouch End," and "Gramma." When Shub-Niggurath, in her incarnation as "Mother," comes bursting into our world through the dead mouth of patient Mary Fay in *Revival*, liquefying flesh and scorching furniture with her insectile touch, there is the joy of being reunited with an old and beloved friend. But there is nothing clever about tagging Lovecraft per se.

Given how tenuous the correlation can be between the horror artist's skill and the horror fan's enjoyment, a Humean account of horror won't work as it stands. All the same, I think this account is getting warm. What it gets wrong, in my view, is that the source of the pleasure we take in horror is not our appreciation of artistic excellence, but the spur to our imagination. We enjoy horror because we like to exercise our imagination, and since strong emotion triggers imagination, we use our feelings of horror as imagination fuel.

As King observes, horror literature makes particularly strong demands on the reader's imagination: "Disbelief is not like a balloon, which may be suspended in air with a minimum of effort; it is like a lead weight, which has to be hoisted with a clean and a jerk and held up by main force" while "the difference in sales between Arthur Hailey and H. P. Lovecraft may exist because everyone believes in cars and banks, but it takes a sophisticated and muscular intellectual act to believe, even for a little while, in Nyarlathotep."[58] Since horror, more than most art, relies on the force of imagination supplied by the audience, horror fans will experience intensely different levels of enjoyment depending on what they contribute. This explains why horror executed with little skill can still be so enjoyable. The art supplies the basics and the audience's imagination does the rest. As King says of the film *The Amityville Horror* (1979), "As horror goes, *Amityville* is pretty pedestrian. So's beer, but you can get drunk on it."[59] Similarly, a group of children sitting around a campfire sharing horror stories can have an intense aesthetic experience—that is, scare the living hell out of each other. It isn't because they are telling their stories with such consummate skill that their art is so powerful. It is because their imaginations have been switched on. The usefulness of horror as an imagination spur applies just as much to mundane horrors like Annie Wilkes as it does to Nyarlathotep. With all due credit to King for how beautifully he drew the character, part of what makes me imagine Annie so vividly is how *awful* she is. She impresses herself on me as a reader because of how negatively I feel about her.

The imagination account explains not just the consumption of junk, but the level of tolerance horror lovers have for major flaws in the work of artists who supply intriguing ideas. It is remarkable how flawed much of the most famous, influential, and best-loved horror fiction is. In *Danse Macabre*, King concludes that "Dracula is a frankly palpitating melodrama"[60] while *Frankenstein* is "a rather slow and talky melodrama, its theme drawn in large, careful, and rather crude strokes."[61] As for Lovecraft, his purple prose is infamous, and King rightly takes him to task for the gross implausibility of his dialogue. Yet Shelley, Stoker, and Lovecraft, all clumsy writers, happened to tell some of the most interesting stories in literature. They were the punk rockers of fiction, making up for their limited skills with some extraordinary sparks of creativity.

King, of course, is a skillful writer: not a punk but a virtuoso. While some horror authors win our affections despite their lack of technique, King stands with the likes of Shirley Jackson, Ray Bradbury, and Peter Straub, as an author who uses good old-fashioned literary skill to draw our imaginations on. But the thrill King is selling us is the same as the one we get from *Frankenstein* or the tale of the Hook: he's blowing our minds by putting the strangest and most terrible thoughts there.

And that's why my love of horror, and of the work of Stephen King in particular, doesn't make me a sick bastard. (It's only those kids I killed that makes me a sick bastard, and we all know Judge Flagg doesn't give a damn about *that*!)

NOTES

1. Noël Carroll is a noticeable exception. For more, get his book *The Philosophy of Horror or Paradoxes of the Heart* (New York: Routledge, 1990).

2. Stephen King, "Lessons from 'Ellen,'" *Entertainment Weekly*, August 7, 2007, http://www.ew.com/article/2007/08/07/stephen-king-lessons-ellen.

3. Plato, *Republic*, in *Plato: Complete Works*, ed. John M. Cooper (Indianapolis, Ind.: Hackett, 1997), 1211.

4. Stephen King, *On Writing* (New York: Pocket Books, 2010), 158.

5. Stephen King, *Danse Macabre* (New York: Gallery Books, 2010), 264.

6. King, *On Writing*, 156.

7. Plato, *Republic*, 1017.

8. H. P. Lovecraft, "The Haunter of the Dark," in *"The Call of Cthulhu" and Other Weird Stories* (London: Penguin, 1999), 354.

9. H. P. Lovecraft, "The Call of Cthulhu," in *"The Call of Cthulhu" and Other Weird Stories* (London: Penguin, 1999), 155.

10. Plato, *Republic*, 1016.

11. Plato, *Republic*, 1017.

12. King has focused even more heavily on spousal abuse, as in *Gerald's Game*, *Delores Claiborne*, and *Rose Madder*. It isn't clear how Plato would take such stories. While he thought that the authority of a father over his children should be complete, he thought that ideally, a woman should only be subject to a man if that man has better sense.

13. Plato, *Republic*, 1211.

14. Plato, *Republic*, 1209.

15. Stephen King, *'Salem's Lot* (New York: Anchor, 2011), 539.

16. Stephen King, *Misery* (New York: Signet, 1988), 259.

17. King, *Danse Macabre*, 421.

18. King, *Danse Macabre*, 435.

19. King, *Danse Macabre*, 184–85.

20. King, *Danse Macabre*, 421.

21. King, *Danse Macabre*, 421.

22. King, *Danse Macabre*, 41.

23. Aristotle, *Poetics*, in *The Complete Works of Aristotle*, ed. J. Barnes (Princeton, N.J.: Princeton University Press, 1984), 2327.

24. Aristotle, *Poetics*, 2337–38.

25. Aristotle, *Poetics*, 2327.

26. Stephen King, "Why Hollywood Can't Do Horror," *Entertainment Weekly*, July 7, 2008, http://www.ew.com/article/2008/07/07/stephen-king-why-hollywood-cant-do-horror/2.

27. H. P. Lovecraft, *Supernatural Horror in Literature* (Mineola, N.Y.: Dover, 1973), 4.

28. Aristotle, *Poetics*, 2327.

29. King, *On Writing*, 189.

30. King, "Why Hollywood Can't Do Horror."

31. Aristotle, *Politics*, in *The Complete Works of Aristotle,* ed. J. Barnes (Princeton, N.J.: Princeton University Press, 1984), 2125.

32. Aristotle, *Politics*, 2122.

33. King, *On Writing*, 199.

34. He left out "bandy legged" and "beady eyed." Aristotle is said to have been both. King, "Lessons from 'Ellen.'"

35. King, *Danse Macabre*, 150.

36. King, *Danse Macabre*, 212.

37. King, *Danse Macabre*, 229–30.

38. King, *Danse Macabre*, 21.

39. Aristotle, *Poetics*, 2323.

40. King, *Danse Macabre*, xiii.

41. King, *Danse Macabre*, 180.

42. King, *On Writing*, 207.

43. King, *Danse Macabre*, 353.

44. King, *On Writing*, 204.

45. King, *On Writing*, 205.

46. King, *Danse Macabre*, 211.

47. Stephen King, *It* (New York: Signet, 1987), 518.

48. King, *Danse Macabre*, 13.

49. King, *Danse Macabre*, xiii.

50. Stephen King, foreword to *Night Shift* (New York: Anchor, 2011), 5.

51. King, *Danse Macabre*, 186.

52. David Hume, *Of Tragedy*, in *Essential Works of David Hume* (New York: Bantam, 1965), 441.

53. King, *Danse Macabre*, 5.

54. Hume, *Of Tragedy*, 442.

55. King, foreword to *Night Shift*, 9.

56. King, *Danse Macabre*, 3.

57. King, *Danse Macabre*, 217.

58. King, *Danse Macabre*, 128.

59. King, *Danse Macabre*, 152.

60. King, *Danse Macabre*, 50.

61. King, *Danse Macabre*, 52.

12

"YOU WEREN'T HIRED TO PHILOSOPHIZE, TORRANCE"

The Death of the Author in *The Shining*

Charles Bane

Stephen King's 1977 novel *The Shining* provides an excellent opportunity to examine one of the more frustrating and often confusing philosophical concepts of the twentieth century, the so-called death of the author. Taken from the title of a 1968 essay by French philosopher and linguist Roland Barthes (1915–1980), this concept continues to baffle students and general readers of literature who grapple with the idea of a text having no author. In fact, a cursory search on YouTube will bring up numerous examples of such readers who alternately try to explain and defy Barthes's concept as mere nonsense. But Barthes brings up difficult questions about authors and texts, including what authorship means, who controls a text—the author or the reader, how much context should be considered when attempting to understand the "meaning" of a text, and so on. As interesting as many of the questions and their resulting discussions can be, Barthes did not completely originate this idea but was working within an established critical tradition. In order to fully understand Barthes's concept, we must first look at the origin of the concept as laid out by literary critics W. K. Wimsatt and Monroe Beardsley in 1946. Once we understand the tradition, the concept becomes much clearer and can easily be illustrated by the various iterations of King's novel, including the 1980 film adaptation by Stanley Kubrick and King's own 1997 adaptation for television.

THE INTENTIONAL FALLACY

In 1946, Wimsatt and Beardsley published an essay titled "The Intentional Fallacy" in which they declared that "the design or intention of the author is neither available nor desirable as a standard for judging the success of a work of literary art."[1] In the essay, the critics note that the idea of an author's "intention" has been the subject of "a number of recent discussions," the most famous of which was a debate between literary scholar E. M. W. Tillyard (1889–1962) and scholar and novelist C. S. Lewis (1898–1963) published as *The Personal Heresy: A Controversy* (1939).[2] Since the concept of "intention" was such a hot topic, Wimsatt and Beardsley set out to clear up the controversy once and for all. They define "intention" as the "design or plan in the author's mind."[3] They then set up several propositions to frame their discussion. The most important of these propositions for our purposes asks how a critic or reader can "find out what the poet tried to do."[4] First, it is important to note that Wimsatt and Beardsley were dealing exclusively with poets and poetry. Second, they were focusing almost entirely on *dead* poets. One point they wanted to make clear was that since the poets are dead, we simply cannot ask them what they *intended*. All we have is the poem or "text," and since an author cannot be summoned or reconstructed from a piece of writing, the text is and can be the only source of meaning. To discuss the "intent" of an author is a fallacy since it uses invalid reasoning to make its argument, namely, it appeals to the intention of an author no longer accessible to us or those attributing intention to that author in order to discern the meaning of that author's text. While Wimsatt and Beardsley do go on to praise literary biography as "a legitimate and attractive study in itself," they immediately argue that "there is danger in confusing personal and poetic studies."[5] Even if we can know something about the author's life, this knowledge should not interfere with a reading or interpretation of a poem.

The theory can be reduced to an analogy about Shakespeare, an author about whom we know very little. Simply put, if *Hamlet* is truly great, then a reader with no knowledge of Shakespeare's life or times can still recognize the play's greatness. The text will speak for itself. Wimsatt and Beardsley's analysis did not remain limited to poetry but soon extended to all other literary genres and to all authors, living or dead. For two decades after its publication, Wimsatt and Beardsley's essay became standard reading for students of literature. Its ideas became generally accepted. The focus on "textual" studies dominated the field of literary studies, with author psychology and biography considered secondary, though still of importance.

THE DEATH OF THE AUTHOR

In 1968 Roland Barthes took literary studies a step further by claiming that we shouldn't simply remove references to the life of its author from the study of her text; rather, we should accept that once a text is written, the author actually ceases to exist in any mode at all. Barthes opens his essay with a quote from Honoré de Balzac's *Sarrasine* (1830) and a series of questions raised by the quote: Who is speaking? The hero of the story? Balzac the individual? Balzac the author? Universal wisdom?[6] Barthes then gives a single answer to all of the questions: "We shall never know. . . . As soon as a fact is *narrated* . . . this disconnection begins, the voice loses its origin, the author enters into his own death, writing begins."[7] Though the study of the text alone was dominant in literary studies, no one had gone so far as to claim that authors were figuratively "dead" and simply didn't exist. But this was exactly what Barthes was arguing.

Barthes argues that author psychology and biography are not helpful, but harmful to literary analysis and criticizes contemporary literary studies for claiming to study the text alone while still attaching "the greatest importance to the 'person' of the author . . . [who] reigns in histories of literature, biographies of writers, interviews, magazines, as in the very consciousness of men of letters."[8] Furthermore, Barthes argues that by placing emphasis on the "person" of the author, the study of literature is focused on "the author, his person, his life, his tastes, his passions" and that the "explanation of a work is always sought in the man or woman who produced it, as if it were always in the end . . . the voice of a single person, the author 'confiding' in us."[9] This focus becomes more problematic when the author is living and can enter the conversation. Barthes believed that literary critics and scholars should follow the lead of linguists, Barthes's primary occupation, and accept that the author represents an "empty process" that serves a function, much like the first-person subject ("I") of a sentence.[10] The subject makes possible the enunciation, but doesn't actually give the utterance any meaning. The listener must infer the meaning. Similarly, an author produces a text, but the reader gives meaning to it.

For Barthes, the emphasis on the author creates a godlike entity that is "always conceived of as the past of his own book. . . . The Author is thought to *nourish* the book, which is to say that he exists before it, thinks, suffers, lives for it, is in the same relation of antecedence to his work as a father to his child."[11] This deification of the author leads Barthes to propose a new word for writers, *scripteur* (scriptor), not a creator of words but simply the recorder of them. Barthes argues that the idea of authors as godlike creators is a myth created to "to impose a limit on that text, to furnish it with a final signified, to close the writing . . . when the Author has been found, the text is 'explained.'"[12] Though reducing a text to one meaning may have a certain appeal, it ultimately limits what the text is and will be, as well as undermines the many cultural facets that the writer consciously and unconsciously embedded in the text. But if we remove the author, then a text is transformed into a living document "made of multiple writings" that draws on "many cultures" and enters into "mutual relations of dialogue, parody, contestation."[13] By accepting a text as its own entity, we actually begin to see how it borrows from and comments on other texts. Once we see a text for what it is, we understand that a writer, not an author but scriptor, can only "imitate," is "never original," and has the power only "to mix writings, to counter the ones with the others."[14] The fact that a scriptor is never original leads Barthes to proclaim, in the most famous quote from his essay, that a text is nothing more than "a tissue of quotations drawn from the innumerable centres of culture."[15] Barthes's comment sparked a controversy still alive today, as many writers and readers argue that new books are wholly original and spring from the minds of their creators. A look at Stephen King's novel *The Shining* and the two film adaptations of it—one Kubrick's and one King's—can demonstrate Barthes's claims as well as the current debate regarding authorial intention.[16]

THE SHINING

In 1977, Doubleday published "a new novel by the author of *Carrie* and *'Salem's Lot*."[17] That novel was *The Shining*, and the author was Stephen King. The first two novels had been best sellers, and *Carrie* had been adapted into a hit film (a television adaptation of *'Salem's Lot* was still two years away). *The Shining* followed suit by becoming a best seller and cementing King's place as America's literary bogeyman. The film rights were quickly sold and a big-budget feature film followed in 1980. To date, the novel remains one of King's most popular among both fans and critics.

But what exactly is *The Shining*? To return to our hypothetical readers at the beginning of this chapter, *The Shining* is a novel, and Stephen King is its author, that is to say, its creator. In fact, the blurb on the book jacket clearly proclaims this fact. However, a few years ago, inspired by the upcoming release of the long-awaited sequel to *The Shining*, *Doctor Sleep* (2013), I wanted to reread the novel. I had a long drive coming up and decided to pass the time by listening to the audiobook. I heard the stock, company announcement stating the publisher, title, and reader, but when Campbell Scott began reading, he did not say, "*The Shining* by Stephen King, chapter 1," to announce the beginning of the actual book. Rather, Scott simply began, "It was in this apartment, also, that there stood a gigantic clock of ebony. Its pendulum swung to and fro with a dull, heavy, monotonous clang."[18] Did I begin at the wrong spot? Was my copy defective? I clearly remembered the clock in the novel signaling that it was "time to unmask," but I knew that episode was much later in the book. I knew the novel opened with Jack Torrance being interviewed for the position of winter caretaker. I attempted several restarts, but finally relented and let the audio play. When Scott finally reached the end of his long opening paragraph, he paused and said, "E. A. Poe, 'The Masque of the Red Death.'" I realized that Scott was reading the epigraphs at the beginning of the novel. There are three total before we get to "prefatory matters," which opens with the job interview.

As I continued listening, I couldn't help but think of Barthes's "tissue of quotations." The three epigraphs, chosen by King to frame "his" novel, appear at the beginning of every edition of *The Shining*. Even when King penned the author's introduction for the 2001 edition, the epigraphs preceded that introduction rather than coming after it. They are the first words that greet the reader, and though King didn't write them, they set the tone of the novel. Furthermore, these three references are not the only "quotations" in the book. There are also popular song lyrics ("*I see a bad moon a-rising. I see trouble on the way*"),[19] radio and television jingles ("*The Shadow knows*"),[20] product taglines ("*All my men wear English Leather or they wear nothing at all*"),[21] medicine slogans ("Excedrin Headache Number Vat 69"),[22] poetry ("*In the room the women come and go*"),[23] additional references taken from the epigraph sources ("*The Red Death held sway over all!*"),[24] and numerous other pop culture references. King did not author any of these words but wove them into his work, creating a "tissue of quotations." In fact, he did not even create the story's premise. At its heart, *The Shining* is a simple haunted house tale, an example of what King refers to as "the bad place," an archetype of horror.[25] Many versions were written before King's, and many were, and continue to be, written after.

These observations are by themselves not that revolutionary, but when we consider the backlash from both fans and King himself over Stanley Kubrick's 1980 film adaptation of the novel, the validity of Barthes's argument becomes much clearer.

STANLEY KUBRICK'S *THE SHINING*

Though *The Shining* was King's third novel, it was Kubrick's eleventh film. King was at the beginning of his career, but Kubrick was nearing the end of his. In fact, he would go on to make only two more films before his death. Kubrick had already been nominated for and won numerous awards. His films tended to perform well at the box office and were well received by critics. So, when it was announced that such a prominent filmmaker would be adapting the novel, expectations were high, especially considering that there was a built-in audience. However, the film was derided by fans of the novel and generally dismissed by critics. King himself openly attacked the film . . . occasionally. In *Danse Macabre* (1981), King praises the film as one of his "personal favorites."[26] In a 1983 interview, King is less enthusiastic, but still impressed: "Parts of the film are chilling, charged with a relentlessly claustrophobic terror, but others fall flat." In the same interview he admits to being

"deeply disappointed in the end result."[27] In the 2001 author's introduction to the reprint of the novel, King mentions that according to a
conversation he had with Kubrick during production of the film, the
novel's blurring of "the line between the supernatural and the psychotic" is what had appealed to Kubrick.[28] King disagreed with that reading,
stating that "Kubrick and [he] came to different conclusions" about
what is "impelling Jack Torrance toward murder."[29] According to King,
Kubrick believed Jack was haunted by memories and King believed he
was haunted by "malevolent ghosts."[30] However, King concedes that
"perhaps those different conclusions are, in fact, the same."[31] This
statement implies that although Kubrick's interpretation of the novel is
different from King's own, they are both equally valid. In later years,
however, King became far more critical of both Kubrick and the film,
citing Kubrick's *The Shining* as the only adaptation of his work he
hated.[32] In an interview with the BBC to promote his new book *Doctor
Sleep*, the sequel to *The Shining*, King took the chance to openly criticize the adaptation:

> I think one of the things that people relate to in my books is there's a
> warmth, there's a reaching out and saying to the reader, "I want you
> to be a part of this." And with Kubrick's *The Shining*, I felt that it was
> very cold. We're looking at these people, but they're like ants in an
> anthill. Aren't they doing interesting things, these little insects?[33]

He again refers to the film as "cold" a year later in *Rolling Stone*,
saying, "The book is hot, and the movie is cold; the book ends in fire,
and the movie in ice." In this same interview, he criticizes the characterization of Jack Torrance, arguing that in the novel, "there's an actual
arc where you see this guy, Jack Torrance, trying to be good, and little
by little he moves over to this place where he's crazy," but in the film
version, "Jack was crazy from the first scene."[34] We'll discuss this claim
of King's in more detail later. By the time of the author's note at the end
of *Doctor Sleep*, King refers to the original novel as "the True History of
the Torrance Family," completely dismissing Kubrick's film.[35]

Fans of King and his novel often cite these very same "mistakes" and
argue that Kubrick simply got the adaptation wrong because he "missed
the point entirely."[36] This perception demonstrates how readers of *The
Shining*, and King himself, consider King to be the *author*ity on the
novel. King is Barthes's "Author-God," acting as a father protecting his

child. He has "limited" and "explained" the text, and his explanation is the only, *autho*ritative reading of the novel. For King, *The Shining* is a "warm" story about a "good man" who is led by "malevolent ghosts" into a downward spiral of madness that almost destroys his family. But, being the good man that he is, he sacrifices himself to save his family and is thus redeemed.

STEPHEN KING'S THE SHINING

King's frustration with Stanley Kubrick's *The Shining* led King to write and produce his own 1997 made-for-television miniseries. I often teach *The Shining* in a horror class, and when I do, I show Kubrick's film version. Every time I teach the film, students who are fans of the novel often ask why I don't show the 1997 version, citing that it is *exactly* like the book. I have always found this claim to be interesting, given the fact that the ending of King's television adaptation appears nowhere in the novel. While *The Shining* ends with Dick Halloran visiting Wendy and Danny at the Red Arrow Lodge and Danny catching a fish, *Stephen King's The Shining* ends many years later with Danny graduating from high school as his mother and Dick proudly look on from the audience. Danny is visited onstage by the ghost of his father, who shares an intimate moment with his son, reminding viewers that Jack wasn't such a bad guy after all. Why this change? Perhaps King simply wanted to revise Kubrick's reading, or perhaps he had begun to suspect, like Kubrick, that maybe Jack wasn't such a good guy. This additional scene rings false and betrays everything that came before it in the film in order to support King's explanation of the novel. Maybe there is more psychosis at work than supernatural, malevolent spirits. Maybe King is wrong, and Kubrick is right. Or maybe Barthes is right and a text "is made of multiple writings, drawn from many cultures" and this "multiplicity is focused" in the mind of an individual reader. [37]

THE BIRTH OF THE READER

For Barthes, the true interpreter of any text is not its author but the reader who brings together all of the quotations and inscribes them with meaning, or as he states, "A text's unity lies not in its origin but in its destination."[38] Readers can see in a text what the author cannot. King saw a haunted house that "possessed" a good man for its own evil ends. Kubrick, on the other hand, saw a man already teetering on the edge of insanity who just needed a little push.

King has spent over three decades explaining why he doesn't like Kubrick's adaptation. It seems that King was destined not to like the film. When King states that "Jack was crazy from the first scene," we can wonder: "Which Jack? Torrance or Nicholson?" According to King, the moment he saw Nicholson, he thought, "Oh, I know this guy. I've seen him in five motorcycle movies, where [he] played the same part."[39] Was it really Kubrick's film that suggested Jack *Torrance*'s madness or the fact that Jack *Nicholson* was playing the role? In 1975, Nicholson had won an Oscar for playing an inmate in an asylum in *One Flew Over the Cuckoo's Nest*. This, along with his "five motorcycle movies," led to his being typecast as crazy. King could not objectively judge the film because Nicholson is a part of the film's "tissue."

Whether King or his fans like it or not, King's novel and Kubrick's film are forever part of the same tissue. During King's interview with the BBC, various clips from Kubrick's film, not King's, were shown. Why? Because the blood gushing from the elevator, the two little girls in their powder blue dresses, and Jack Nicholson shoving his face through the bathroom door and exclaiming, "Here's Johnny!" are images that have become inextricably linked with *The Shining*, even though none of them appear in the novel. They are "original" to the film.[40]

If we, as readers, become consumed with, to quote Barthes, "the 'person' of the author," we might be inclined to read King's *On Writing: A Memoir of the Craft*. In this memoir, King tells of an intervention his family had in 1985, during which his wife Tabitha dumped "a trashbag full of stuff from [his] office out on the rug: beer cans, cigarette butts, cocaine in gram bottles and cocaine in plastic Baggies, coke spoons caked with snot and blood, Valium, Xanax, bottles of Robitussin cough syrup and NyQuil cold medicine, even bottles of mouthwash."[41] He goes on to describe the pain he was causing his family and how he still cannot remember even writing some of his books while he was "under the influence." Based on such evidence, a psychoanalytic reading of *The Shining* might argue that the novel is actually about a writer, husband, father, and addict who is struggling with his own inner demons that manifest themselves as spirits. In short, the same reading that Kubrick arrived at without knowledge of King's personal addictions. The same psychoanalytic reading might perhaps argue that King's belief in Jack Torrance's redemption might be hope for his own. However, such a reading is guilty of what Wimsatt and Beardsley refer to as the "danger in confusing personal and poetic studies." Though it is interesting to note, it is only one possible reading, a part of the tissue of quotations. But under a Barthes-influenced reading, it does not matter that King himself was, while writing the novel, an alcoholic. For Barthes, the tissue is too complex to be pinned to a single identity or author; if the author's wishes are dead, more interesting interpretations are possible as new readers continue to be born. The death of the author benefits both the reader and the text. For readers, it expands the possibilities of a text by opening up multiple interpretations rather than a single, authoritative reading. For texts, we must consider Ben Jonson's famous quote about Shakespeare being "not of an age but for all time."[42] In order to remain vital and valid, a text must have a life outside of its author. If the text is limited, it becomes no better than a moralistic tale or one that is frozen in time and, therefore, dead. But there is no single way to read *The Shining*, nor does King have more authority over the novel than anyone else who reads it. By allowing herself to die, figuratively, that is, not limiting the reading of her text, an author gives life to her creation.

NOTES

1. William K. Wimsatt Jr. and Monroe C. Beardsley, "The Intentional Fallacy," in *The Norton Anthology of Theory and Criticism*, 2nd ed., ed. Vincent B. Leitch (New York: Norton, 2010), 1233.

2. Wimsatt and Beardsley, "The Intentional Fallacy," 1232.

3. Wimsatt and Beardsley, "The Intentional Fallacy," 1233.

4. Wimsatt and Beardsley, "The Intentional Fallacy," 1233.

5. Wimsatt and Beardsley, "The Intentional Fallacy," 1239.

6. Roland Barthes, "The Death of the Author," in *The Norton Anthology of Theory and Criticism*, 2nd ed., ed. Vincent B. Leitch (New York: Norton, 2010), 1322. The questions are here simplified for summary purposes.

7. Barthes, "Death of the Author," 1322.

8. Barthes, "Death of the Author," 1322.

9. Barthes, "Death of the Author," 1322.

10. Barthes, "Death of the Author," 1323.

11. Barthes, "Death of the Author," 1324.

12. Barthes, "Death of the Author," 1325.

13. Barthes, "Death of the Author," 1325.

14. Barthes, "Death of the Author," 1324.

15. Barthes, "Death of the Author," 1324.

16. From this point on, the novel will simply be referred to as *The Shining*, the 1980 adaptation as Stanley Kubrick's *The Shining*, and the 1997 adaptation as *Stephen King's The Shining*.

17. Tagline on the original hardcover edition of *The Shining*.

18. Stephen King, *The Shining*, read by Campbell Scott (New York: Random House Audible, 2012), audiobook, 15 hrs. 49 mins.

19. Stephen King, *The Shining* (New York: Pocket Books, 2001), 221. Originally from the 1969 single "Bad Moon Rising" written by John Fogerty and performed by Creedence Clearwater Revival. The italics are King's.

20. King, *The Shining*, 52. The Shadow was a vigilante who first appeared in pulp novels in the 1930s. Its popularity led to it becoming first a radio show and eventually a series of films and a television series. Each episode opened with the line "Who knows what evil lurks in the hearts of men? The Shadow knows!" The italics are King's.

21. King, *The Shining*, 4. The tagline for a popular men's cologne. The italics are King's.

22. King, *The Shining*, 197. The "Excedrin Headache Number . . ." was a popular ad campaign that began in the 1960s.

23. King, *The Shining*, 178. A line from the T. S. Eliot poem "The Love Song of J. Alfred Prufrock" first published in 1915. The italics are King's.

24. King, *The Shining*, 2001, 173. King slightly alters the final line of Edgar Allan Poe's short story "The Mask of the Red Death: A Fantasy," first published in 1842. The original read, "And Darkness and Decay and the Red Death held illimitable dominion over all." The italics are King's.

25. Stephen King, *Danse Macabre* (New York: Gallery Books, 1981), 278.

26. King, *Danse Macabre*, 226.

27. "Stephen King: The *Playboy* Interview," *Time*, June 1983.

28. Stephen King, introduction to *The Shining* (New York: Pocket Books, 2001), xvi.

29. King, introduction to *The Shining*, xvi.

30. King, introduction to *The Shining*, xvi.

31. King, introduction to *The Shining*, xvi.

32. "Writing Rapture: The *WD* Interview," *Writer's Digest*, May/June 2009.

33. Stephen King, interview with Will Gompertz, *BBC Arts*, BBC online, September 19, 2013.

34. Andy Greene, "Stephen King: The *Rolling Stone* Interview," *Rolling Stone*, October 31, 2014.

35. Stephen King, author's note to *Doctor Sleep* (New York: Scribner, 2013), 530.

36. Stephanie Early Green, "Book Review Monday: *The Shining*, by Stephen King," *Stephanie Early Green* (blog), May 27, 2013, http://stephanieearlygreen.com/book-review-monday-the-shining-by-stephen-king/. I chose this blog solely as a representative example. A quick Google search will bring up any number of similar complaints about Kubrick's adaptation.

37. Barthes, "Death of the Author," 1324.

38. Barthes, "Death of the Author," 1325.

39. Greene, "Stephen King: The *Rolling Stone Interview*."

40. Though the "Here's Johnny!" quote isn't exactly original. It is yet another quotation woven into the tissue. This phrase was used by Ed McMahon to introduce Johnny Carson during his run as host of *The Tonight Show*.

41. Stephen King, *On Writing: A Memoir of the Craft* (New York: Pocket Books, 2000), 90.

42. Ben Jonson, "To the Memory of My Beloved the Author, Mr. William Shakespeare." The poem was appended to the beginning of the First Folio of Shakespeare's collected works that appeared in 1623.

13

WHAT HAPPENS TO THE PRESENT WHEN IT BECOMES THE PAST

Time Travel and the Nature of Time in *The Langoliers*

Paul R. Daniels

In *The Langoliers*, a few passengers aboard a commercial airline flight wake to find that they've mysteriously traveled a few minutes into the past . . . a few minutes *behind* everyone else. They find that the world still exists, after "the present" has moved on, but only for a short duration before the langoliers—the timekeepers of eternity—arrive to remove everything that remains permanently from existence. Bob Jenkins, one of the main characters, theorizes that their plane happened to travel through a rip in the temporal fabric of reality. Where they end up, as Bethany Simms laments at one point in the story, is out of step with the present. They find the past is empty in an important sense: while it has our familiar artifacts—like tables, chairs, buildings, and trees—there are no people; it's vacant and lifeless. Dinah Bellman, the young blind girl, describes the world that remains as having the feeling of being *over*. This story prompts a few interesting questions.

First, are the characters in *The Langoliers* really time travelers? There's a sense in which it might seem as if they are, but there's also a sense in which they aren't—after all, they don't seem able to do anything that might change history and nobody else is around when they're in the past. At the very least, this depiction of time travel differs from others found in science fiction. Think of *Doctor Who*, *The Terminator*, or *Back to the Future*. In those stories, the past and future are no different than the present—when the time travelers arrive at their destination time, everyone and everything is there, just as it's supposed to be. This isn't what it's like in *The Langoliers*. Whether or not we should consider them time travelers will, it turns out, depend on what we mean when we say someone's a time traveler. Drawing on the work of philosophers like David Lewis, we can better understand what it means to say someone's a time traveler and, with such an understanding in mind, gain greater insights into the rich world depicted in *The Langoliers*. A second interesting question is: How should we understand the nature of time in *The Langoliers*? When the main characters find themselves outside of the present, the world seems to be a very strange place—things don't sound or look the same; food and drink have no taste; colors are muted; matches and fuel won't burn—the past has no causal "oomph," no life to it. As Bob Jenkins describes it, they find themselves in a dead world, a world after the present has moved on without them. There are a variety of theories of time we can lean on to better understand the experiences of the main characters.

By looking at these questions we can gain a deep level of appreciation of the world Stephen King created in *The Langoliers* and, in the process, reveal insights about the nature of the real world. So we'll come away from this discussion with, on one hand, an understanding of what it takes for a story to count as a *time-travel* story and, on the other hand, an understanding of the nature of time. These insights are, to be sure, no trivialities: the role of time is, after all, omnipresent in our lives; together with space, time is the backdrop against which everything happens.

TIME TRAVEL IN *THE LANGOLIERS*

What's the deal with time travel? We see a lot of depictions of time travel in fiction, and we can often tell pretty easily that the characters are time travelers. For instance, they might travel to past times where younger versions of themselves are running around doing memorable things. Or they might travel to future times, where familiar faces have grown old. Typically, when time travelers travel to the past, we see the past as it was. When the Terminator, for instance, traveled back in time to try to kill Sarah Connor in the *Terminator* films, we see Sarah Connor as she was in the 1980s, even though the Terminator came from a very different time in order to change things. But this isn't the sort of experience that the characters in *The Langoliers* have. In *The Langoliers*, no one else is around when they arrive at Bangor airport; the place is deserted. It's not readily apparent that anything they do there, in the past, will affect the future in any way. In virtue of this, *The Langoliers* isn't your typical run-of-the-mill time-travel story. And so, we can ask: Should we consider *The Langoliers* a time-travel story at all?

Despite the differences, we still have good reason to consider *The Langoliers* a time-travel story. To see this, consider the following question: How do we distinguish time travelers from non-time travelers? After all, as someone might playfully point out, we're all time travelers in a rudimentary way—that is, we're all time travelers at least insofar as we exist at one time, and then we subsequently exist at later times. Here I am, now, sitting with a warm cup of tea. And there I was, a few minutes ago, boiling the kettle in the kitchen. How did I get from that moment to this one? Surely I traveled from then to now. That is, surely, we're all gradually traveling into the future as we travel from one moment to the next. But this isn't what we mean when we say someone's a time traveler. To call me a time traveler is to misuse the notion of time travel, even if it's true that I travel through time in some way; time travelers differ from us regular folk in an important way.

The crucial difference between a time traveler and a non-time traveler is that there's a discrepancy between the "personal time" of a time traveler and the "external time" of the world, which is not true of non-time travelers. Let me connect the dots here in a few steps. First, what do we mean by personal time and external time? This distinction comes from the twentieth-century American philosopher David Lewis (1941–2001).[1] Personal time and external time aren't different temporal dimensions or anything like that; that's not what we mean when we talk about personal time and external time. Instead, Lewis argues that personal time and external time are merely different ways we can measure the amount of time that elapses between two moments—such as the moment a time traveler begins her journey, and the moment her journey ends. First, everyone and every object—you, your car, Albert Kaussner, his violin—has its own personal time (which is precisely why it's called *personal* time). Personal time corresponds to the amount of time it takes that object to get from one moment to another; it's, roughly, what would be measured by an imaginary perfectly functioning watch traveling along with the object. Whereas, in contrast, external time corresponds to the amount of *actual time* that elapses from one moment to another.

We can illustrate this with an example. Think of me again, five minutes ago, getting ready to boil the kettle for my cup of tea. And think of me now, sitting here with my warm cup of tea. These two different events take place at two different moments; how long did it take me to travel from the one to the other? We can now see that there are two ways we might make that measurement: by my own personal time, and by external time. In this case, though, both measurements will come out the same—roughly five minutes. It's because they're the same that we can identify me as a non-time traveler. Our assessment would be different had I, instead, gone on a time-travel journey while the kettle was boiling. Imagine that after starting the kettle, a time portal appeared in the kitchen and sucked me through to the year 1885, where I stood dazed and confused for an hour before another time portal appeared and returned me to the kitchen just as the kettle came to a boil. In this case, the amount of external time that elapses between when I turn on the kettle and when I sit down with my warm cup of tea is still the same: five minutes. It's the same because nothing has changed about time itself, or the kettle boiling (it didn't come with me on my trek through time). Only *I* went on a strange journey. Here, in virtue of my trip to 1885, my personal time measurement will be just over an hour. It still took five minutes for the kettle to boil, but *I* had to wait an hour before it was ready! I had to wait this long because I spent that hour in 1885, between starting the kettle and sitting down to drink the cup of tea. So, we call me a time traveler because there's a discrepancy between my personal time measurement and the external time measurement. All this is to say that the external time measurement will always be the same as the personal time measurement for a non-time traveler, and that we'll always be able to find a discrepancy between the personal time measurement and the external time measurement of time travelers.

So what about *The Langoliers*? Think of "The Event," as the passengers call it; this was the moment their plane first passed through the anomaly, while they were all asleep, and separated them from the present. Consider the moment The Event occurs as their departure event. And think of the moment they return to the present at the end of the story as their arrival event. It took the characters the bulk of a day to travel to Bangor, refuel the plane, fly back over the desert, and land at LAX—this is the personal time duration of their journey. But when they return to the present they learn that it's merely a few hours after they left—this is the external time measurement between when they left the present and when they rejoined it. Because there's a discrepancy here, we are justified in calling them time travelers. And so, we're justified in calling *The Langoliers* a time-travel story, despite all the ways it differs from more run-of-the-mill time-travel stories.

THE NATURE OF TIME IN *THE LANGOLIERS*

Let's turn to our second question: How should we understand the nature of time in *The Langoliers*? Because the characters travel to a different time, they are able to learn a lot about the nature of time in their world. We'll proceed here by first considering two prominent theories of time that aim to explain the nature of time: Most people seem to intuitively think that a theory of time called "presentism" is the correct theory of time for our world, that this theory rightly characterizes the way time works in the real world. Most philosophers, on the other hand, reject presentism and favor a rival theory of time called "eternalism." However, I'll argue that neither of these accurately capture what's going on in *The Langoliers*. So I'll then argue that there's an alternative theory of time that more accurately accounts for the experiences and observations of the passengers in *The Langoliers*.

Let's start with presentism. Presentism is characterized by two claims about the nature of time.[2] First, according to presentism, only the present moment exists. The "now," or "the present" is privileged in an important way, and only things that are around in the now are real. For instance, you and this this book exist because they're both part of the present. Julius Caesar, though, doesn't exist. Why? Because he's not around *right now*. If you freeze the entire universe right now, and searched high and low, you would not find Julius Caesar. And because he doesn't exist anywhere right now, he doesn't exist *at all*. This is the core claim of presentism: if something isn't part of the present moment, it doesn't exist in any sense. Of course, while Julius Caesar doesn't exist anymore, he used to exist. And this brings us to the second key claim about the nature of time that the presentist endorses: the moment of time that is privileged in this way changes; this is the familiar notion that time flows, or progresses. Think about a past moment when Julius Caesar did exist—for example, when he took his legions across the Rubicon River in 49 BCE. At that time, he and everything around him existed. You and this book did not. But the privileged present gradually flowed and progressed into the future, eventually reaching the point where Julius Caesar didn't exist anymore, and finally coming to when you and this book came into existence. In virtue of this, most people intuitively think presentism is true. When you tell people about it, a common reaction is for them to say, "Of course I exist and Julius Caesar doesn't, that's obvious!" or "Of course there's something special about *right now!*"

So, what's the problem with presentism, and why isn't presentism true in *The Langoliers*? It has to do with the fact that *The Langoliers* is a time-travel story. Many philosophers think presentism is incompatible with time travel.[3] That is, if presentism is true, it's not possible to be a time traveler. So, if presentism and time travel are incompatible, presentism cannot be true in *The Langoliers*. Many think presentism is incompatible with time travel because of the "nowhere" problem (as it's often called). The nowhere problem is this: since, according to presentism, only the present moment exists, no other "places in time" exist. So, would-be time travelers have nowhere to travel to. That is, their destination in the past doesn't exist anymore. And since it's impossible to travel to a place that doesn't exist, it's impossible to time travel if presentism is true. But in *The Langoliers* the characters do travel to the past. And, crucially, the past exists when they arrive. Granted, the past is different than the present—there's no "oomph" or life in the past— but the past still exists (at least until the langoliers get there). But according to presentism, only the present moment exists. And the characters have clearly left the present when The Event happens. So, because the past and future still exist when not part of the present moment, and presentism requires that only the present moment exists, presentism cannot be the right theory of time for the world depicted in *The Langoliers*.

Having ruled out presentism, let's turn our attention to eternalism. The eternalist rejects both claims asserted by the presentist—that is, the eternalist denies that only the present exists, and she also denies that there's anything special or privileged about the present.[4] Eternalists consider time to be very much like space. By that I mean, according to eternalism, all times are equally real in the same sort of way as how all (spatial) places are equally real. The eternalist will say things like: "Look, Melbourne is no more real than Pluto. One is here, the other is not. But that difference doesn't make a difference about whether or not either place really exists. So, too, with times. Pluto may not be 'here,' but it still exists; and 49 BCE may not be 'now' but it still exists." What the eternalist is doing here is claiming that indexicals like "here" and "now" are the same: it'd be a mistake to conclude that Pluto doesn't exist merely because it's not here, and likewise it'd be a mistake to conclude that Julius Caesar doesn't exist merely because 49 BCE isn't now. Thus, just as there is nothing special about *here*, there is nothing special about *now*. Put differently, according to the eternalist the world is merely a static space-time block, extended in time just as it's extended in the more familiar three dimensions of space. A lot of philosophers think that insights from physics, especially from relativistic physics, provide compelling reasons to think eternalism is the right theory of time for our world (but we won't get into those technical reasons here).

So, what's the problem with eternalism, and why isn't eternalism true in *The Langoliers*? One reason is that there's clearly something special about the present in *The Langoliers*. This is tension with the eternalist picture since, according to it, there's nothing metaphysically special about any moment (any "now") just as there's nothing special about any place (any "here"). In *The Langoliers* the characters theorize that they've gotten out of step with the privileged present, and they're desperate to get back to it. And their experience of rejoining the present is an amazing one . . . sights, smells, sounds are vibrant; the world in the present is alive and dynamic. This feature of the story means that eternalism cannot be the right theory of time for *The Langoliers*. So, because there is a time in *The Langoliers*—the moving present—which is special, eternalism is ruled out. In short, it's not enough that other times exist. It would *also* have to be true that no time is special. So eternalism doesn't fit *The Langoliers*, either. Those who reject eternalism as the correct theory of time for *our* world, as presentists do, often do so because they think that in our world there *is* something special about the present. Our own experiences tend to suggest this—after all, the stuff that's happening right now seems different in a very important way from stuff that happened in the past.

Since neither presentism nor eternalism can accommodate what we know about the world in *The Langoliers*, let's consider a third option: the moving spotlight theory.[5] This theory of time is less prominent than presentism and eternalism, but it fits better with the observations of the characters in *The Langoliers*. In a sense, the moving spotlight theory combines aspects of both presentism and eternalism. The moving spotlight theorist will endorse the following claims: First, that all times (past, present, future) are equally real. Like the eternalist, the moving spotlight theorist maintains that all moments in time exist just as all places in space exist. And, second, that there is a privileged present— the now—which changes as it moves into the future. That is, only a single time is ever part of the now and only that time shines with a special metaphysical status. This theory of time gets its name from a classic analogy used to explain it: Imagine a police car is driving down a suburban street at night and shining its searchlight on the houses, one at a time, as it gradually drives along. Think of the houses as moments in time, ordered from earlier to later, just as the houses are ordered from lower to higher street numbers. And think of the light being shone as the present. The houses that have already been illuminated represent past times, and the ones that have not yet been illuminated represent future times. And the light moves along, in a fixed direction, just as we imagine the "now" moves from earlier times to later times. The previously illuminated houses (past moments) still exist, but aren't privileged as the light from the police car (the privileged status of the "now") doesn't shine on any of them. The same goes for the houses farther up the street (future moments). Only the current illuminated house is lit up, and this changes as the police car drives along.

The crucial difference between the privileged present according to the moving spotlight theory, and the privileged present according to the presentist, is that the special metaphysical status featured by the present is not about what exists according to the moving spotlight theorist (whereas it is with presentism). So, then, what kind of special metaphysical status does the moving spotlight theorist have in mind here, and how does the present differ from other nonpresent times? The difference we have in mind here with respect to the moving spotlight theory is something very much like the difference the characters notice when they rejoin the present—the past was, as Bob Jenkins describes it, a dead world; the present is alive like everything is active or just *on*.

Advocates of this theory of time tend to argue that it combines the best features of both presentism and eternalism. On one hand, the moving spotlight theorist doesn't conclude that things far away in time are unreal merely because they aren't now—a claim that seems foolhardy when we switch and say parallel remarks about things which are spatially far away from here. The moving spotlight theorist avoids this as she agrees with the eternalist about how different times exist. And on the other hand, the moving spotlight theorist can say that there *is* something unique about the present; something the eternalist cannot say. Both these features are found in *The Langoliers*. We see this in the experiences had by the characters as they travel to the real-but-dead past, and then to the real-but-not-yet-born future, as well as the uniqueness of the moving "now" as it catches up with them. Because of the observations and experiences had by the characters in *The Langoliers*, we can recognize that the nature of time in the world Stephen King has created here is best characterized by the moving spotlight theory.

THE CURIOUS CASE OF THE LANGOLIERS

While the moving spotlight theory does a pretty good job of matching the observations of the characters in *The Langoliers*, some might have reservations. Someone might say something like this: "Okay. So the moving spotlight theory tells us that there's something special about the present moment, and that that privileged status changes as it flows along into the future. And this seems like a feature of the world in *The Langoliers*. Moreover, the moving spotlight theory tells us that past and future times exist even when they aren't part of that privileged present. And this does seem to be a feature of the world in *The Langoliers*, too— the world exists while they're at Bangor airport, but it has no life or 'oomph.' But what about the past *after* the langoliers have eaten it? *Nothing* exists after they've been there! So, there's no sense in which, for instance, Julius Caesar exists." That is, there's nothing left after the langoliers have been there, and this looks like a problem. But the fact that there's nothing left in the world after the langoliers have been there shouldn't worry us here. Why? Because our question was about the nature of time in *The Langoliers*. The langoliers, and their effect on what exists, is a separate and additional feature of the world Stephen King created—this is beyond our question about the nature of time. That is, while the langoliers eat everything around them, this is not a feature of the nature of time, but rather a feature of the langoliers themselves (it is a monster story, after all). Think about it this way: we've been at risk of equivocating between different senses of *nothing*. On one hand, we might mean *absolutely nothing at all*, while on the other hand we might merely mean *no objects* (no things). What exists after the langoliers have been there is nothing in the latter sense. So even though the langoliers consume all the *content* in the world, they don't have any effect on time itself (or space). No *things* remain in the world, but *space-time* still does. That is, it's still there—like a backdrop or clean canvas—even though it's not populated with anything.

So, then, what's the upshot here? What have we learned? For one, we've revealed some further details about the rich world depicted in *The Langoliers*. That is, we know that the nature of time in *The Langoliers* doesn't conform with presentism or eternalism (i.e., we've learned that neither presentism nor eternalism are the right theory of time here); instead, the moving spotlight theory is the right theory of time. And we've also come away with an explanation for why the main characters in *The Langoliers* are properly understood to be time travelers, even though this story differs in crucial ways from most other time-travel stories. These are not trivial insights; on one hand, they enable us to better appreciate the setting envisaged by Stephen King, but they also further our own appreciation of the real world. Time can seem like a very tame topic, at least until we start thinking about it explicitly. Does time flow? We might naturally think it does, but the eternalist will disagree (and contemporary science may very well support her here). Everything we do takes place in time; it's central to all our experiences. So, we should care about the nature of time because of how pervasive it is to us. Being mindful of the nature of time, by critically examining the sorts of theories of time discussed here, allows us to better appreciate the ubiquitous role time plays in all our lives. *The Langoliers* serves as a nice example through which we can illustrate and test these ideas.

NOTES

1. David Lewis, "The Paradoxes of Time Travel," *American Philosophical Quarterly* 13, no. 2 (1976): 145–52.

2. Craig Bourne, *A Future for Presentism* (Oxford: Oxford University Press, 2006).

3. William Godfrey-Smith, "Travelling in Time," *Analysis* 40, no. 2 (1980): 72–73. See also William Grey, "Troubles with Time Travel," *Philosophy* 74, no. 1 (1999): 55–70.

4. David Hugh Mellor, *Real Time* (Cambridge: Cambridge University Press, 1981).

5. Ross Cameron, *The Moving Spotlight* (Oxford: Oxford University Press, 2015).

14

NOTES ON FOREKNOWLEDGE, TRUTHMAKING, AND COUNTERFACTUALS FROM *THE DEAD ZONE*

Tuomas W. Manninen

I've seen the future and it will be; I've seen the future and it works.—
Prince, "The Future"

Johnny Smith, the protagonist in Stephen King's *The Dead Zone*, is a clairvoyant: just by touching people (or objects belonging to them) he can know matters of fact not known by them. Some of this knowledge pertains to events in the present that are unknown to the individuals he touches, while some other items pertain to events yet to come. Each of these aspects of Johnny's clairvoyance is problematic for different reasons.[1]

In regard to what Johnny knows about the present, consider the following examples: just by touching the hand of Eileen, his physical therapist, Johnny knows that her house is on fire because she forgot to turn off the burner that morning;[2] just by kissing Sarah, Johnny is able to tell her where she could find the wedding ring she thought she had lost.[3] Yet, if the individuals he touched don't know (or wouldn't know) these matters, then how could Johnny? Where does he get his knowledge from? What makes it knowledge, anyway?

When it comes to what Johnny can know about the future, examples abound! Johnny knows that Chuck will die in a fire if he attends the graduation party at Cathy's,[4] and that Greg Stillson, once elected president, will start a nuclear war.[5] But are these matters of fact? And if they are, then is the future predetermined? Can it be altered? And what of human freedom, our ability to choose?

To start our inquiry, we need to get clear on what *knowledge* is. For a long while—dating back to Plato's *Theaetetus*, written circa 396 BCE—philosophers accepted the following definition of knowledge: knowledge is *justified true belief*. Although Edmund Gettier wreaked havoc with this definition in his (in)famous essay, causing many alternative definitions to be proposed, we will not cover all of them here.[6] Regardless, most current definitions of knowledge require *both* that what is known is *justified, and* that what is known is *true*. We can call these the *justification condition* and the *truth condition* for knowledge.

The *justification* condition is significantly challenged by Johnny's clairvoyant skills: If the individual Johnny touches has no knowledge about the state of affairs (like Sarah about the whereabouts of her wedding ring), is Johnny justified in believing what he perceives? Maybe—just to speculate here—Johnny is able to tap into subconscious memories that Sarah has; she has a visual memory—and maybe even a tactile one—about her wedding ring falling off, but she did not pay any attention to it at the moment. When Johnny touched her hand, he was able to access this recording of the event in her memory. Or something along those lines; I will leave this question for epistemologists to sort out. This is because the discussions in epistemology, post-Gettier, largely focused on the *justification* condition. In contrast, the focus of this chapter will be on the truth condition, of how only *true* events can be known. But even if we set aside the vexing questions about the *justification condition*, we cannot escape questions arising from the *truth condition*.

Put briefly, if we claim that only *true* events can be known, we run headfirst into the following problem when we try to reconcile this definition with *The Dead Zone*. If we suppose that for every true statement, there has to be some state of affairs that makes it true (or, serves as its truthmaker), we face very few problems in the present. At the moment, the statement "I am reading a chapter about the metaphysical questions raised by Stephen King's *The Dead Zone*" is made true by the fact that you (the reader) are, in fact, reading just such a chapter. To put this more formally, let us call statements *truthbearers* (meaning that *statements* can be either true or false). As for the question "What makes a truthbearer *true?*" we need to consider truth*makers*, which are some-thing outside of the realm of statements, namely, reality. Because there is a considerable disagreement among philosophers as to how to cash out the truthmaker theory, my goal is to merely outline the bare bones of such an account. So, consider this: for each truthbearer (a state-ment), there needs to be a truthmaker, be it some event/state of affairs and so forth, that renders the truthbearing statement true (or, converse-ly, the absence of which renders the truthbearing statement false).[7] For example, the statement "Charlie Norton and Norm Lawson discovered a dead body on January 1, 1975," is made true by the fact that the two aforementioned boys did discover a dead body on that very day.[8] So far, we seem to have satisfied the requirements about statements made in the present, whether about the present or past. The world either was a certain way or not, something either is the case or it is not. Thus, statements about the past or present are clearly true or false depending on whether something did take place, is taking place, or not.

But what if we tried to apply this account about truthmaking to *future* events? That is, what if we applied this account to statements about events that have not yet occurred? Consider *The Dead Zone* again, particularly the events of that fateful night in October 1970, when Johnny took Sarah to the "Absolutely Last Agricultural Fair of the Year in New England" where Sarah fell sick. The truthmaker for the statement "Sarah fell sick at the agricultural fair" is the *fact of Sarah's falling sick at the agricultural fair*.[9] Looking at the events of that night retrospectively—like, by Sarah, when she visits Johnny's grave about a decade after the night at the fair—the aforementioned truthmaker re-mains fixed, Sarah's wishes to the contrary notwithstanding: "Every-thing was supposed to be different, wasn't it! It wasn't supposed to end like this."[10]

But what about *future* events? That is, if future events have truth-makers (which is what they would need to have, if claims about the future are to be true), are these truthmakers obdurate (as some turn out to be with Jake Epping's travels to the past in King's *11/22/63*) to the point that they cannot be changed at all? The problem outlined above is one of those venerable ones in philosophy that dates back to the times of ancient Greece. Aristotle (384–322 BC) offers one of the first state-ments of knowledge about future events in his *De Interpretatione* (On Interpretation) where he speculates on whether or not a sea battle will take place tomorrow: "A sea-fight must either take place tomorrow or not, but it is not necessary that it should take place tomorrow, neither is it necessary that it should not take place, yet it is necessary that it either should or should not take place tomorrow."[11]

So, if there is to be a sea-fight tomorrow, there is going to be some event, state of affairs, or whatnot that makes the statement "There is a sea-fight" true. Although this may seem like a trivial issue, in this case, the appearance is quite deceiving. More generally, some future event— call it X—is either going to take place tomorrow (or, at some time at a more distant future), or it is not going to take place. Either Greg Stillson gets elected as the president of the United States, or not; either Johnny Smith gets a job with the Phoenix Public Works Department, or he does not; and so forth. But if X (for *any* value of X) occurs *and* someone knows that X will occur *before X actually occurs*, there is a problem, especially in light of the foregoing analysis. If you know something, then it has to be true, it has to be the case. And so if you *know* the future, that future has to be certain, which means it is necessarily the way you *know* it to be, or rather, it will be. Thus, the future is determined. Johnny knew that he was in a car accident that put him in the hospital for the reason that he did end up in the hospital for being in the car accident. But did Johnny really *know* that Greg Stillson was going to be the president of the United States and, subsequently, going to start a nuclear war? On our analysis of knowledge—which requires truthmakers for true statements, if he did *know* it, then the future appears to be just as fixed as the past.

In light of our foregoing discussion, we can reformulate Aristotle's problem, as it applies to Johnny's situation—and his talents—as follows: If Johnny knows the statement "Greg Stillson, once elected president, will start a nuclear war" to be true, then there must be a truthmaker for this claim (e.g., the series of events including Stillson's winning the election, being sworn in as the president, and subsequently his instigating a nuclear war). This would entail that there is no way of changing these events. Or, in Aristotle's words, we could say that "that which was truly predicted at the moment in the past will of necessity take place in the fullness of time."[12]

In other words, this is our problem. Although you (the reader) *could* have picked up some other title than the one that you are presently reading (like, *Roald Dahl and Philosophy: A Little Nonsense Now and*

Then), you cannot change things—or your choices—after they have taken place, which means that you are kind of stuck with reading *Stephen King and Philosophy*. Put more generally, we can alter *neither* the truths *nor* the truthmakers about the past—so why should we be able to alter *future* truthmakers? Johnny could have refrained from taking Sarah to the fair—but only up until the point when he took Sarah to the fair. In other words, the future would be locked in—or, in the words of wisdom that Dorrance Marstellar offered to Ralph Roberts, "Done-bun-can't-be-undone."[13]

ABOUT THE FUTURE (AND SIMILAR MATTERS)

At this point, it is time to contemplate our options, just as Johnny ended up doing once he had his visions of what the future would bring—or what Stillson's presidency would entail. Ours, however, is a problem of metaphysics. Assuming for the sake of the present argument that Johnny's visions about the future are accurate, how could he have known what the future would bring? More precisely—and more poignantly: How could statements about future events have truthmakers? Here, we could think about future contingencies, or events that could happen but need not to happen. For instance, although Sheriff Bannerman decided to contact Johnny Smith to solicit his help in tracking down the Castle Rock Strangler, he did not have to. Although Sarah Bracknell could have stayed home instead of going to the fair with Johnny, she did not have to, and so on, and so forth.

So here is our problem. If we want to know something, what is known must be true—and therefore have a truthmaker. But if something is true, or has a truthmaker, then it cannot be otherwise. So if we are to know something about the future, it appears that the future event has to be locked. Thus, if one can have knowledge of future contingencies, there appears to be nothing one could do about them. In order to make sense of all this we have a few alternatives to consider. Here is our list of potential answers to the question "How can Johnny Smith *know* the future, and also change it?"

Option 1: Johnny can't really do this. His alleged clairvoyant abilities are but a fraud, just as Dees's *The Inside View* reported.[14]

Option 2: At best, Johnny is just guessing about future events without any guarantee that any of his visions will materialize despite the fact that his guesses turn out correct with an uncanny frequency.

Option 3: There are no truthmakers for future contingent events, as the future is yet to unfold. Contingent statements about the future are neither true nor false, up until the time the future becomes present.

Each of the above three alternatives could resolve the issue at hand—but that is not quite the same as *solving* the question. After all, we did assume that Johnny could *know* about the future. Hence, we haven't really solved the matter with options 1 or 2. As for option 3, although it would—again—sidestep the original problem, we would only face further ones. Suppose that there were no truthmakers to the statements revealed by Johnny's visions about the future. If this were the case, we would seemingly have to abandon the possibility that Johnny has clairvoyant abilities. Here the real question is, is there an independent reason for rejecting the claim that future contingencies have truthmakers—that is, independent of this particular problem? This rejection conveniently abolishes the problem, not through offering a solution, but by rejecting it. The question now becomes, can we not do better?

Option 4: Johnny can know about the future, and there are truthmakers to future contingent events. However, he is not able to change these.

This alternative is even less desirable than the alternatives above. If we maintain that Johnny's visions reveal to him the truth about the future (and, along with those, the truthmakers about the same) we must endorse some version of fatalism. That is to say that the future is fixed; Johnny is just among the very few who can see how things will shape up to be.

If Johnny's visions about the future meet the truth condition for knowledge (so that we can speak of him knowing what will happen in the future) there would seem to be no way for Johnny to try to change what will come. Worse, he could not even *deliberate* about the future events he knows will happen, any more than he could have deliberated about taking Sarah to the agricultural fair after the fact.

Even if this alternative explains the truth of statements about the future, it would also fix things beyond alteration. This option would effectively preclude the possibility of deliberating about future events.[15]

After all, you cannot deliberate about the choices you made in the past, even if you regret some past action ("I should never have __!"). Likewise, were this the case for future contingents, you could not deliberate about future actions, either ("I will never __ again!"). In short, in order for deliberation, and choice, to be possible, it must be the case that future events remain open.

In light of this—especially if we want to allow that Johnny can know the future in the sense that he knows what follows from some choices, the future must remain open. The monologue[16] where Johnny considers the options he could—or should—take to thwart Greg Stillson from becoming president is indicative of this. This leads us to our final alternative:

Option 5: Johnny *can* know about the future—but he doesn't know which one will materialize.

Basically, this option allows that Johnny has knowledge of possible futures, along the following lines. Consider the statement: *If Stillson were president, he would start a nuclear war.* Now, Johnny does not know that Stillson will become the president; at the very most, Johnny knows that if Stillson *were* to become the president, a nuclear war would follow. This type of knowledge is called *counterfactual* knowledge—or *middle* knowledge, according to the person who came up with this theory, Luis de Molina (ca. 1535–1600).[17] Although middle knowledge has most commonly been offered as a way of reconciling human freedom with divine foreknowledge—the problem that if God knows everything, then God knows what I will do tomorrow as well as that Stillson will start a nuclear war, so the future is set and human freedom is illusory—it can be applied here as well. Although Johnny may not have all the divine powers—given how his knowledge of future events is often partial—it is worthwhile to pursue this alternative, in particular because it is related to the general problem of counterfactual knowledge—knowledge about contingent future events, of events that may happen, but not out of necessity.

When applied in Johnny's case, we can construe the situation as follows: When Johnny touches Chuck and warns him what would happen if he attends the graduation party at Cathy's, he is not describing what will happen. Johnny's vision is captured by the statement "Chuck will die *if* he attends the graduation party at Cathy's," which would be made true by the fact of *Chuck dying at Cathy's after the fire breaks out*. However, Johnny's vision is conditional, and the status of the statement "Chuck will attend the graduation party at Cathy's" is undetermined; in Johnny's terms, it's in the dead zone. For philosophers, it's a future counterfactual. The result, or consequent, may or may not happen depending on whether the antecedent, the preceding event, occurs. So if Chuck goes to the party, he will die. But this only tells Johnny what will happen if Chuck goes. Chuck may very well decide not to go, at which point Johnny doesn't know what will happen to him. But by preventing the antecedent, Chuck attending the party, he can prevent the consequent, Chuck dying in the fire, at least insofar as they are linked. Chuck may very well still die in a fire, but it won't be because of the antecedent Johnny prevented. But futures can unravel in many ways. Stopping one preceding event doesn't guarantee the consequent won't arise by other means. Despite the fact that the above statement— "Chuck will die *if* he attends the graduation party at Cathy's"—has a truthmaker, namely, Chuck's dying in the fire once in attendance, so do the statements that capture possible alternatives—including "Chuck will not attend the party at Cathy's because he was convinced by Johnny's warning" or "Chuck will not attend the party at Cathy's because his ride there broke down," or . . . The conclusion we have reached is not entirely unlike the one that Johnny Smith reaches. All said, we have found a way for Johnny's knowledge about the future to be possible. But as for the question that still remains, at what cost?

CONCLUSION

In sum, we can conclude that Johnny *does not* know how future events will unfold, but that he knows how they *may* unfold. By virtue of knowing this, we need not abandon the truthmaker view, and we can also allow him to deliberate about the future. This is because Johnny's knowledge about the future is—not in the *dead zone* (as suggested by his own analysis) but *counterfactual* knowledge. That is, Johnny knows that if Chuck *were* to be at the graduation party at Cathy's, he *would* perish in the fire that subsequently took place.[18] Similarly, Johnny knows that *if* Stillson were elected as the president, a nuclear holocaust *would* follow. And so on. Johnny knows how the future may be, that is, how it will turn out should certain events come to pass. So he can alter the future, albeit in unpredictable ways, insofar as he can prevent those antecedent events from occurring. He can prevent the nuclear war Stillson would cause by preventing Stillson from becoming president, although there may be other ways in which a nuclear war begins, and Stillson may even still have a hand in that. Johnny merely prevents the possible future linked to Stillson being president.

Now, there is no Castle Rock, as it does not exist in the real world—and neither do Johnny Smith, or Herb and Vera Smith, or Sarah Hazlett (nee Bracknell). Still, the problems raised by the fictional account offered in *The Dead Zone* (as well as in *Insomnia* and *11/22/63*), as depicted by Stephen King, certainly do. After all, if the truthmaker account outlined above is to hold when it comes to future contingencies, we could do worse than to test it against fictional accounts and translate those lessons here. In other words: even in a world without clairvoyant abilities we are hardly content with the notion that the future is fixed—or that it's all just a guessing game. When we claim that some future event (e.g., the fact that the sun will rise tomorrow morning) is going to happen, we are positing truthmakers to those statements.

There is a further reason as to why some of the questions above are important. After all, if we suppose that there is—say—an omniscient deity, one who knows (accurately, truthfully, etc.) what the future will bring, then what do we—including you, I, or anyone else—have left of our supposed freedom? The question raised by Johnny Smith's fictive ability to tell how the future will unfold—or, from his perspective, how it *may* unfold—pertains to a genuine question about human free will and divine omniscience. If God knows the future, not Johnny, and God is perfect and never errs, then is the future determined? So, instead of thinking about Johnny Smith and his being able to predict what future will unfold, suppose that it was some deity who had the same ability, and who was inerrant in its visions. How might this fact change your perception of the situation, the future, and human freedom?

At this juncture, we could expand our analysis beyond *The Dead Zone*, and still draw from the works by Stephen King, For one such instance from *Insomnia*, Ralph Roberts is shown a vision of the future by Atropos (one of the "little bald doctors") wherein Ralph sees his neighbor's child being run over by a car. For this situation—when the vision about the future is courtesy of a supernatural being—other resolutions may have to apply.

And from those cases, we will just walk away.

NOTES

1. There are very few philosophical discussions that explore questions about clairvoyance and other paranormal forms of perception. One of the exceptions is Jane Duran, "Philosophical Difficulties with Paranormal Knowledge Claims," in *Philosophy of Science and the Occult*, 2nd ed., ed. Patrick Grim (Albany: SUNY Press, 1990), 232–42. Even so, Duran's discussion is more related to the justification question.

2. Stephen King, *The Dead Zone* (New York: Signet, 1979), 146–47.

3. King, *The Dead Zone*, 134–35.

4. King, *The Dead Zone*, 333–35.

5. King, *The Dead Zone*, 302–5.

6. The argument that upended the "knowledge-is-justified-true-belief" definition was presented in Edmund Gettier, "Is Justified True Belief Knowledge?," *Analysis* 23 (1963): 121–23. For further analysis on the "Gettier problem" (and the responses thereto), see Matthias Steup and Jonathan Jenkins Ichikawa, "The Analysis of Knowledge," in *Stanford Encyclopedia of Philosophy* (Spring 2014), ed. Edward Zalta. For present purposes, we will employ the following general definition for knowledge: "knowledge" is nonaccidentally true belief.

7. For a comprehensive—and succinct—introduction to truthmakers and truthbearers alike, see John Bigelow, "Truthmakers and Truthbearers," in *The Routledge Companion to Metaphysics*, ed. Robin Le Poidevin, Peter Simons, Andrew McGonigal, and Ross P. Cameron (New York: Routledge, 2009), 389–90. As an added benefit, this piece is quite accessible with only minimal previous exposure to philosophy. For a more in-depth introduction to the issue, see Robert C. Koons and Timothy H. Pickavance, *Metaphysics: The Fundamentals* (Malden, Mass.: Wiley, 2015).

8. King, *The Dead Zone*, 88–90.

9. To bypass another set of objections, I am ignoring the fact that the events depicted in King's *The Dead Zone* are fictional, and I am treating the narrative as if it pertains to real events (even if just to make my point . . .).

10. King, *The Dead Zone*, 401.

11. Aristotle, *De Interpretatione*, in *The Basic Works of Aristotle*, ed. Richard McKeon (New York: Random House, 2001), 48 (19a.30–33).

12. Aristotle, *De Interpretatione*, 47 (18b.33–36).

13. Stephen King, *Insomnia* (New York: Penguin, 1994), 368.

14. King, *The Dead Zone*, 210.

15. For a thoroughgoing exploration on why the ability to deliberate about future events is not just needed in the present, but why it would be precluded if the future events were fixed, see Richard Taylor, "Deliberation and Foreknowledge," in *Free Will and Determinism*, ed. Bernard Berofsky (New York: Harper & Row, 1966), 277–93.

16. King, *The Dead Zone*, 352–56.

17. De Molina's writings are somewhat hard to come by, but there has been a recent resurgence of interest on the topic of middle knowledge. For further information, as well as a list of sources, see Linda Zagzebski, "Foreknowledge and Free Will," in *Stanford Encyclopedia of Philosophy* (Fall 2011), ed. Edward Zalta, §2.5.

18. King, *The Dead Zone*, 333–44.

15

TIME BELONGS TO THE TOWER

Randall Auxier

Edward Bulwer-Lytton wrote the turgid line "It was a dark and stormy night . . . ."[1] If he hadn't, no one would know his name today. It's a hard legacy, being the poster child for bad writing. But in Victorian times, this man's praises were on the lips of every critic and his books were pirated throughout the British Empire.[2] Meanwhile, Herman Melville gave up writing prose on account of his *failure* as a novelist.

Similarly, Harold Bell Wright was regarded as the greatest American writer of his age, that being the 1910s through the 1930s. No one now knows his name. At the same time, F. Scott Fitzgerald really couldn't make much of a living from his books and stories and resorted to Hollywood. Come to think of it, most of the writers we still read from that era did the same thing. There may be a different chapter to be written about the little "pick-me-up" writers got (and still get) from the movies. Certainly Hollywood has done plenty for Stephen King. But Wright's books spawned some fifteen movies (you've never heard of), and plainly it didn't do much for him, in the long run.[3]

Is Stephen King our Bulwer-Lytton, our Harold Bell Wright? Are we currently overlooking our Melville and our Fitzgerald? We should be circumspect. I wonder whether King's work may wilt and wither when time has moved on (if indeed it really does move on; see my other chapter in this book). Or, perish the thought, is it possible that Stephen King really *is* the best we have, but is perhaps only the most memorable writer in a forgettable period? Surely not, but one seeks a more expanded perspective, some distance and some light.

THAT MOMENT WHEN . . .

Well over thirty years ago, trying to impress a girl who adored Stephen King, I read *The Shining* (wow), then, reading backward in time, *'Salem's Lot* (not so good . . .), then *Carrie* (much better), and then . . . *The Stand*. And I was hooked. I read the latter three times. I had never done a triple read with any writer, except Tolkien and Poe. I began to form the immature notion that King might be a sort of mixture of, well, Poe and Tolkien.

In college I had one of those *refugee-from-the-sixties-perennial-ABD-literature-professors-who-will-never-be-tenured* for my modern American fiction class. (There were lots of them treading academic water back then; some are still with us, but most finally disappeared into their water pipes.) We were reading the standard fare of that day— Vonnegut, O'Connor, Faulkner, Hemingway. At that time, Stephen King had just published *Different Seasons*, the collection of four novellas that contained the nascent movie scripts for *The Shawshank Redemption*, *Apt Pupil*, and *Stand by Me*, but this Hollywood trifecta hadn't happened yet. In my sophomoric arrogance, I informed this professor, the one with the alcohol on her breath for an early afternoon class (detectable from the second row), that *Different Seasons* was as good as anything we were reading. She hadn't read any Stephen King, but she humored me. "What about these stories *convinces* you that they are so good?"

I said, "Err, ummm. Geez, I like 'em." I think I may have done slightly better than that, but not too much. Somehow the simple sentence "He's like a cross between Poe and Tolkien" was not quite within my cognizance at twenty. Today I can certainly sling verbal chitterlings at you, but I have come back 'round to affirming my earlier judgment about the quality of King's work: I think he might be, well, "Tolkien meets Poe," but of course, less pretentious than the *haute culture* writers of earlier days. We just wouldn't read stuff in that style today. We like our culture low and real.

I want to hand you King *as* "Tolkien meets Poe," both as literature and as psychology in this chapter and to present it as a question of *time*. The reason I need both literature and psychology is that the "time" of literature and the "time" of lived individual experience are really very different from (and subordinate to) the "time" of the Tower (and there is more to the Tower, *always* more, than we can really grasp, but we can make a start). We have to see how literary time and psychological time work for King before we can really appreciate the time of the Tower, since it sucks all time into itself, rather Darkly.

I mention my old professor because of Robbie Henderson. He is the character who, at age twenty,[4] sits in the Intro to American Lit class taught by Wesley Smith, the main character of King's 2009 novella *Ur*. Initially this book was released only on Kindle (and as an audiobook on Audible). Between 2009 and 2015, you couldn't even get *Ur* on *other* e-readers like Nook; the whole story was one big advertisement for Kindle (and for Amazon).[5] A print version is available in *The Bazaar of Bad Dreams*, but it isn't quite the same story.

It's a shame that the original *Ur* is going to be missed by so many King followers. For my money, there is more information about the workings of the Dark Tower packed into that story, those "sixty-one pages" (except they aren't really "pages," are they?) than in any other source of similar length in King's whole corpus. *Ur*'s main character, Wesley, teaches literature at a smallish college in western Kentucky, and his young student Robbie Henderson has a similar outlook and set of questions as I had, lo those many years ago. This scenario of "the kid and the English teacher" comes from King's own experience in college when (as legend has it) he had an instructor who actually recognized his talent. The class apparently devolved into a discussion between King and the instructor, pretty much bypassing the needs and interests of the other students. This general scenario of "the kid and the English teacher" repeats itself a few thousand times every year in colleges all over the United States, and perhaps beyond.[6] Later, King was that instructor.[7]

There is something magical about that moment in our young lives when we first experience something like *aesthetic urgency* in the presence of excellent writing. This kid-and-the-teacher scenario is also the frame for *11/22/63*, with variations and reversals. The "kid" is no *kid*, but Harry Dunning, an older adult student, the school janitor, brain damaged from childhood head trauma, and trying to get his GED, while the teacher, Jake Epping, is a thirty-something high school English teacher who also teaches such adults at night—and admires them. All the action in *11/22/63* is motivated by this teacher-student relationship.

Some part of King still wants to *be* that teacher he commonly depicts. But having students does take away from one's time to write. Hence, being "that teacher" comes at the expense of being "that author" whose books are being taught by "that teacher," and bringing "that student" to an experience of aesthetic urgency. I think of the long list of successful novelists who began as English professors and quit teaching as soon as they could afford to—Wallace Stegner depicts it poignantly in *Crossing to Safety*, and Bernard Malamud does it comically in *A New Life*.

Yet, the *authors* who give us this gift, this awakening of aesthetic urgency, are not so very numerous—every generation has only a few who can do it, at least on a broad scale. King has now done it for several new generations of readers, just as Salinger or Harper Lee opened millions of minds in the early sixties. As I write this, Lee's second novel is newly published, to a great hue and cry. The controversy *derives* its vehemence from "that moment when . . ."—that is, from the sheer weight of millions of minds not wanting that precious moment altered by a sequel or prequel (or whatever Lee's second book really is). People are very fussy about the past, when it is personally meaningful. They want nothing to mess with their perceptions of it. Later we will discuss King's theory of the "obduracy" of the past, but this obduracy may have as much to do with our psychological attachment to the past as with the past itself. We will also be returning to *Ur*'s Wesley Smith and Robbie Henderson, but first, a bit about the past of the Tower.

ALL THINGS SERVE THE TOWER

From a physical point of view (as distinct from psychological or literary), the Dark Tower is no longer a sort of *place*, in the more recent writings; King's thinking about the Tower has evolved beyond that. For decades the Tower was more spatio-dimensional, holding to time's irreversible arrow (more or less), in a loose mixture between Hugh Everett's many-worlds quantum hypothesis and the cosmologists' ideas about the existence of a stacked "multiverse."[8] The Tower has evolved, however. It still involves space, but it's also about time these days, perhaps as a result of King's inability to resist the urge to write *11/22/63*.

Before about 2005, King really wasn't a "time-travel" sort of author. He also prefers actual science to science fiction, and somehow time travel just seems to cross that line. But saving JFK from Oswald's bullets was something he couldn't resist. He isn't exactly known for his literary temperance, after all. Now, as a result, the Tower has become an n-dimensional temporal labyrinth that combines the warping effects of gravitation with the chance effects of quantum dynamics and the stacked multiverse across parallel worlds—or something like that.[9]

But there is something more than this metaphysical mix in King's temporalized Tower; now we find something literary and psychological, more experiential and down to earth. This "something more" is *like* gravity, but the gravity of the Tower ain't Newton's falling apple. It is something closer to the original meaning of that word: gravitas, whatever pulls us downward, into seriousness. This kind of concentrated gravity messes with meaning and borders on chaos. It isn't evil, precisely, but evil is grave business, as are many other things that lurk in the gloom. It is the sort of gravity that makes the House of Usher fall.

We will come to these characteristics of the Tower in due course, but *as* a "tower," it surely symbolizes the Tolkienesque side of King's work. Somehow, the centers of concentrated gravity always live in towers, don't they? It is not as if King's explicit allusion to Tolkien is subtle, like his occasional use of Tolkien's language.[10] And, as "dark," we also find in this archetypal tower the Poe influence. We need not dig six feet down to unearth King's love of Poe. One of the first things Wesley Smith does when he discovers he has a special "Dark Tower Kindle" that will show him writings from parallel universes is find an "Ur" in which Poe lived twenty-six years longer, and Wesley then reads Poe's "unwritten works" until dawn. I expect that is what King himself would do.

So what *is* this Dark Tower? In the first place, and for decades now, it is the product of an imagination so lively that it possesses multiple versions of every story King tells, with differences wavering on single choices at crucial junctures, and even on chance arrangements of space and time. King repeats throughout *11/22/63*, "Life turns on a dime." He said early in his career that his characters go where they will and he follows them with his pen. He *feels* their choices and realizes they can make different ones. And he wants to tell those stories, *too*. King can't resist giving us *some* of the alternative paths. He needed to create the

Tower to hold them all, in a kind of topological suspense, so that we never really know how the story comes out—because there is no such thing as "the" story. In the author's note to his *Bazaar of Bad Dreams*, he makes this explicit: "Some of these stories have been previously published, but that doesn't mean they were done then, or even that they're done now. Until the writer either retires or dies, the work is not finished."[11] And as if to prove the point, he changed *Ur* the Kindle novella into "Ur" the short story, and several of the others in *Bazaar*.

In equally real levels of the Tower, our own real present "floats," is suspended for just a moment, and then the flimsy events went *both* as we see them and also went otherwise, creating an otherwhen, a parallel to our time thread. To keep this floating and splitting under control, King has clusters of relative constants that serve as narrative nodes, which you might think of as the parasympathetic ganglia of these trans-dimensional, transtemporal nerve centers, through which most (or perhaps all) intelligibility courses. But it's the moments of chance and choice that mark the thin dimensional separations. To *disrupt* a node, by some kind of transtemporal action, is to risk the abyss, or, as the low man in the yellow coat puts it in *Ur*, "The tower trembles, the worlds shake in their courses, the rose feels a chill, as of winter."[12]

Tolkien built two towers as the twin loci, the positive and negative poles of one amazing world, existing in its own *linear*, irreversible time, with a single, complex, expansive history, a history that converges at crucial points and hangs upon the courage and the decisions of unlikely actors. King does like the brave underdog upon whom all depends as a literary device. But King simultaneously builds thousands (nay, millions) of time threads, crisscrossing in parallel courses, in which those same sorts of unlikely characters both *do* and *don't do* what both they should and shouldn't do, yet, all relative to a single Tower, to which time "belongs."[13] Hence, the past isn't "the" past, it is only "a" past, from a literary perspective. But that is a fundamental ambiguity that will have to be massaged if the readers are expected to pass by it in fear or fascination. Let's look at it.

"THE" PAST

Even *a* past *wants* to be *the* past, which is to say, it doesn't want to be changed, as Jake Epping repeats without surcease in *11/22/63*. He is mistaken to refer to it constantly as *"the"* past, a lesson he finally learns when his presence in the past has nearly destroyed all meaning for the world, or the universe or, even "reality itself" as the mysterious Zack Lang puts it in a poignant exchange.[14] By the end of the novel, our hero has become unwilling to act in "the" past so as to ensure it remains "the" past. He concludes that he can do no *good* in the past; all is dark.

Unbeknownst to Jake, initially, each time he passes through the "rabbit hole" from 2011 into 1958, he is actually stepping into a 1958 that had not (until he stepped through) *divided* from the other possible 1958s. He consistently interprets the time and place of his arrival as having been "reset" (and all his earlier interventions erased) because when he steps *back* through, everything looks just as it did the first time. But in King's world of the Tower, Jake is probably leaving one Ur and stepping into another. When he goes back to "the" future, he remains in the latter Ur he has now "created." If this is right, he never really gets "home," so to speak.

Yet, by stepping through and doing *nothing*, Jake can get a new path nearly identical to the one he was living in to begin with, in 2011, and this seems to be a convergence that makes Zack Lang and his "gatekeeper" colleagues more comfortable. Left to itself, apparently the past converges, in "the" future, on the arrangement of events in "the" present, it *would have produced* if left undisturbed. This possibility is floated by King late in *11/22/63*; King's Tower is a topological labyrinth in time, not exactly in space. Its past, then, while not settled, has a sort of *ideal* arrangement we can name "the" past.

PASTS

Ur offers over ten million versions of "the" past, and no gatekeepers to go insane over them. In that story, our hero, Wesley, that youngish professor (but old-school lover of books), orders a Kindle for various complicated reasons. Wires get crossed somewhere in the Tower such that the device that arrives by mail gives Wesley access not only to the novels written in his own time continuum, his own "Ur," but also novels and stories from over ten million other "Urs"—with different pasts. For example, there is an Ur in which Hemingway lived an extra four years and finished two more novels. There is an Ur in which Shakespeare died in 1620 rather than 1616 and finished two more plays. And as I mentioned earlier, there is an Ur in which Poe lived to 1875 and wrote six novels.

In addition to contrasts, there are constants among these Urs. These are the "nodes" or "ganglia" like I mentioned above. Hemingway "always writes *A Farewell to Arms*," in every Ur, and almost always writes *For Whom the Bell Tolls* and *The Old Man and the Sea*. Wesley dimly supposes that there are these anchoring moments that embody something essential in the unfolding of all times, and they might be political events (such as JFK's assassination) as well as literary ones, but we don't really know, at the time they occur, which events will be the essential ones. Jake Epping is paralyzed by this uncertainty by the end of *11/22/63*. I guess that messing around with these nodes is what makes the gatekeepers insane.

In *Ur*, then, Wesley eventually gets in trouble when he discovers an experimental "Ur function" on the Dark Tower Kindle that allows him to read the *future* local newspapers of his own Ur. As such temptations always go, he sets about changing "the" future (a rather different project from changing the past, since "the" future is, presumably, less obdurate). Wesley has very good reasons, largely unselfish ones, for what he does. Still, he violates what are called the "paradox laws," and some Dark Tower regulators come to make decisions about Wesley's punishment in the climax of the story.

These enforcers are actually the "low men in yellow coats" from *Hearts in Atlantis*, the same ones revealed in volume 6 of the Dark Tower novels as "can-toi," ratlike beings who believe they are becoming human. Wesley has to argue for his life, or freedom, or something he knows not what, against the paradox of time disruptions he has created. I won't spoil it, since it isn't necessary here, but I will say that it is in this scene that the low men utter the phrase "All things serve the Tower," twice. And in so saying, they touch their badges in reverence—badges that bear a symbol of a red eye (as if we don't recognize Sauron when he is alluded to).[15] And so they do. We'll return to this.

"THE" PRESENT

The list of influences on King is well known, and long.[16] He has always been a voracious reader, and he loves to include reading recommendations for all of us within his own stories. By choosing to emphasize Tolkien and Poe, I don't intend to start an argument or to play down how crucial Lovecraft or Shirley Jackson or Ray Bradbury (or a couple dozen others) are in goading King one way rather than another. Still, King's relation to Poe is more permanent and more intriguing than these others, I think. King is well below Poe (and Tolkien, for that matter) as a prose stylist, but both really know how to tell a story. *That* gift transcends all sins or graces of style. Poe was a master of story structure and of how readers *experience* the unfolding of it, viscerally, below the level of conscious awareness. King has that same power, but not every story is equally excellent in the employment of this "authorial sense" of the reader's precognitive near past, present, and near future.

The philosopher Susanne Langer discusses "literary time" as a fundamental aspect of what she calls the "primary illusion" of imaginative fiction. When we hold a novel in our hands, we have a piece of wood pulp and as a literary form, a *completed* story, right there, in our hands, in *the present*. When we read, it is still complete at every point along the way—the ending has, after all, already been written, and we cannot truly forget the fact of the "real present" at any point, which is *not* finished. Yet, we *suspend* the fact of the present flowing moment and give ourselves over to the semblance of narrative time, creating a *virtual* present over the ontological and physical framework of actual time flowing.[17] We thus *choose* the virtual present, the novel's time and its passage, as a substitute for our real, flowing present, and we defer the sense of the real future except as a vague, impending je ne sais quoi.

From the materials of this virtual present we have decided to "believe in," and from the subconscious flow of feelings and minutes, the author must create in us a *feeling* of a *virtual* past (what has gone before this moment in the world of the novel—both explicitly and implicitly) and a *virtual* future (the histories and destinies of the characters, both in and beyond the time frame of the novel) which we accept as *integral* with the virtual present. We *believe* in these histories and destinies *together*, using the materials of present experience.[18] And we prefer the unreal world to the real at a very deep level.[19] Without it, there is no

aesthetic urgency, no moment between teacher and student, no immer-
sion in unreal time. All the words are lifeless. Our "positional act" of
believing all this virtual time at once costs us a good deal of psychic
energy, and we become more heavily invested in the narrative than we
have intended; we find that we care about the events and characters we
have chosen to believe in because of the energy we have put into believing in them.

King's device of the "floating present," that moment of chance and
choice, is an explicit instance within a narrative of what we *all* do when
we read. In reading the narrative, we *possibilize* the actions described,
treating them as contingent and open to many futures on some sort of
general trajectory (even though we know the later events have already
been written and are settled). In reality, as well as in the book we are
actually reading, there is only one future, of course. But *that* limitation
is for the *normal* author. No one ever accused Stephen King of being
normal.

King violates these sorts of rules gleefully. He reserves the right to
revise along the lines of parallel universes, even after the story is written, and until he is dead (and maybe he'll still be revising in the afterlife, or in some Ur in which he dies later). Normally we treat the action
we are reading at the moment as a *promise*, immanent in the virtual
present (instead of an actual past, something already written), in order
to experience that vital relation *as if* it were not yet settled. The critics
call this the "willing suspension of disbelief," but I think it is closer to
the "will to believe," as William James styled it. This is why we (usually)
resist the urge to skip to the last page. We don't want to disrupt the
illusion we have chosen and *believed* (at the cost of some energy). But
King promises us nothing final, even if the book is finished. We find
ourselves obliged to carry his characters, even dead ones, with us into
new adventures, ones than might turn out differently than those we
have stored as memories.

Much has been written about this aspect of reading, this suspension
of disbelief, by psychologists, phenomenologists, as well as literary critics and the like. I won't belabor it, but I will point out that the phenomenon of "virtual time" explains why it is so difficult for an author to
finish a narrative, to *write the ending*.[20] A satisfactory ending has to
allow the *virtual* present to release its promise and to converge upon,
and then to *become*, the reader's *actual* present again, as the cover is

closed. With King, we're never really sure, even when we close the cover, that we've *left* the story or that it's over—in fact, we are sure it *isn't*, at this point in his career.[21] He seems to think this is fun. Or maybe he thinks it's necessary. It isn't *just* play, in any case, even if its presentation is playful. These characters may appear again, especially the deadest (and deadliest) ones.

Psychologically, viscerally, emotionally, intellectually, this belief in what sort of doesn't exist is complicated stuff. The ability to tell a story, and especially to *finish* a story (even proximally), belongs to those with an amazing ability to project and control this semblance of a virtual present, to anticipate and feel, psychologically and phenomenologically, how each moment will affect readers as they *give themselves to* the temporal semblance.[22] There is no formula for succeeding at this task. Both King and Poe, as virtuosos of this semblance, will push a reader to the point of even losing confidence in the author's power to bring it off at the end, and then they manage to do it, over and over (even if not absolutely always). It is for the sake of this kind of experience of convergence (or occasionally of just letting go of the semblance itself) that we, whose discovery of aesthetic urgencies persists, *give over* our real present to a virtual present and ride the ride.

OF CASTLE ROCKS AND CRIMSON KINGS

The Tolkien/Poe influence is important not just due to the similarities with King, but also because, really, he is so different from both in so many ways. There is an "advance" with King in imaginative engagement with "the possible." He stands on their shoulders and then sees further. Since this literary kinship with both is more phenomenological than stylistic, it has to do with a gnawing impression one gets, reading King, of a world, nay, of many worlds, *beyond* the story being told. Those other worlds come in flashes of intuition and corner-of-the-eye glimpses, and they portend far more than any single story can actually carry. A lifetime is not long enough to tell us the truth of the Tower, or its chaotic fringes, the domain of King's Crimson King.

For many of us, the first hint of this imagined world was the recurring Castle Rock Killer. He was first featured in *The Dead Zone* but morphed and skulked in the shadows of so many later stories. He just kept showing up, nebulous and relentless, and he's still "out there," both dead and unkillable. We really can't ever catch or stop the killer because he isn't quite like us; his crimes cross the barrier of the past, run through the fringes of the present, and may await us in any future we choose—that sense is like the feeling we get contemplating the House of Usher or the Land of Mordor. But Tolkien's universe vibrates with the ancient, the linguistic, the mythic, the eschatological. Poe's mindscape is made of the animal, the vengeful, the sinful, the stolen, and all on the edge of sanity and insanity. He occupies the present only—*our* world, *its* history, *its* future. Poe conceals our willing suspension of present time by enticing the reader to treat his or her actual present as being one with the virtual present of the story.

King does not invoke the power of the past as a settled piece of history, whether fantastical or factual, that creeps forward, taking down innocents in its path. Rather, he abuses the past as something that just didn't have to be as it was, and he toys with making it other than it was. Tolkien's universe doesn't allow this. It wouldn't even occur to Poe. Time bending and space shifting is King's "advance" on these heroes of his. Some would see it as squandering his literary inheritance, and I couldn't disagree, but if King is a sort of literary trust-fund kid, at least he invited everybody to the big party.

But then there is this: King lacks Poe's command of the power of present sanity as it edges toward insanity because King assumes that our sanity can be held together under even unreal, impossible shifts in time and dimension.[23] Why, pray tell, doesn't Jake Epping just lose his sanity as he shifts between 1958 and 2011? King allows that the shifts are hard on Jake's psyche, but the persistence, or perhaps just the *insistence, of personality* is stronger than time for King. For Poe, personality usually cannot successfully negotiate the simplest endurance of the past into and through the present. His protagonists often cannot negotiate a single temporal continuum and remain sane. One simply gets no sense from Tolkien or Poe that time is flexible. With King, *it bends*—both the strings of time and the mind.

In works through the nineties and into the present, King exploits the thin places that divide *our* Ur from its "neighborhood" (to use the topological term), that being all those possibilities that almost happened but didn't. The problematic clown Pennywise of *It*, and the shapeshifting Leland Gaunt in *Needful Things*, and the traveling caravan of soul-sucking demons in *Doctor Sleep* show us the places in Maine, or Colorado, or New Hampshire, or particular places like the Kitchener Iron Works in Derry, or the Texas School Book Depository, spots where the Dark of the Tower oozes into our Ur, and where the Urs almost touch, where they place our lives within the reach of Crimson Kings and Castle Rock Killers. But even the deep connections with Maine and its spookiness—Castle Rock, Derry, Jerusalem's Lot—are just examples of "thin places." The slipping between and among Urs is looser and more mysterious in the writings from the nineties, as King sifted through the shifts and splits more carefully.[24] The issues had come to a fuller definition by the time King wrote *Ur* (2009). In still more recent writings the idea of moving among Urs has become closely defined, as has the cost of doing so. The sense of solemnity that accompanies each transition has become explicit. Time travel isn't child's play.

AMAZINGLY ADMIRABLE

Immanuel Kant (1724–1804) says that "amazement" is the experience of seeing something that does not conform to our sense of what is *possible* for the world as we have experienced it, whereas "admiration" is what persists when we have released our doubts and vexations about what we see or hear. When we admire something, we accept that what we *believed* was impossible is indeed actual, and we cannot really doubt it. Moving from amazement to admiration is a taxing transition, psychologically. It threatens the unity of personality.

Additionally, time travelers *know* things that we who are stuck in a single linear time cannot know, and that commits them to a divided condition. They have to decide whom to tell, if anyone, and if so, what should and shouldn't be told. It is very stressful, and the more so as they come to care about people they meet in the past—as Jake puts it, "Time travelers lie a lot." But in time-travel stories, they always hold the center of their personalities. Otherwise, well, no story. The only question is, how does an author communicate the psychological cost?

In King's case, his characters seem to hold the center while time traveling with (comparatively) minimal effort. And the same is true for his other characters as they face a thousand instances of "the amazing" and try to achieve "admiration." I don't find this quite believable, which is also part of the reason that King's "insane" characters are not very convincingly insane, to me—nothing like Poe's, or, if one considers Gollum and Saruman insane, Tolkien's. Poe and Tolkien are *convincing* when it comes to depicting insanity. But they don't try to negotiate the literary and psychological challenges of time travel. For the sanity of a literary character, having one's personality "unstuck in time," to use Vonnegut's happy phrase, does not require the navigating of just a single future, but of many.[25] For most of us, I think the *singularity* of "the" future may be a condition of maintaining sanity. But rather than have his main character go insane in *11/22/63*, King has his "gatekeepers" bear the cost. King does understand this; he just displaces the cost.

Thus, while Poe also creates feelings of what impends, what awaits, what cowers and cringes in the corner (only to find its courage and come back doubly dangerous), he doesn't want any heroes, let alone transtemporal heroes, and he doesn't brook any defenders, whether flawed or flawless, of the good, the right, and the just. His central characters struggle for their sanity, and they don't need the special pressures of time travel and dimension shifting to fail at it. Poe doesn't mind cleverness, chance, scientific understanding, and the like, but he apparently doubts that anyone is genuinely brave.[26] He looks into our souls and then makes us look, too, and there is naught but creeping corruption, even if some of it is less putrid than some other. But for Poe, the unity of personality hangs on its capacity to deal with the way its sole present must become its one future. The psychological structure of "The Pit and the Pendulum" is the epitome of this trope.

This is not King's take on human nature or on the intensity and inescapability of the present. He prefers ordinary guys and gals and thinks that plenty of them will hold up quite well under even extreme pressure, including transtemporal shifting.[27] King especially "admires" the stupendous courage and tenacity of children—think of characters from *The Shining*'s Danny Torrance all the way to his niece Abra Stone in *Doctor Sleep*, in the same spot almost half a century later, and including a hundred kid-heroes in between. King makes this explicit in his main character in "Mile 81": "If Pete Simmons had been twenty, he might have asked a lot of bullshit questions that didn't matter. Because he was only half that age, and able to accept what he had just seen, he asked something simpler and more pertinent."[28]

This characteristic of childlike (if not quite child) heroes is also present in Tolkien, but utterly missing in Poe. Hobbits seem able to deal with amazement, and to accept it just as children do. It is good to remember that children, having seen little of the world, are frequently "amazed" and are obliged to transform experience into admiration. Adults become much more rigid about what is genuinely possible and hence are worse off when required to *accept* what they thought impossible. But in *Ur* and *11/22/63*, King had to have adult heroes. And he had to deal with heavy fallout, both literary and psychological, from sacrificing the unity of time.

King's understanding of time shifts is subtle enough to make an effort toward granting that Kant is right: the shift *in us*, subjectively, from amazement to admiration requires tremendous effort and is shot through with doubt. H. G. Wells had no such insights, as far as I can see. His heroes were Victorian manly men; they were more like Theodore Roosevelt than Danny Torrance. Roosevelt would have arrived in a different time and pronounced the whole adventure "bully," but I doubt many people could pull that off.

The psychological dimension to King's writing also expresses our contemporary popular scientism in ways that would be impossible for Poe, and would be a real stretch for Tolkien. King's universe needs to look like our current scientific understanding of things (and their limits). The Tower needs to be *believable*. For this reason, I have never found King's understanding of human psychology to be very profound or provocative; I think psychology is closer to being an art than a full-grown science, at this point. But at least his view of the unity of personality becomes transtemporal or transdimensional only at a cost to the unity of the character's psyche. King does get that much right.

King favors strictly physiological explanations of psychology in his grasp of our common "disorders," and there is nothing creepy about this kind of psychology, in my opinion. Freud and Jung (and Lovecraft) are much creepier. The King characters who are supposed to be on the edge of insanity—from the brain-damaged Trash Can Man (in *The Stand*) to the alcoholic, middle-aged Danny Torrance (in *Doctor Sleep*)—are unconvincing to me, as cases of insanity. They are just you and me, plus brain damage or a couple of different chemical turns in their lives. There is always an easy-to-understand reason why they are as they are, *unless* they come from the Dark Tower (and then, all bets are off and it ain't physiological psychology anymore, it's proximity to evil that crazes us). *Convincing* literary insanity needs to be uncanny, unfamiliar, unexplained.

So, King's people from our world (i.e., our Ur) don't really seem darkly psychotic like, for example, Poe's Montresor in "The Cask of Amontillado" or the unnamed narrator of "The Tell-Tale Heart" (who anticipates the physiological interpretation of insanity beautifully, but is still very creepy in our own day). To explain Danny Torrance, for example, one only needs the old idea from William James (and indeed, Poe before him) that some people's bodies are just *more sensitive* than others, just as some people are *taller* than others. People with sensitive bodies perceive things that people with numb bodies can't understand or process in their brains. Combine that with the difficulty we all have sometimes in getting our brains to *slow down* and you have Danny Torrance. Yes, he sees dead people, but its causes are found in brain science. He struggles to keep it together, but it isn't precisely a struggle for sanity. If King has a weakness relative to grasping insanity, it might derive from his *strength* in navigating transtemporal personality limits more or less believably. This brings us to the meat of the matter.

"THE" FUTURE

What if? King is just the sort of incubus who whispers such words in every ear. What about . . . a *different* future growing from an altered past? Who can really just let go of that? Is there a living person who hasn't got a moment in the past when he'd like to take a metaphysical mulligan? If ever there was a man with the right shovel to go ghoulishly about *that* cemetery of stubborn speculation, it's King. He invented ten million Urs in order to study his way through his planned story about JFK—*11/22/63*, King's epic contribution to *the might have been*. As he says in the epilogue, he first attempted to write the book in 1972, but only now have time, distance, and maturity made it possible. In other words, only now will the Dark Tower hold this story (and its millions of variants). Relative to King, however, we sort of don't want to believe that one person has so many stories, and no matter how many he slings out at us and no matter how many loop back into the Tower, we still take the Tower to be merely a literary device.

But I think *the Tower is real*. I am not saying it exists in the physical sense; I am saying that your life, the way you tie *your* possibilities to your *actual life*, past, present, and future, *is* "the" Tower, from your perspective. You *believe* in your possibilities, and you believe in the reality of "the" past ones you left undone, and you hold them close, however impossible they are now, for the sake of "the" future ones you cannot yet give up. And in touching this, a precious human moment, so familiar and yet so neglected in philosophies and sciences, King has achieved perfect command of his gift. You create your virtual present and extend it over "the" past and future because you *believe* in the Tower. King restrains himself at a thousand pages (give or take), but how many pages would *you* like to tell the stories of what you didn't do, but almost did?

In the event you haven't read *11/22/63*, I think the slow pace of the book builds the right empathy between protagonist and reader. You are allowed time to create the time frames you need to care what will happen to what has already happened. King says:

> I'm a novelist by nature I will grant you that, and I have a particular liking for the long ones that create an immersive experience for writer and reader, where the fiction has a chance to become a world that's almost real. When a long book succeeds, the writer and reader are not just having an affair, they are married.[29]

That "almost real" world is what Langer called "virtual." And after all, if Langer is right, the entire value of time in a novel derives from the semblance it creates that, somehow, impossibly, the future isn't yet accomplished, determinate, intelligible, and already tied up in a neat package. We are so picky about "the" future, aren't we? When we give ourselves to the literary semblance, we won't settle for the future we can *see*, composed of the possibilities that lay as straight as railroad tracks before the trajectory of the past. We insist that our author, whether it be Bulwer-Lytton or Scott Fitzgerald, pull from the material of "a" present, that we *never* actually experienced, an ending, "a" future, we never foresaw, or at least not too clearly. And yet, that ending must have been there all along, as a possibility. We want virtual time to be at our mercy, and we stand over it, whip in hand, and say, "Go ahead, surprise me; I'll let you know whether you do, at the end of my critical lash."

Our author has to make our reading experience converge on our actual present, and that is why it is so hard to write the end of a novel. As the possibilities we have felt, in the virtual future of the pages, begin to narrow toward an ending, they also converge on our present reading experience, and they do so until they become an experience of closing the book. The author must make us *willing* to come back to the real present, even if we are reluctant about it. As we close the book, the reading becomes an enclosed experience that never really was, except as it rode along the actual flow of time we expended in reading.

But if the Tower is real, *that* time belongs to the Tower, too—the Tower becomes real when we *feed* it real time, *our* time, a piece of our lives we can't reclaim. That *counts*. And who can finally tell the difference as to whether any of the Tower's own time has not oozed into ours?

NOTES

1. The full line is actually: "It was a dark and stormy night ; the rain fell in torrents—except at occasional intervals, when it was checked by a violent gust of wind which swept up the streets (for it is in London that our scene lies), rattling along the housetops, and fiercely agitating the scanty flame of the lamps that struggled against the darkness." Jesus that's awful. Bulwer-Lytton actually began the novel *Paul Clifford* with this purple sentence. It led finally to a wildly popular contest beginning in 1983 (and continuing to this day). People try to outdo one another at writing badly, in Bulwer-Lytton's style. See http://www.bulwer-lytton.com/2015win.html.

2. Typical of this renown is the estimation of John Lord, who was a popular lecturer and whose lectures eventually became the widely read *Beacon Lights of History*. He says:

> In the brilliant constellation of which Dickens and Thackeray were the greater lights was Bulwer Lytton,—versatile; subjective in genius, sentimental, and yet not sensational; reflective, yet not always sound in morals; learned in general literature, but a charlatan in scientific knowledge, worldly in his spirit, but not a pagan; an inquisitive student, seeking to penetrate the mysteries of Nature as well as to paint characters and events in other times; and leaving a higher moral impression when he was old than when he was young.

Lord goes on to list lesser lights whose literary genius falls below these three. These include such aspirants as Henry James, who was not Bulwer-Lytton's equal, and George Eliot who, because she was a woman, had to be treated separately as a novelist, as surpassing the expectations of her sex (with no suggestion that she might be the equal of a man). See John Lord, *Beacon Lights of History*, vol. 7, *Great Women* (New York: James Clarke, 1886), 347–48. On the other hand, at least Lord did include a full volume on great women in his ramblings, which many Victorian gentlemen might have regarded as beneath considering.

3. For a hilarious screed on Harold Bell Wright and his success, see Bill Bryson, *One Summer: America 1927* (New York: Anchor, 2014), 384–85.

4. Rarely can one be so precise, but Robbie's birthday is April 12, 1989. The day on which he makes the comments is November 19, 2009; see Stephen King, "Ur," in *The Bazaar of Bad Dreams* (New York: Scribner, 2015), 241, 248.

5. Since the initial Kindle version and the physical book are different in a number of crucial ways, I will adopt the convention of referring to the first Kindle edition of 2009 as *Ur*, and the paper version of the story as "Ur"—in quotation marks, followed by page numbers. Interestingly, the initial audio version of this story and the audio version that is supposed to be the audio of *Bazaar* are the same (i.e., not edited). Thus, if you want to *hear* the original story, you can get the audio of *Bazaar*. I suppose they didn't want to go to the trouble of making whole new recordings, especially given that the recording of *Ur*, along with others that had been released independently, such as "Mile 81" and "Drunken Fireworks," were such good recordings.

6. I hesitate to generalize beyond the United States and Canada because it seems to me that this odd concurrence of the study of great imaginative literature with the study of one's own language (the phenomenon of the "English Department"—where lit and grammar and poetry and creative writing and sometimes rhetoric all congregate, somewhat to the detriment of each, and have technical writing and the like tacked on) may be peculiar to the North American education systems. Yet, it is also the *way* that this stuff is *delivered* in the United States and Canada—small classes, writing intensive, reading great authors to *learn* to write—that sets up this magical moment so well. Our odd way of mixing things in North America brings the proletarian kid face-to-face with Hemingway and Faulkner, and, appropriately, Steinbeck, in community college as in the Ivy League, and is associated often with such mundane matters as learning to write a business letter (or e-mail). Does that happen elsewhere? I honestly don't know.

7. King indulges himself by describing this moment briefly but beautifully in a passage of *11/22/63: A Novel* (New York: Scribner, 2011, 285–86, where

the main character, Jake Epping, is working as a substitute teacher in Florida and tells his students about *Catcher in the Rye* in 1959 or 1960, when the (new) novel is "banned" from almost every respectable library and school. One supposes that Jake's love of teaching, and of this moment, just *is* King's undisguised autobiographical feelings.

8. Google it.

9. I take up the physics and metaphysics of this change in chapter 16 in this volume.

10. I noticed last week that in King's recent novel *Revival*, in which he creates his version of the mad scientist, this character's first appearance (which is recalled several times in the course of the story) casts a shadow that blots out a "westering sun"—one of Tolkien's favorite phrases. King is playfully allusive like this with the language of many authors, but Tolkien is certainly among his favorite.

11. Stephen King, "Author's Note," *The Bazaar of Bad Dreams* (New York: Scribner, 2015), p. v.

12. This is very near the end of *Ur*. I cannot cite a page for this or other references to *Ur* because it is published on Kindle and as an audiobook only. According to the reviews there are 1,700 "locations" and sixty-one pages on the Kindle edition. There are fifty-five pages in "Ur" and this quote survived the revisions, so I can give you that; it's p. 262. I will not pursue the "rose feels a chill" portion of this passage, but I assume it has something to do with the rose petals that surround the Dark Tower.

13. The phrase "Time belongs to the Tower" comes from the story "Everything's Eventual," from the 2005 collection of the same name. That story contributes very little to our grasp of the Tower's time, but the suggestions of writings to come are certainly there.

14. See King, *11/22/63*, 798. Zack Lang is some sort of gatekeeper of the time portals. He is surely there as a tool of exposition, so that King can explain to readers (and his characters) what is happening, but beyond that it isn't easy to tell what these gatekeepers are. Readers have many theories as to what kind of being Zack is and how he came to be stationed at the portal. We are told very little except that he was once from Seattle. His predecessor, called only "Kyle," was unable to bear the psychological strain of keeping the gate, and so turned to drinking and finally committed suicide. These beings are charged with keeping all the time strings in their heads/minds at once, and it drives them insane if too many variations are introduced, evidently. So they seem to be coal mine canaries of some sort and some readers theorize that they are like lesser "keepers of the beams" of the Dark Tower.

15. See King, "Ur," 263.

16. See the brief but revealing discussion of how King imitates whoever he is currently reading, and a list of some imitations in King, *Bazaar*, 51–52.

17. See Susanne Langer, *Feeling and Form: A Theory of Art* (New York: Scribner, 1953), ch. 16.

18. Jean-Paul Sartre describes this process very clearly in *The Psychology of Imagination* (New York: Citadel, 1991), esp. pp. 13–14, 18–21.

19. See Sartre, *Psychology of Imagination*, part 4, pp. 171ff.

20. King remarks that on rare occasions when an ending comes to him first, as inspiration, the story has to be written very carefully in that case.

21. The Dark Tower series ends with this promise. Roland's quest will begin again, but it may be different, this time.

22. I don't mean anything fancy here by "phenomenology." I mean that just as there is an *immediate* psychological and visceral effect of reading, a *what-it-feels-like-to-read-this-in-the-moment-I'm-reading-it*; there is also a *reflective* sense of an author, a *what-it-is-like-to-have-read-this-book* (and any number of other books by this author), when we reflect on the experience as a whole. This latter is the phenomenological *sense* of a story and/or an author. It's what we appeal to as evidence when we say "Geez, I like 'em."

23. See the comic chapter in "Ur" titled "Wesley Refuses to Go Mad," 228–37, in *Bazaar*.

24. The experiment in time bending we find in *The Langoliers* in 1990, in *Four Past Midnight*, is an abortive temporal hypothesis, relative to the Tower. If beasties consume the past a few minutes after it passes, then obviously the past isn't "still there" for the likes of Jake Epping to explore.

25. The principal characters of the Dark Tower novels, coming as they do from different times, would seem to indicate how blithely King approaches this problem. These characters do bring their times into the settings of the Tower, but the psychological cost seems small.

26. I cowrote with Salwa Khoddam a psychologico-literary (mainly Jungian) study of one of Poe's main characters that I can recommend to anyone interested in this point. See Randall E. Auxier and Salwa Khoddam, "Reading the Maelström: Narrators, Texts, and Language in Edgar Allan Poe's 'A Descent into the Maelström,'" *Short Story* 7, no. 1 (Spring 1999): 115–32.

27. One thinks of the study of psychological pressure under extreme physical conditions in *The Long Walk*, written as Richard Bachman, in which King examines every possible variation of the dissolution of personality under the near certainty of impending death in an ever-narrowing future. It is Poe's "Pit and Pendulum" times a hundred. Interestingly, the dystopia in which this story is set is an alternative future Ur in which, apparently, the Germans won the Second World War and initiated a "culture of death" to sustain their authority with rituals and public spectacles. Thus, the many-worlds aspect of King's

imagination is hard at work even in this (relatively early) experiment. On the other hand, King was hiding under a pseudonym at the time and so felt free to stretch himself a little more than he might have under his own name, with regard to time and the Tower.

28. King, "Mile 81," in *Bazaar*, 46.

29. King, introduction to *Bazaar*, 1.

16

UR 88,416

Randall Auxier

People say Stephen King has a vast imagination, but what does it mean? At the very least, imagination is our power to create before our "mind's eye" (whatever *that* means), or our consciousness (whatever *that* is) images of things that are not presently in our senses. It seems like magic. If something isn't in your senses, how can it be before your mind? The answer is both simple and impossibly complicated: time. Whatever imagination is, it *defies* time—that is, present time, the *now*, as it flows by—and it puts our minds or our consciousness (or whatever) in touch with that which is *not now* and is *not here*.

Whatever time really is (an even bigger mystery), it *can* be treated this way: defied, or transcended, or transgressed, or subdued, or divided and quarantined. Time can bend, stretch, twist, and slow down. But I doubt that physical force alone can do that bending. The power has to be subtler. It is about stranger, nonlocal energies that we don't understand—perhaps even something like the "secret electricity" that possesses and ruins the mind of Reverend Charles Jacobs in *Revival*. And yet, we possess a power that goes into that multifarious flow. Imagination is the mistress who persuades time to yield this or that aspect of itself and to cough up images that are somewhen else, even if they aren't necessarily some*where* else. We routinely imagine what never existed anywhere, and never could. The only reason we know these images are somewhen else is not because we know when they are, but because we know they are not now, not presently in our senses. They may not be anyplace in the universe, but they hold a moment of duration between our last image and our next one, even without belonging to the physical flow of time through our senses and nervous system. That is what you do when you imagine heaven—it's mainly about its current absence from your senses, deferred in time until . . . eternity, I suppose, which is another word for nowhen.

IMAGINE THERE'S NO HEAVEN, I WONDER IF YOU CAN

That ought to be enough to chew on for a while. But of course there is more. Imagination has a deep relationship with the past—when we remember, we bring images to mind of things not presently before us, but that we treat as having belonged to our senses at some point in our past. So every time we remember, we use our power of imagination to call to mind images of what our senses once had in a different present moment. But imagination doesn't stop with that. You can imagine things you never experienced at all—I have imagined many times the accident that almost killed Stephen King. And I can imagine it from different perspectives—I am across the road and down a bit, and I see the truck coming and I want to yell. Or I can see it from above, as though I were in a helicopter hovering over the scene. Why can anyone do that? And we can also take things we really *did* experience and see them as if we were outside our bodies, looking on.

So, to put it mildly, this is a pretty weird ability we humans have. We bend the where and the when until we have quasi experiences of what we never experienced, and sometimes, what never happened at all or, and I repeat: *never could happen.* And here, friends and neighbors, is the rub. Not only will your imagination take you elsewhere and else-when. It will take you to nowhere and nowhen, but that trip is a little bit dangerous to your mental stability. You don't want to send your mind away for too long to, well, that nowhen that includes what isn't even possible. I have commented in detail about the psychological cost of time bending in another chapter. Here I am interested in what that is, in physical terms, and in terms of knowledge. How can we have knowledge of what doesn't exist? I wonder if we can.

LIFE TURNS ON A DIME

That is one of Jake Epping's favorite phrases in *11/22/63*. In that other chapter, I described Stephen King's Dark Tower as "a loose mixture between Hugh Everett's many-worlds quantum hypothesis and the cosmologists' ideas about the existence of a stacked 'multiverse,'" and I said that with the combined stories of *Ur* and *11/22/63*, "the Tower has become an *n*-dimensional temporal labyrinth that combines the warping effects of gravitation with the chance effects of quantum dynamics and the stacked multiverse across parallel worlds—or something like that." I think King's Tower comes closest to being a mix between what Brian Greene calls a "quantum multiverse" in which a new universe is created with a diversion of events that leads to a split, and a "quilted multiverse" where infinite space permits the actual occurrence of all genuinely possible events infinitely many times.[1]

King began exploring the ideas of parallel dimensions of space long ago. The dimension shifting in *The Talisman* and also the development of the alternative reality of the Dark Tower series experimented with the idea of multifold space, with thin places, but presumably the same time structure, or closely connected time flow. But in *Ur* (2009), King really began temporalizing the Tower. The question of how many dimensions the Tower holds was answered in the sense that *at least* 10,438,721 parallel time threads called "Urs."[2] Each of these seems to have split off from an UR Ur, some primal font of Urs, and each new Ur is created by some event that is special—in quantum physics, these events are called "observations," upon which waves collapse into particles, and what was indeterminate becomes determinate. But King chooses historical moments rather than neutral acts of observation, and in these moments, life turns on a dime. A new Ur springs into being, with at least two branches, each following out the consequences of the "dime" moment, and its fundamental ambiguities. The context is something like this: everything that genuinely *can* happen, actually *does* happen. There may be far more threads than those enumerated in *Ur*, but there are not fewer.

"Dime" moments can come in any cultural form—politics, music, literature, military conflicts, and so forth. Discovering that he can read the *New York Times* for *any* Ur on his Dark Tower Amazon Kindle (sent to him from somewhere in the Tower due to some sort of processing error), our hero Wesley Smith checks politics and finds that Hillary Clinton actually won the 2008 election in most of the Urs, but Barack Obama wins a fair number in some other Urs—so this is a nonessential moment, evidently. But importantly, Sarah Palin shows up as a player only in Wesley's own Ur (which is, FYI, Ur 117,586). He thinks to himself that this made sense; she "had always been an outsider."[3] This is the work of chance in a given Ur, which King allows, as a sort of counterbalance to the nodes that serve as near constants.[4] So, in these "pasts" there is the operation of both constancy, or, as he calls it later, "obduracy," and of chance. Obviously, chance is what brings the Dark Tower Kindle to Wesley to begin with—the reversing of two digits in his MasterCard number, he theorizes. So these are the fundamental factors in how King imagines the temporal ontology of the Tower: chance and obduracy. Later I will try to provide the "laws" of King's universe, but that will take some imaginative work on *our* part to reconstruct. King gives enough hints, but it's not like he wrote a treatise on this.

THE BIG CASINO

Wesley Smith is an English professor at a small college in western Kentucky. A telling moment in *Ur* occurs when his student Robbie Henderson suggests that Wesley should "check the big casino" on his special Kindle. Wesley doesn't understand. But it's obvious to Robbie: *the Kennedy assassination*. He counters Wesley's blank stare by citing his history professor (Wesley's colleague).[5] One assumes King hadn't quite thought this through. Robbie wouldn't think of the assassination as "the big casino." Remember, the setting for *Ur* is rural western Kentucky in 2009. Robbie is twenty years old. I have lived in this same region most of my life, half of it spent teaching students just like Robbie Henderson. I can personally assure every reader that these students were *not* thinking about whether history would have been better if Kennedy had lived.

This Kennedy "thing" is a fantasy pondered by Yankee baby boomers and isn't terribly meaningful to the rest of the world, and especially not in the rural South half a century later. Robbie would have been *much* more likely to ask if Wesley could find an Ur in which General Lee didn't order Pickett's charge at Gettysburg. But New Englanders, in my experience, often carry the poignant feeling of having been robbed of something beautiful and morally good when Dallas took Kennedy away from them (and us). At least Jake Epping, in *11/22/63, is* a New Englander.

The revealing aspect of this awkward "big casino" moment in *Ur* is that it shows King's imagination actively at work in 2009 on the problem of how to pull off the time-bending part of the epic tale of *11/22/63*. In *Ur* he is working out the temporal metaphysics of the Tower. He postulates what I would call a "floating present," which is a requirement for maintaining the "unity of action" (to use the literary term). Given that, the unity of past time, and to a lesser degree, the unity of place, will have to be sacrificed or occluded in the epic story. Perhaps *one* of Aristotle's three unities (time, place, action) *can* be sacrificed to a significant degree without damaging the intelligibility of the narrative, but the loss has to be shored up by a strengthening of one or both of the others.[6] In *11/22/63*, King realized he had to put all three aspects of time, that is, past, present, and future, on the chopping block. The question was how to handle the effects on the unity of place and action. The tight focus on first-person narrative is one thread of continuity King uses to shore up the breaches in unity. It comes as no surprise that narrating time travel raises hosts of difficult questions that can't be answered. They must be met with devices and strategies that satisfy or gently befuddle the inquiring reader. The reader must be made passive to the paradoxes, somehow.

EPISTEMIC PRIVILEGE AND THE SPREADING EFFECT

One localized (but telltale) problem that crops up in *11/22/63* is that our hero, Jake, goes back to change the past, and then, arriving again in 2011, finds that his transtemporal companion, Al Templeton, who has *not* gone into the past on this trip, still "knows" the alternate future which (now) "never occurred," due to changes Jake made in 1958. Jake has saved a family from being murdered, and has prevented the original lone survivor (a kid named Harry Dunning) from being permanently damaged, and Jake does so in such a way that neither Jake nor Al would ever have even *met* that survivor in the "new" 2011 to which Jake has just returned. Remember, Al has been in 2011 all along. (This stuff *is* confusing, isn't it?) Jake speaks first to Al: "Explain to me how you can remember Harry Dunning if he was never a janitor at LHS [Lisbon High School] and never bought a Fatburger from you [in your restaurant] in his whole life. Second, explain to me why you don't remember [Congressman] Mike Michaud visiting the diner when that picture [on the wall now, in place of Harry's] says he did?" After some puzzling, to this query, Al theorizes: "You [Jake] remember him [Harry] in his life as a janitor and as your student because you're the one who went down the rabbit-hole."[7] In short, in the same way that we can carry small items from one time to another in pockets, wallets, and so forth, we can also carry our memories back and forth. There is something transtemporal about the person, and personality and memory is a part of that, but it isn't necessarily any different from carrying a key or a coin or a cell phone through the "thin places." But keys and coins and cell phones don't have to remain sane. The cost of having more than one "present" is psychologically high, and King recognizes it. Both Al and Jake have to find verifications in the altered 2011 that they *really were* back in 1958 (and not dreaming it or something), and that they had causal power *in* 1958 to bring about a slightly or even greatly altered present in 2011. Only *seeing* the results of, in the simplest case (a name carved in a tree in 1958), and finding it fifty-three years later in the altered 2011 relieves the doubt that extorts such a high psychological toll for Al. Seeing is believing and the psychological pressure begins to dissipate, but not entirely.[8]

Epistemic privilege for the time traveler is, therefore, a narrative necessity but comes at a cost to deep characterization. The conversation between Jake and Al continues. Al says:

> "I remember him [Harry Dunning] either because I've used the rabbit-hole myself, or just because I'm near it." He considered. "That's probably it. A kind of radiation. The Yellow Card Man [a half-crazy drunk "gatekeeper" named Kyle in 1958] is also near it, only on the other side, and he feels it too. You've seen him, so you know."[9]

In short, the proximate theory is that "thin places" radiate epistemic privilege, allowing those "within range" to remember what *didn't* happen (anymore at least) in their current present, but *did* happen on an alternate line (another Ur) that they somehow no longer occupy. We all know the paradoxes of time travel. There is no need to list them here.

What is interesting is that the paradoxes increase as one imports more and more difficult psychological and epistemic baggage across Urs.[10] It is hard on the minds of time travelers or dimension shifters. My point is that, initially, King has his characters toy with the idea that spatio-temporal proximity to a time bubble will carry with it a radiating epistemic privilege, a capacity to know what those not near the bubble don't know and can't know. Of course, the privilege is transported beyond the bubble along with the person who has once gotten the privilege. In this sense it becomes more "entangled" than local, so the privileged person becomes a sort of mobile host of epistemic privilege.

WHAT ARE THE CHANCES?

Like Al Templeton, Jake Epping *believes* he steps into the "same moment" in 1958 whenever he passes through the rabbit hole, and he believes he can return to 2011 two minutes later, no matter how long he remains in "the past." This two minutes that elapses in 2011, no matter how long a person is "in" the past, is what I called "the floating present." That ratio of infinity to two minutes is important, since it allows Jake to change bits of the past and return to the present to see the "effects," without losing much time in the "present." But each time he resteps through the portal, history *apparently* reverts to its default setting, the original 1958, to give him "another shot." So Jake believes he can correct mistakes, repeat (apparently) successful labors, and add to them as he remains for longer periods. (We find out in the end that this isn't what is really happening.)

After some minor successes in improving some lives, he goes for what Robbie Henderson improbably called "the big casino": saving JFK from Oswald. In *Ur* we have been informed that in every Ur in which JFK was assassinated, it was always Oswald and he always acted alone.[11] As King reports, in the voice of Wesley Smith, the Warren Commission was actually right, to everyone's astonishment. Admittedly, no one, I mean no one *alive*, knows whether King's hypothesis about Oswald's role in the assassination *is true*, but again, *he* is the author and *we* are the readers, after all. He can assert that Hemingway wrote A *Farewell to Arms* in every Ur and that Oswald always acted alone if he damn well pleases. A cute paradox does arise that King probably foresaw, but with the bigger paradoxes he had to confront, this one goes below the radar for most of us: Jake Epping hasn't read *Ur*, apparently, since he is unsure whether Oswald acted alone, even though King has clearly made up *his* mind about it, and Jake is one of his characters.[12] *Ur* is available in 2011, and Jake surely knows of Stephen King—he's an English teacher.

I think pretty much every English teacher today reads *some* Stephen King, and certainly every single such teacher *in Maine* does. Jake would know about the Dark Tower, too. He would have to. I'm thinking Jake might find *Ur* in a Google search, if he had time to do one in 2011 (which King cleverly precludes by rushing the 2011 events due to Al's failing health). Even assuming Jake doesn't realize that *he* is a Stephen King character himself, you would still think he might do a little re-search, if given time, and discover Oswald really did act alone, accord-ing to Jake's maker, and save himself five years by finding him and killing Oswald in 1958. I don't think Jake is allowed to argue with King about this, although King does suggest in *Danse Macabre* that his char-acters get up and walk on their own. Not very many authors would encounter such a paradox, since few ever become so very widely read in their own home ground as to have to decide whether their own charac-ters have actually read their earlier novels. It isn't believable that Jake hasn't read King. That's my point. And it's kind of a game changer, as you will see.

In any case, although it will cost Jake five years of his life to pull off the trick, he goes back to give us, heroically, the future of which we were deprived. When Jake goes back, he knows his efforts may create more despair than happiness. I think this fact about changing the future *by* changing the past is why King had Robbie Henderson (however improbably) call the Kennedy assassination "the big casino." Chance is clearly involved. And this factor would demotivate most people more strongly than motivate them. The "save Harry Dunning" frame is now necessary, since Jake has nothing about his own life that can be "fixed" in temporal proximity to 1958. King employs this chance relation of past to future to motivate Jake Epping to try "the big casino." Jake discovers that to save Harry Dunning, *really* save him, he actually has to stop the Vietnam War, since Harry will die at Khe Sanh in 1968 if he is unhurt in his father's murderous rampage in 1958. Stopping Vietnam means saving Kennedy, since it is commonly believed that he wouldn't have escalated the war as Johnson did. Would *you* spin that wheel and put, say, five years of your life on red or black?

MOTIVES AND MOTIFS

That is the question King was obsessed with for forty years. He thought about it very seriously off and on, I think, and decided that the kind of person who would save Kennedy needed to care about Kennedy more than is normal, and even *that* sort of person would be daunted by the prospect of giving up five years of a future in 2011 to live them between 1958 and 1963, just on a chance of succeeding in stopping Oswald and having a better history. King depicts Al Templeton as a Kennedy fanatic, and a betting man, and one who very craftily finances his journey to save Kennedy with wagers on sports, and Al doesn't get greedy. But Al is much older, and he is a smoker, and the past is obdurate. So he loses a bigger lottery, the cancer lottery, and that clears the path for a more sympathetic protagonist—a mild-mannered English teacher who is not a betting man.

Yes, *that's* the key to the story, King must have realized. Chance must play a role—it always has in King's multiverse-ish Tower labyrinth. The chance things might be better, along with the confidence of an accomplished gambler, like Al Templeton, might be enough to try a spin at the big casino; and for Al, at least, that might be a fair wager even if he never gets back to 2011. Still, it was easy enough for King to create a protagonist who had no special reason to return *to* 2011—Jake has no children, a failed marriage, and is at the back side of thirty without writing his novel. But English teachers, even divorced, childless ones, still prefer books and cats and quiet evenings and glasses of not-too-expensive wine to, say, time travel and killing people. Jake wouldn't spin that wheel even if only *he* were at risk, let alone when other people's lives are stacked up on every number. Something more is needed.

Jake also belongs to the wrong generation. He is a Gen Xer, born long after Kennedy was dead. It was an accepted fact of his life. Al grew up in the aftermath of it. The easy thing would have been to make a man like Al Templeton the protagonist, someone who was a child when

Kennedy was killed, who lived through the subsequent assassinations and wars and Watergate, someone who could feel in his bones that it all turned on a few bad decisions by a handful of people. And *that* protagonist could easily be a huge Kennedy partisan and a sportsman with a good aim and a knowledge of guns, and perhaps also the kind of person who could pull the trigger with another human being in the crosshairs, so, perhaps also a veteran, even an officer. Why not just build into your protagonist the personality needed to make it believable that he would spin the wheel?

THE BEST POSSIBLE WORLD

And here, at last, we come to Ur 88,416. In the same section in *Ur* when Robbie calls the Kennedy assassination "the big casino," Wesley, Robbie, and Don Allman are looking at the Kennedy assassination by perusing the *New York Times* from various Urs. The "special" Dark Tower Kindle has the available Urs simply numbered, and these boys are choosing "Ur numbers" to examine somewhat arbitrarily, mainly by turning their birth dates and their girlfriends' and mothers' birth dates into long numbers (remember, there are over ten million Urs in the Kindle). Comparing Urs, they discover that sometimes Kennedy gets away, sometimes he doesn't go to Dallas at all, and so forth. So this is not a necessary "node" in the Dark Tower universe. It is in this context that they find that Oswald always acted alone in all the Urs in which Kennedy was assassinated.

But then there is Ur 88,416, which is the future where Kennedy lives, is reelected in 1964, and Edmund Muskie succeeds him in 1968 (yes, King is even so shameless as to make the senator from Maine his fantasy president in place of Nixon); there is no Vietnam War and RFK and MLK live; and the Beatles actually play for Kennedy's final party at the White House in 1968. The whole story has only one hiccup: Pete Best is still the Beatles' drummer (and no one wants *that*, but hey, no world is perfect). This is the scenario Jake Epping wants, minus Pete Best, plus Ringo, but close enough. The desideratum is Ur 88,416.[13] Of course, this dreamy utopia disappeared from the print version of "Ur." Kind of a shame, since many of King's faithful followers desperately want this fantasy. But Jake is a practical person and he knows this is a one-in-ten-million shot, at best, even if he hasn't read *Ur*.

This raises the issue of genuinely *likely* futures had Kennedy lived. King explains in the afterword to *11/22/63* that he discussed with the famous Harvard historian Doris Kearns Goodwin and her spouse Dick Goodwin (who was a Kennedy aide) the probable scenarios had Kennedy lived, and they seemed to think a George Wallace presidency was likely (*not* Edmund Muskie!). But I would infer, from the depiction of the world, the Ur, of 2011 to which Jake returns *after* stopping Oswald, that King turned over the possibilities and realized a number of things. For example, the West might lose the Cold War if Nixon didn't go to China. And being, shall we say, not exactly an *optimist* about the human prospect, King felt obliged to depict a pretty awful future.

In sum, my point is that it just doesn't look like Jake Epping, or anyone like him, would actually undertake this quest. So why not send Al Templeton, or someone even more likely? What about some soldier of fortune, some Bruce Willis–type avenging angel? I think I know the answer to this question. Apart from the obvious power of having Jake be "just an ordinary guy," so that lots of people can identify with the hero, it is really *King* who wants to take this trip, *himself*. He says very clearly that he first tried to write this novel in 1972, but "I dropped the project because the research it would involve seemed far too daunting for a man who was teaching full-time."[14] King also admits that "even nine years after the deed, the wound was still too fresh," meaning the assassination was too close in time for any perspective to be had.[15] He was asking himself all along, I surmise, "What would it take to motivate *me* to go through that rabbit hole and give this a try?"

A METAPHYSICAL MULLIGAN[16]

That question is surely what brought about the idea of the "reset." This literary device is utterly unsupported by any theory of plural universes or multiverses I have ever encountered, but I do have a suggestion about it, which I hinted at earlier. Still, its first motive is clearly literary. King needs to find some set of circumstances that would persuade him, or someone like him, to spin the wheel, for those of us who aren't gamblers (and Jake Epping is not). People like King and Jake (and you and me) need a *hedge*; we need at least *some* security against losing. Otherwise, we won't play. So what if you believed that you could undo any damage you had done simply by stepping through the portal one more time, and then turning around and coming directly back, without doing anything in 1958? The reset, the metaphysical mulligan appears. Without it, King can't have the English teacher he wants, *and was*, for a hero.

As cosmology or quantum physics, or even for the Tower, there is no reason at all to imagine it possible to "reset" the past,[17] nor is there anything in relativistic time dilation to compress infinite past time into two minutes of elapsed time in 2011, which is how the rabbit hole works, what I called "the floating present."[18] Is it *only* literary convenience? I don't think so. I think King plays a trick on his readers and his characters. We find out near the end that there really *isn't* a reset when Jake returns to 1958. He creates a new and parallel course every time he steps through, but he doesn't know it. Finally he learns the truth, talking to Zack Lang, the guardian of the rabbit hole. Zack begins:

> "And what did he [Al Templeton] tell you? Each trip was the first time?"
>
> "Yes, A complete reset."
>
> He laughed wearily. "Sure he did. People believe what they see. And still, he should have known better. *You* should have known better. Each trip creates its own string, and when you have enough strings, they always get snarled. Did it ever cross your friend's mind to wonder how he could buy the same meat over and over? Or why things he brought from 1958 never disappeared when he made the next trip?"
>
> "I asked him about that. He didn't know, so he dismissed it."[19]

King has indeed thought this through—to the extent one can. Al's hypothesis about epistemic privilege due to proximity radiated from the bubble (Zack Lang says it isn't a rabbit hole, it's a bubble), is simply inadequate. King lets the reader believe it until page 796. Still, he finally points out that even if the person can carry the knowledge back and forth between times in his nervous system and brain (which is a huge paradox in its own right, and we'll take it up in the end of this chapter), the process of moving physical items from one time to another is more complicated—perhaps this is why some time-travel fiction requires the traveler go naked.

But Lang is pointing to something even tougher. Al Templeton has been buying meat and selling it forty years later for a long time. He goes through the bubble, across the street, buys hamburger meat at 1958 prices, and then heads back through to sell it in the future at prices that his competition can't match. Each time he goes back, he buys *the same* meat, in his way of thinking. The first law of thermodynamics is somewhat hostile to this habit of Al's. Energy cannot be either created or destroyed, it can only change forms. On Al's theory (and granted, he's not a physicist), that meat, repeatedly consumed in the future by real physical beings (energy changing forms), would have to be *created* from nothing to be *re*bought and *re*consumed, providing *real* energy repeatedly in the future. It isn't physically possible, as King has Zack Lang point out. So this isn't a metaphysical mulligan. But does the "dime" moment, creating a new string, solve this problem?

IMAGINE ALL THE PEOPLE LIVING FOR TODAY

What Jake is really doing, I think, is trying to find Ur 88,416, even though he knows nothing of the Urs. He is *imagining* that one Ur, and imagining it as the one future we would all share. Imagination has an ambiguous relation to knowledge, just as it has to time. Without the power of imagination, we would have no knowledge, but imagination doesn't seem to be bound by the rules we impose on images that we call knowledge. Imagination will bring us fantasy, the never was, the never will be, and worst of all, *error*, like Al's and Jake's regarding the reset. If Jake *knew* about the Urs, he wouldn't go through the hole. That's why he can't learn the truth until the end. I suppose it's a good thing Jake didn't read *Ur*. If he had, he might have suspected that each time he steps into the past he creates a new Ur, and *that* new Ur is the one he "returns to"—not to the one he left. Still, the less stuff he changes in the past, the greater the overlap of the new Ur with the one he exited.

This appears to be a principle of the Urs, similar to what the "continuity" assistant does for film sets through multiple takes, so that film editors can choose from different takes without having objects suddenly appear and disappear in the background. Thus, there is no reset, but there is continuity among courses of time. King gives us adequate clues to grasp this, especially with the changes in the Yellow Card Man to the Orange Card Man to the Black Card Man, as Jake repeats his trips. King offsets the epistemic and psychological effects of new Ur creation with the device of the radiation theory—the later Al *is* the same Al who was standing by the rabbit hole when Jake leaves the first two times, and doesn't have his memory erased or augmented because he was near the rabbit hole. But it doesn't work any better than the meat-buying paradox. I wonder what would have happened if Al used the two minutes to go pee and get a cup of coffee. King knows he has to have more. In any case, since the characters are deceived about the reset, and *must remain* unaware, of what they are doing, they *believe* in the impossible reset. Their belief surely convinces many readers that there *is* a reset. But King still has a problem.

THREE (OR SO) KEEN IDEAS ABOUT TIME

At the relevant level, then, which is neither literary nor psychological, nor phenomenological, but cosmo-temporal, physical, epistemological, and metaphysical, King brings together several keen ideas about time in an attempt to address (if not solve) these paradoxes that he recognizes.[20] He is keen on doing his best to avoid cheap tricks, and really think through the implications.[21] His metaphor is the time string, but his version isn't anything like the well-known string theory in physics. His time "strings" are akin to vibrating *guitar* strings.

If you think of the "stretch" between 1958 and 2011 as a guitar string strung across the cosmic Stratocaster (and after all, King is a guitarist), Jake plucks that string every time he steps through the portal. He also *adds* strings, increasing the tension on the instrument. The plucked string vibrates the whole time he is displaced, and in so vibrating, it tries to come back to rest, but keeps echoing. And Jake has a cosmic guitar pick, which is his *intention* toward the past: the plucked string vibrates more violently the more he *intends* to alter "the past." If Jake goes after a genuine node in the Tower's vibratory structure, his actions threaten the order, the instrument itself, but not all nodes are created equally; "Oswald always acted alone" may not be the biggest one, but it's bigger than "Hemingway always writes *A Farewell to Arms*," in *Ur*, since more related events depend on it. The King cosmos, then, is really more like a sitar with droning strings and sympathetic strings and playing strings, but the point is that the cosmic order will bear only so much dissonance before, well, "the Tower trembles, the worlds shake in their courses, and the rose feels a chill, as of winter" as the low man in the yellow coat says in *Ur*.[22]

King imagines and favors the analogy of strings bending because of their remarkable obduracy, their insistence upon returning to their original tuning and coming to rest. This was an idea he didn't yet have when he wrote *Ur*. He hadn't thought through the implications of Ur 88,416. On reflection, he realized that there has to be greater unity among the Urs than simple dime splitting allows, or at least a heavy unity has to exist if one aims to *travel* among the Urs. Whence this unity? How can an author or an agent of physical causation gain the Archimedean point? I will get to this, but for now it is enough to note that saving JFK is, then, a string bender that even Clapton couldn't manage. It will break the instrument. So the time string *resists* and returns to its original shape with the resoluteness of silvered steel. As King puts it, "The past is obdurate. . . . The resistance to change is proportional to how much the future might be altered by any given act."[23]

I think we have now reached a full understanding of this characteristic of Tower time, with this "law," which we might call King's *first law of Dark Tower dynamics*, with a nod to Sir Isaac Newton. In fairness to Newton, King also asserts "balance." The obduracy of the past is balanced with the "flimsiness and maliciousness of events," which is the quantum counterpart of the first, and a close cousin of the butterfly effect.[24] Jake Epping avoids even slight interactions with Lee Harvey Oswald for fear of altering his course, since saving Kennedy requires saving him from just that moment of just that fateful day. Otherwise Oswald, or some other assassin, might kill JFK elsewhere, elsewhen, and Jake would lose his epistemic advantage. The implications of the *first law* are that the past is *easy* to change in ways you *wouldn't* prefer, but hard to change according to the paths you *would* prefer. Ur 88,416 is infinitely delicate and turns on a dime.

King's second idea is that "the past harmonizes." Coincidences among Urs are not accidental. If you notice a 1957 white-over-red Plymouth Fury in Lisbon Falls, Maine, and you see another one in Florida, and a third one in Texas (or maybe a fourth one being driven by Arnie Cunningham in Pittsburgh in 1978), this is a "harmony." Harmonies are the means by which the past creates its convergence on *a* present, with maximal overlap and minimal variation across many strings, like a series of overtones, a sort of temporal guitar harmonics, converging on a rich tone. These are the strings vibrating in sympathy with an order that sort of meshes with the gravitas and magnetism of the "must be."

This harmony analogy is better with a Martin D-28 than a Stratocaster. A Stradivarius might be better still. Everyone knows that the *way* a guitar (or a violin) has been played, over decades, even centuries, contributes to its sound in the present—it's as if all those past tones are preserved in the wood and the varnish, and the very tension of the instrument, the way its pieces press against each other, its seams and joints. The sound you hear, now, unites with the continuous, physical existence of the instrument. When you pluck a string or strum a chord, you are hearing the echoes of every previous pluck, faint though they are. You are also contributing to the next sound, and every possible sound the instrument can make thereafter. And physically speaking, this idea may not be simply an "as if." It may have a genuine basis in the way time really passes. It is hard to say what happens to past time, but every theory of physics requires that it at least persists in some way into the present. There is a harmonization here, something like the compatibility of the past with every genuinely possible future.

These harmonies, faintly contributing in the present act of plucking, set off echoes that we can *interpret* if we listen rightly, King believes. But it is delicate business. You cannot unplay that chord (hence, no real reset), and you cannot prevent its conservation and its effect upon the next. The good news is that you wouldn't want to live in a cosmos that wasn't cumulative in this manner. The bad news is that the sour chords persist, too. But in King's cosmos, the sour chords never get control because the sour notes will be drowned out by the convergence of the harmonies and overtones.

A lot of people don't realize that all the violins in an orchestra are playing a bit out of tune—it is the nature of the instrument. Perfection isn't a possibility. One needs a full section of violins and violas in an orchestra to counteract the problem.[25] But the effect of many bows upon the many strings is an almost magical convergence upon a rich and thick unified tone. The characters and histories of all the various violins pile into a convergence that sounds far better than any single one of them can sound alone. Hence, King's later idea, after *Ur*, is that although we might create a new string with each trip through the rabbit hole, these "temporal strings" could (in principle) converge upon a single overall order so long as we don't break the instrument. Let us call this King's *second law of Dark Tower dynamics*: the conservation of harmony. Jake Epping discusses it throughout *11/22/63*. Harmony confounds the Crimson King.

That sets up the third idea. As the day of reckoning (November 22, 1963) approaches, Jake Epping is pondering time and he provides one correlate of the second law: "*It's all of a piece*, I thought. *It's an echo so close to perfect you can't tell which one is the living voice and which is the ghost-voice returning.*" But then he pushes onward in his thinking:

> For a moment everything was clear, and when that happens you see that the world is barely there at all. Don't we all secretly know this? It's a perfectly balanced mechanism of shouts and echoes pretending to be wheels and cogs, a dreamclock chiming beneath a mystery-glass we call life. Behind it? Below it and around it? Chaos, storms. Men with hammers, men with knives, men with guns. Women who twist what they cannot dominate and belittle what they cannot understand. A universe of horror and loss surrounding a single lighted stage where mortals dance in defiance of the dark.[26]

This is the *third law of Dark Tower dynamics*, which long ago he named the danse macabre. I feel confident that King sees this as the best he can do with the Tower as a temporal labyrinth. This view of time is much like the account given by the philosopher F. W. J. Schelling (1775–1854) in his unfinished book *The Ages of the World*. I'm not saying King has been wading through old tomes of German metaphysics (although he got the word "Ur" from such sources, almost certainly), but the resemblance here to Schelling is uncanny. Maybe "great minds think alike," or maybe it's just a "harmony" between King and Schelling, but Stephen King is no metaphysician. He belongs with writers like Anne Rice and Kurt Vonnegut who have these gnawing suspicions about time, life, and existence that they can only work through narratively— they don't build systems, they tell stories. It's better than building systems.

King's final idea about time, then, is that the dimensional thinness among resonances creates transient "bubbles" of dissonance. The time portal itself is an unstable dissonance. This is suggested by Jake's thoughts about it at a number of places in the text, and indeed, the portal *does* seem to move, to float, on the 1958 side, and Jake fears it may pop like a soap bubble. The present floats like a bubble, then, and is never quite where you left it. When time travel is used as a literary device, there has to be a point of reference so that readers (and characters) can track the "real" sequence of events. The device of epistemic spreading counteracts narrative chaos; it is a spotlight on the dance so that Jake *remembers* every "reset" he lives through. His body continues to age, as a residuum of his *original* Ur, and so serves as the locus of "absolute time"—the ground of the required unity of time, as Aristotle insists. If everything serves the Tower (see my other chapter), then so does time, finally. But what a slippery servant! And what a strange optimism this is. You don't *want* Ur 88,416. That is King's point. You just want the dance.

JUST MY IMAGINATION, RUNNIN' AWAY WITH ME

So there we have three "laws" that King uses to hold his universe together while characters cavort in time. But what sorts of laws are they? They are not laws of physics. And they are not *like* laws of physics. They don't even approach solutions to the paradoxes raised by time travel, and this, dear reader, is a subject about which you may have been misled by well-meaning scientists. Time travel is not physically possible, in the familiar literary sense, in which a character preserves his or her physical body, memories, thoughts (and sanity) across time frames. If time travel in some other sense is "possible," I cannot see how it would benefit us to be able to do it. But King's time travel must preserve not only what physical reality will permit, it must also preserve the conditions that are needed for biological life and the conditions that preserve historical order, along with the integrity of our psychology, knowledge, and moral existence. That is a tall order.

Physicists who talk about time travel often forget that the process would have to preserve biological life *and* the still more delicate and subtle processes that ride along with biological life, such as consciousness and personality. We know with fair assurance that biological life can be maintained only within a very narrow and quite exceptional range of gravitational and electromagnetic interaction. Earth gravity, earth electromagnetism, earth temperature, earth chemistry: these provide conditions under which beings like ourselves can live. Getting a time bubble that bends time while preserving these conditions requires far more than physics. And when we add the requirement that the subtle, even subquantum arrangement of energies that hold our consciousness and thought and synesthesia in balance must also be maintained, the challenge of creating a time portal becomes impossible. We have to skip all of the intermediate steps and simply *imagine* the portal, or bubble, or machine, or device, or what have you.

Yet, that is one of the things imagination can do. Immanuel Kant (1724–1804) assigned three principal functions to imagination: (1) it brings to our minds those aspects of the sensible world that we can use to present objects to our minds; (2) it schematizes and holds objects before the mind while we renew our act of consciousness; and (3) it provides comprehensive symbols of that which we cannot think clearly and in detail and in all its parts. This is difficult language, but what it means is that when we have a hunch or a feeling or a suspicion, imagination can synthesize from all that we think and feel a symbol that is whole, comprehensible, interpretable to us, and we allow that symbol to stand in the place of an experience we *don't have*. But sometimes the symbol is so vivid that we feel we have experienced the real thing it replaces. Unfortunately, there is no way at all to ensure that the symbols our imaginations synthesize are experiences that *could be had*, by us or by beings like us.

Kant also indicated, as he noticed that imagination can bring us symbols of which we must beware, that this power of ours seems to have *its own* immediate relation with possibility itself—and I would add, with the *im*possible, too. Imagination *must* outrun all our thinking and understanding and reasoning and judgment in order to bring back to our simplistic, mundane thought processes, to our nervous impulses and energies that developed to help us survive and negotiate the world, these amazing gifts, these *symbols* of the nowhere, nowhen that *seem* to make sense.

But these symbols only make sense so long as we don't analyze them too closely. They fall apart under scrutiny. And the kind physicist who tells you time travel is possible is, I'm sorry to say, imagining a symbol. You *can* imagine it, yes. But you cannot do it, and we have absolutely no evidence to suggest that *even if* it were physically possible to "travel" in time (which I doubt), a human body, let alone a human mind, could survive the transition.

Yet, we have now arrived at our destination. King's "laws" are really rules about how to imagine time travel so as to generate maximum *believability*. And in this regard he does better than any physicist I've heard of. King's laws are original as far as I have seen, although we all have to admit that some *very* creative stuff has been dreamed up by writers in this genre. Still, King's laws permit some kinds of analysis that other approaches do not. His organic combination of laws inspires one to scratch the head a little bit more, and that happens because it all seems so plausible. It is a thermodynamics of time travel, added to the basic idea of the music of the spheres. The epistemology is full of holes and requires us to suspend our disbelief, but the real driving force is moral. I think that reaching Ur 88,416 is the goal of all this dreaming, but in the end, King's pull toward realism, toward real physical science and believable narrative, led him to abandon that attractive Ur and settle for what Walt Disney so aptly called "the plausible impossible." He'll settle for the dance, because to dance is to live and to live is to dance. He wants you to join him for a dance.

NOTES

1. See Brian Greene, *The Hidden Reality: Parallel Universes and Deep Laws of the Cosmos* (New York: Vintage, 2011), chs. 2 and 8. I really must go on record as insisting that this is all complete nonsense in my view. There is no chance that any of it is anywhere close to being an accurate story about the cosmos. There are commonsense alternatives to these wild assertions cosmologists are making these days, apparently with serious intent. They need to learn the difference between problems generated by mathematics and problems generated by concrete experience. They also need to learn when they do and do not have enough information to form a viable physical theory. Presently, we don't know enough to be attempting grand theories of everything.

2. See Stephen King, "Ur," in *The Bazaar of Bad Dreams* (New York: Scribner, 2015), 224.

3. King, "Ur," 241.

4. In an act of perfect gratuitousness, King asserts that Al Gore usually won the election of 2000 in almost every Ur. It was a node that got messed up by hanging chads, one supposes, leaving our current Ur in a poorer condition than it had to be. King took this part out of the print edition of "Ur." See below.

5. From 2009 to 2015, the only way readers could get *Ur* was as a Kindle download or on Audible. I refer to the 2015 print version of the story as "Ur," while the novella of 2009 I cite as *Ur*. King revised the story for the print version. Most notably, he left out all mention of the Kennedy assassination in "Ur," but it played a prominent role in *Ur*, which is what I am summarizing here. A few minutes after calling the Kennedy assassination "the big casino," Robbie doesn't know anything about the Cuban Missile Crisis. This was a flaw in the story, and perhaps that is why King removed it. After all, either Robbie's history professor covered Kennedy or he didn't, but leaving out the Cuban Missile Crisis in the former case is not an option. In the revised "Ur," the Missile Crisis material remains in the story, but I don't think King cut the stuff on the assassination just to remedy this incoherence. He had since completed *11/22/63*, which handles time differently and in a more developed way. In any case, to get the Kennedy assassination material from *Ur*, one has to get either the Kindle or the audiobook.

6. Aristotle's famous theory is in *Poetics*, books 5–7. He never expressed "the unities" as absolute demands. That habit of thinking of the three unities as absolute demands is a characteristic developed among much later followers, especially French neoclassical (i.e., pre-Romantic) purists. The French of that age had the audacity to think of Shakespeare as inferior because he doesn't always maintain the strictness of all three unities.

7. Stephen King, *11/22/63: A Novel* (New York: Scribner, 2011), 228.

8. See my discussion of "amazement" and "admiration" in my other chapter in this book.

9. King, *11/22/63*, 230.

10. Shortly after the conversation quoted above, Jake breaks down when he discovers he has saved Harry Dunning from being damaged in his father's murderous rage only to condemn him to a different, early death in Vietnam. In Jake's Ur, Harry lives a full life with mental and physical impairments but is happy.

11. Again, this part was cut out of the 2015 print version.

12. King defends his level of conviction about whether Oswald acted alone in *11/22/63*, afterword, 845. For those who may think I'm being silly about the likelihood that King might write Jake such that he had read King, remember that Roland Deschain reads King, and later *meets* him, in the last two Dark Tower novels (not counting *The Wind through the Keyhole*). King even wrote

his 1999 accident into that series as an attempt on his life by the Crimson King, so I don't think that the usual boundaries apply to King's characters.

13. I can't find any secret code in the number 88,416. But knowing King, I doubt very much that it is random. Let this be a puzzle for fans with time to kill. There is an entry on it at the King Wiki, so please share with all of us if you figure anything out. See http://stephenking.wikia.com/wiki/UR_88416.

14. King, *11/22/63*, 846.

15. King, *11/22/63*, 846.

16. A mulligan is what golfers call it when one makes a perfectly awful shot, retrieves the ball, sets it back where it was, and hits it again without counting the poor stroke.

17. Kurt Vonnegut explores the complexities of the "reset" in *Timequake* (New York: Putnam, 1997), and I have analyzed the paradoxes in my essay "Reading Whitehead," in *Whitehead: The Algebra of Metaphysics*, ed. Michel Weber and Ronny Desmet (Brussels: Les Éditions Chromatika, 2010), 61–92. The paradoxes discussed here apply one and all to King's reset. But they are too complicated to explain here—and there is, in the end, no reason to do so, since King's reset doesn't actually occur.

18. Even if Einstein were correct regarding the idea that gravitation warps space-time, there still wouldn't be any way to step twice into the same past by somehow "warping" across a curve. One of King's weaknesses in dealing with time is that he entertains ideas about it that have their roots in general relativity. See Jimena Canales, *The Philosopher and the Physicist: Einstein, Bergson, and the Debate That Changed Our Understanding of Time* (Princeton, N.J.: Princeton University Press, 2015). Canales's book shows convincingly that Einstein was better at self-promotion and intrigue than he was at physics. For the problem that defeats general relativity, with finality, see Gary L. Herstein, *Whitehead and the Measurement Problem of Cosmology* (Frankfurt am Main: Ontos Verlag, 2006). Nor is Einstein's theory necessitated by mathematical considerations. See Hans C. Ohanian, *Einstein's Mistakes: The Human Failings of Genius* (New York: Norton, 2008).

19. King, *11/22/63*, 796.

20. Stephen King's son Joe Hill may be responsible for some of the ideas about time travel in *11/22/63* as King acknowledges in the afterword (847). I will treat them as King's here and leave the future to decide.

21. Speaking of keen, in the literal and literary sense, Philip Pullman has done some outstanding imaginative thinking about the Everett hypothesis of world splitting, and how one might move among these worlds, using a very keen knife, one with its own will and cosmic orientation. See the Pullman trilogy *His Dark Materials*, especially volume 2, *The Subtle Knife*. I have analyzed his approach closely in my essay "Cuts Like a Knife," in *The Golden*

Compass and Philosophy, ed. Richard Greene and Rachel Robison (Chicago: Open Court, 2009), 101–20.

22. See my citation on this quote in the previous chapter.

23. King, *11/22/63*, 232.

24. See King, *11/22/63*, 294–95.

25. It is easier to play "in tune" on a cello or double bass because the strings are longer and the region on the fingerboard that will sound "in tune" is larger. The violin is quite unforgiving in this regard, since even the tiniest misplacement of the finger will provide a tone noticeably different from the intended one. This is one reason (in addition to volume) that violin sections need to be larger than cello and bass sections for most orchestral music.

26. King, *11/22/63*, 615–16.

FROM DESPERATION TO HAVEN

Horror, Compassion, and Arthur Schopenhauer

Jacob M. Held

The world is sunk in evil, and men are not what they ought to be; do not let that lead you astray, and see that you are better.—Arthur Schopenhauer[1]

There is something about the worlds Stephen King creates—Haven, Castle Rock, Mid-World—that speak to a fundamental aspect of human existence: life is full of suffering. We are immersed in a world of loss and define ourselves by how we respond. The horrors King paints, although often supernatural, are more often mirrors of the mundane world of banal human existence. Sure, vampires are scary, but 'Salem's Lot wasn't pleasant before they arrived. And although Tak decimates Desperation, David Carver had known loss before he ever entered that small Nevada town. In fact, for most of King's stories the supernatural merely augments the amount of suffering his characters experience, but not the fact that they suffer fundamentally. We are always already awash in evil, in pain and suffering. This is the human condition, and it is a problem we have collectively been seeking to rectify since we had the intelligence to recognize it.[2]

Given that so much of life is painful or otherwise disappointing, we may begin to wonder why we bother at all. Why try to be good, or do the right thing? Does it matter? If the world is sunk in evil, and we're bound to drown, why struggle so hard to stay afloat? The situation seems especially dire if even a God can't save us.[3] If an appeal to the divine can't assure us or afford our lives some greater meaning or significance, then it seems we may be destined to devolve into nihilism, the belief that nothing matters.[4] But this seems an unsatisfactory conclusion. Life does matter, so we persist and seek to find value in it, to ground meaning in our lives. This may be why King's stories, and his protagonists, resonate with us. They are mired in pain, they are awash in evil, yet they don't give in. They find meaning. They find value. They struggle, and they do so admirably. King clearly perceives the problem, for he paints "a universe of horror and loss surrounding a single lighted stage where mortals dance in defiance of the dark."[5] It is this "defiance of the dark," this response to a universe of "horror and loss," with which I am interested. How do we defy the dark? How do we eke out meaning and craft praiseworthy lives for ourselves in a world defined by suffering? It is the existential problem posed by pessimism, the philosophical belief that life is essentially just not worth it. So we should turn to the authority on pessimism, Arthur Schopenhauer.

HAVEN IS SUNK IN EVIL

Arthur Schopenhauer (1788–1860) claims, "Life swings like a pendulum to and fro between pain and boredom, and these two are in fact its ultimate constituents."[6] Although I am not sure if this accurately reflects his take on the matter, Stephen King does paint a bleak picture of life in his stories, even before the really bad supernatural, evil stuff happens. Stephen King's worlds are always already sunk in evil. As 'Salem's Lot opens, even before Barlow arrives and wreaks havoc on the poor town, we are given a glimpse into a dismal existence, life in provincial Jerusalem's Lot. Father Callahan sees it clearly. Thinking back on having taken Sandy McDougall's confession, he recalls her "saying in her breathy little voice that she had hit her baby and when he asked how often, he could sense . . . the wheels turning in her mind, making a dozen times five, or a hundred a dozen." His response is understandable: "He wonders if she knew or guessed that he would like to reach through the little window with both hands and grasp the soul on the other side as it fluttered and twisted and squeeze it until it screamed."[7] Sandy is wretched. We're afforded one scene in the book where she throws her son, Randy's, bottle at him, hitting him in the forehead, before eventually striking him twice, bloodying the infant's nose.[8] Abusing an infant is an evil act, but one that is human, all too human. And King's worlds are full of examples of the evils with which we are afflicted and that we inflict on one another. We don't need vampires to imagine horrors like child abuse, nor do they fundamentally change the nature of our shared human condition. Vampires just add to, but they do not change the nature of human existence, namely, suffering. And 'Salem's Lot is just one town in one book in King's multiverse.

In Haven, where *The Tommyknockers* takes place, we are presented with similar vignettes, such as the tale of Paul Clarendon, in the early days of Haven, who after suspecting his wife has mothered an illegitimate child with a passing pastor slits its throat with a straight razor, before ending his and his wife's lives. This is human evil, evil we can familiarize ourselves with daily through the news. Paul Clarendon is fictional; child murder is not. In addition, Haven is rife with evils of variable degrees, from spousal murder to adultery, alcoholism, and other banal cases of the wretchedness of the human condition. Add to these literary examples the very real nature of existence including war, famine, disease, and natural disasters, and it becomes pretty clear that this planet is no place to be a human, which may be why Bobbi and the new and improved denizens of Haven want to power up the Tommyknocker ship and take leave of this place. So even though in *The Tommyknockers* you have the element of aliens, the horrific element, the "monster" of the story is human misery, in this case misery caused by shortsighted egoism and exacerbated by addiction, human failings that define us and that the Tommyknockers merely amplify. Ironically, making us *more human*—"becoming"—makes us *less humane*.

King, whether in *'Salem's Lot*, *The Tommyknockers*, or myriad other stories, begins from where humanity always already is, suffering. The supernatural components amplify but they don't redefine what it means to be human. All the worst King can offer, from werewolves and vampires to aliens and ancient demonic forces, seem to highlight a fact about the human condition, that we are defined by our confrontation with evil and suffering, with struggle. Given this, I'd maintain that the most enlightening aspect of King's work is how his characters respond to their struggles. King's characters always face a choice: stay in Mexico or return to 'Salem's Lot; drink oneself into a stupor and die oblivious or save David Brown and resist the Tommyknockers; run or face Tak; run or save Seth from Tak; run away with Susan Delgado and (perhaps) live happily ever after or pursue the Tower; and so forth. So how do King's characters almost always respond? In all these cases, the characters faced with these difficult choices respond with compassion, taking the good of others as their object of action. They think not of themselves, but of others. In the face of grave suffering, in the face of meaningless pain and chaos it is their choice of compassion, not self-interest, that defines them and that effectively saves them, others, and us, at least for a while. In this regard, King's works articulate well our fundamental connection to our fellow human beings, and speak to the value of compassion, our drive to do as much as possible to help, to alleviate what elements of suffering we can. His characters always strive to make it better, at least a little bit, for now.

PESSIMISM IN HAVEN

Arthur Schopenhauer is arguably the most influential philosophical pessimist. But his pessimism doesn't stem from a depressive personality or bad childhood. He is a pessimist because that is the judgment he finds most appropriate given the nature of reality. Schopenhauer's pessimism stems from his metaphysics, that is, how he understands the nature of reality to be fundamentally ordered.

According to Schopenhauer, the one thing that marks the essence of human life, and all life in general, is the will to live. This will is the unconscious motive force that moves us constantly and unrelentingly onward. It is "a blind, irresistible urge."[9] We strive, and striving necessarily brings failure, disappointment, and pain:

> We have long since recognized this striving . . . where it manifests itself most distinctly in the light of the fullest consciousness, is called *will*. We call its hindrance through an obstacle placed between it and its temporary goal, *suffering*; its attainment of the goal . . . *satisfaction* . . . all striving springs from want or deficiency, from dissatisfaction with one's own state or condition, and is therefore suffering so long as it is not satisfied. No satisfaction, however, is lasting . . . it is always merely the starting-point of a fresh striving. . . . Thus that

there is no ultimate aim of striving means that there is no measure or end of suffering.[10]

Or, as noted above, "Life swings like a pendulum to and fro between pain and boredom, and these two are in fact its ultimate constituents."[11] As we follow Gardiner through the eight hundred or so pages of *The Tommyknockers* we can see the pendulum swing from pain to boredom (or a drunken stupor) and back again myriad times. As David and company flee Tak in *Desperation*, or Audrey and her neighbors hunker down in their suburban nightmare awaiting the return of the Power Wagons in *The Regulators*, we see the repeated cycle of horror, death, and destruction and then the calm before the next, inevitable storm. King's readers jump from vignette to vignette with only small respites between horror scenes. Life in Haven, or wherever King takes you, is pain, punctuated mercifully, but only sporadically by boredom, or rather the absence of whatever evil is being inflicted upon his characters. Thinking of life this way, as a series of painful vignettes with only infrequent and minor interludes of boredom in between, Schopenhauer describes children as prisoners. "There are times when children might seem like innocent prisoners condemned not to death but to life and as yet all too unconscious of what their sentence means."[12] Children may, in fact, provide the best window onto Schopenhauer's worldview. And King's children all suffer greatly, and are so often prisoners in their pain, helpless to resist. So King's fictional children bring to vivid realization our shared condition.

Let's consider one of King's fictional children, David Brown from *The Tommyknockers*. David's a young boy, an adoring younger brother to the unfortunate, would-be magician Hilly Brown. David loves Hilly. But as the Tommyknockers grab hold of his older brother, Hilly becomes less than an ideal sibling. Hilly desperately wants to be a successful backyard magician; he wants to amaze his classmates, parents, and neighbors. He becomes so single minded of purpose, so obsessed, that he can't envision his life not being that amazing magician. His myopia foments his egoism: that his fame, his reputation matters most. He'll do anything to be great, and the Tommyknockers assist. They "teach" him how to create a disappearing device, one that "disappears" by sending anything to a distant, dying planet, Altair-4. In his quest for backyard stardom Hilly forces his brother, against his protests and tears, to be his assistant. "[Hilly] looked out at the audience—bored and inattentive . . . and resentment rose up again. He stopped seeing the frightened tears in David's eyes." He doesn't hear, or acknowledge his pleas as his younger brother begs him, "*Hilly, please . . . please, I'm scared. . . .*"[13] Too driven by ego, Hilly proceeds. David is disappeared by the trick the Tommyknockers taught his brother, transported to Altair-4 where he is left cold, alone, and struggling to breathe.

The theme of one's ego grabbing hold, overpowering, and driving one to do the unthinkable, to hurt or violate the most vulnerable among us, is common throughout *The Tommyknockers*. When Bobbi loses her dog, Peter, and we only later learn she turned her beloved pet into a battery, we are appalled. But for Bobbi it's a small price to pay for what the Tommyknockers can offer her. She even disposes of her sister when she becomes a nuisance. But in King's works, as in life, it is often the most vulnerable—children and animals—that suffer the most, prisoners to this life. Yet we all suffer. So Schopenhauer remarks, "From this point of view, it might occur to us that the really proper address between one man and another should be, instead of *Sir, Monsieur*, and so on, *my fellow sufferer*. However strange this sounds, it accords with the facts."[14]

So, my fellow sufferer, given the nature of existence, and considering the poor, unfortunate children among us: "Would not everyone rather feel so much sympathy for the coming generation that he would prefer to spare it the burden of existence, or at any rate would not like to assume in cold blood the responsibility of imposing on it such a burden?"[15] How many parents have had similar thoughts as they watch their children grow up? How many parents have looked at their children and thought, "I'm sorry"? Sure we can find pleasantries in this life, but that won't alter what we know to be true: our lives, and those of our children, will be more defined by loss and failure than pleasure and success. Anecdotal and empirical evidence bear this out. "Our susceptibility to pain is well-nigh infinite; but that to pleasure has narrow limits. It is true that each separate piece of misfortune seems to be an exception, but misfortune in general is the rule."[16] It just doesn't seem worth it. So what would King's characters do? What would Gard do?

The beginning of *The Tommyknockers* presents us with a long vignette about Jim Gardiner, "Gard" to Bobbi. Gardiner is a recovering alcoholic, and a writer whose best days, or at least best poems, are behind him. During one event on his poetry tour he gets drunk, launches into a diatribe against nuclear power,[17] chases the patron of the event with an umbrella, and ultimately passes out on the beach after a several-days-long drinking binge. Gard awakes and after contemplating his place on the planet stands at the end of the pier, staring into the deep, inviting, black water. Here stands Gardiner, with nothing to live for, nothing ahead of him but more failure. Why not jump, why not just end it all? Why wait for the pendulum to swing back to boredom one more time? He we all stand, just one bad day away from lunacy, nihilism, suicide. . . .[18] We are fragile beings, sensitive beings that are both incredibly resilient and remarkably frail. We can endure the gravest horrors, and yet be broken unpredictably by evils that others routinely endure. We are susceptible to disease, addiction, insanity, yet we are capable of great charity and love. Yet too often the difference between endurance and destruction is unpredictable, a function of the irrational nature of our psychological life; we teeter on the edge. This is where Gard stands, at the edge of the pier, on the precipice. So what drives him onward? In what does he find value? Why is Gard not broken? In the end, it's Bobbi. It's his connection to her, his drive to help, his compassion that pushes him forward.

So we ought not let our suffering lead us astray. In fact, that is one of the crucial lessons of Schopenhauer, and one reflected time and time again in King's stories. Even in light of this fact, that life is defined by suffering, we do not, nor do King's characters, lie down and die. His stories are driven by protagonists who, upon learning the depth and enormity of the specific form of suffering they and their community are enduring, respond. So although a happy life may be impossible, it is possible to live a *heroic life*.[19]

KING'S AUTHORS: FROM ALCOHOLISM TO HEROISM

The fear for Schopenhauer, and for all of us, is that pessimism, the belief that the world is fundamentally defined by suffering and redemption or salvation is impossible, will lead us to despair.[20] The problem with despair is that it is often met with either avoidance of the problem or nihilism. We may choose to simply avoid the problem, that life is pointless, through mere distraction. We fill our lives with gadgets, video

games, movies, parties, and other social events, or drugs, alcohol, or
what have you, all in an effort to distract us from the looming specter of
death, and to blind us to the pain that surrounds us. Friedrich Nietzsche (1844–1900) called this type of person the last man. These "last
men" take simple pleasure in everything and anything but truly value
nothing. They treat life ironically, as though it lacks any inherent value,
and in fact would scoff at those that commit themselves to anything
sincerely.[21] On the other hand, despair may lead us to accepting that all
is pointless and worthless and so sapping life of all meaning. This is
nihilism. We can see why Schopenhauer would be, and we should be,
concerned.

If we look to the world and find only suffering and despair, but
realize that we can make it better for ourselves by squeezing what
pleasure we might from it, with our good as our only goal, with our
satisfaction as our primary motive, others are bound to suffer. Examples
from King's corpus are numerous. In the Dark Tower series, we are
offered myriad examples of how narrow self-interest, how egoism, can
foment grave wrongs from the Breakers of Devar-Toi and children
being roont, to the Grays of Lud, human sacrifice, and child rape. In
fact, much of the Dark Tower series is about confronting a world that
has "moved on," which more often than not seems to mean a world that
has devolved into egoism where groups and individuals, in order to eke
out a meager life of banal pleasures, are often sadistic and cruel, and
exploit and abuse all others around them. Once the world moves on all
that are left are the "last men." And so despair drives them to egoism, to
self-service even at the cost of grave pain and suffering for others. The
only other option would be nihilism, or oblivion, and here we'd find the
Crimson King, who seeing no value in this world doesn't seek his own
self-interest or pleasure, but rather nothingness as the preferable alternative to this life. There's either no point to living, or the only point is
self-interest. Schopenhauer is more focused on egoism, that is, blind
self-interest as a problem. (We'll leave nihilism for Nietzsche.)

Egoism is predicated on severing our affective or ethical bonds to
other human beings, thinking only of ourselves and our interests, even
at the expense of others.[22] Thus are sadists, misanthropes, and self-
serving assholes born.[23] Schopenhauer sees the problem clearly. He
claims, "The chief and fundamental incentive in man as in the animal is
egoism, that is, the craving for existence and well-being."[24] Driven by

our will to live, or self-interest, we seek only that which benefits us and see others simply as competitors for scarce resources, or obstacles in our way. Many of King's characters struggle with egoism, with self-preservation before the turning point of the story where they assume the role of hero or savior. We see it with Ben Mears and Mark Petrie in *'Salem's Lot*, as they contemplate returning to the small town from safe exile in Mexico. We see it with Johnny Marinville's sacrifice in *Desperation*, Audrey's sacrifice to save Seth in *The Regulators*,[25] Gard's sacrifice in *The Tommyknockers*, and many more. In each case, the character must overcome the drive to self-preservation, must overcome egoism in order to adopt the role of hero.

Let's recall a particularly poignant scene from *Desperation*. In this book we are presented with a Nevada town, Desperation, set upon by an ancient evil, Tak, unleashed from its underground lair through the unearthing of an old mine shaft. Tak uses human beings as hosts, and once inside, and before his presence completely destroys the host's body, proceeds to wreak havoc, killing and destroying for the mere enjoyment of killing and destroying. Tak is a sadist; he derives pleasure from the pain and suffering of others, and that seems to be his only motivation. Johnny Marinville, an alcoholic writer (imagine that), stumbles into town while on a writing tour, alongside various other characters, including the Carver family, whose daughter—Pie as she is known—is killed by Collie Entragian, the local peace officer and current host of Tak. In the end the entire Carver family will be killed, all except the young boy, David, who seems to have a unique relationship with God. At one point in the story as David and Johnny are facing unimaginable horrors alongside their small group of fellow sufferers, David confronts Johnny. Johnny has grown weary and seems ready to give up. I mean, what's the point? Tak jumps bodies, seems indomitable, and the whole town is dead. They are set upon by snakes, coyotes, vultures, among other horrors, and there's no apparent way out. Johnny's self-interest speaks to attempting to flee Desperation. But David is tired of Johnny's incessant bitching. So he confronts him: "God is cruel . . . but life is more than just steering a course around pain. That's something you used to know, Mr. Marinville. Didn't you?"[26] We see a similar turning point in *The Regulators*, again as a nearly broken person, Audrey, has to decide whether or not to flee. Audrey sees a chance to run, to get away from Tak. But that means leaving behind her nephew,

Seth. Leaving him to Tak. So she stays, just as Johnny also decides to stay. In both of these cases, the characters decide that something is more valuable than mere existence. Life is pain, it is cruel. But the nihilist has nothing, literally. And the egoist only has himself, and in that regard, has very little, since by nature we are communal beings, relying on others for both physical and mental well-being.[27] Schopenhauer paints a grim picture: "Life itself is a sea full of rocks and whirlpools that man avoids with the greatest caution and care, although he knows that, even when he succeeds with all his efforts and ingenuity in struggling through, at every step he comes nearer to the greatest, and total, the inevitable and irredeemable shipwreck, indeed even steers right into it, namely death."[28] Gard knows this to be true, as do all of King's protagonists. Gard knows he'll never escape Haven, even if he can successfully navigate Bobbi and her comrades. He knows he's doomed. So what can we count on in this world aside from the certainty of suffering, disappointment, and death? What matters? An answer is needful.

DON'T SPEAK IN THE LANGUAGE OF THE DEAD

As human beings we are social beings; we are intimately tied to each other for both our physical and emotional needs and well-being. Egoism, therefore, is "a general kind of failure to live as we are capable of living."[29] In this case, egoism, or a separation from others, a separation that dismisses their interests at best and derives pleasure from their suffering at worst, invites callousness,[30] cruelty, and opens us up to becoming more like Tak, more like the Tommyknockers, users and abusers of each other. Egoism is beneath us; it is base or bestial. Schopenhauer notes how man, as egoist is, "at bottom . . . a hideous wild beast."[31] As a beast, man is capable of great cruelty, from the most wretched cases of child abuse to slavery.

Cruelty is the most offensive thing to humanity. "Nothing shocks our moral feelings so deeply as cruelty does. We can forgive every other crime, but not cruelty."[32] Schopenhauer notes horrific real-life examples of cruelty, such as a mother who murdered her five-year-old son by pouring boiling oil down his throat.[33] We can forgive those that do wrong, but cruelty is inhuman, a perversion of our essence. King presents us with myriad illustrations of such cruelties, always rooted in the breakdown or rejection of our affective ties to each other. When we fail to appreciate each other, to consider each other's interests, we become harsh, callous, and capable of the gravest evils. These evils stem from egoism.

If we go back to *Desperation*, when David confronts Johnny we get an inkling of what is wrong with egoism. First, we should be concerned that all too often we define happiness in terms of pleasure and seek only to feel contented, as if we were merely animals. Alasdair MacIntyre laments the evolution of the concept of happiness, from something akin to eudaimonia or excellence to the current usage where happiness simply means "a subjective appreciation of life."[34] In discussing philosophical education, MacIntyre notes that too often we operate under the idea that happiness, as contentment or satisfaction, is seen as the end of life. This attitude, he fears, destroys a drive toward excellence. He observes that we rarely ask, "Do [I] have good reason to be pleased, contented, or satisfied?"[35] Instead we are given the expectation of happiness, and the notion that we're all owed contentment. But David is right, and Johnny knows it. Life is about something more than just steering a path around pain.

Here we may speak of purpose, a goal beyond ourselves that defines us, that anchors our lives in a meaningless world to some value greater than ourselves. Schopenhauer states, "A happy life is impossible; the best that man can attain is a heroic life, such as is lived by one who struggles against overwhelming odds in some way and some affair that will benefit the whole of mankind, and who in the end triumphs, although he obtains poor reward or none at all."[36] A better description of King's protagonists is not possible, from Ben Mears in *'Salem's Lot*, to Johnny in *Desperation* and of course Gard. One can witness the brutality of the world, its nature as intractable, endemic suffering, one can note our natural disposition and drive toward egoism and respond not with despair or selfishness, but instead note that we are more than mere beasts, that we can be better, and ought to be held to a higher standard.

THE KID MATTERS OR...

Being held to a higher standard is about being held to a standard of excellence. This focus on excellence, or flourishing, is the crux of virtue theory; the idea that certain character traits when formed into habits promote our flourishing, they facilitate greatness. "The virtuous person is someone whose character inclines her towards right conduct and who chooses what is the right thing to do in the particular circumstances through the judicious exercise of practical wisdom."[37] Virtue is about right conduct that leads us toward our good, our welfare as human beings, beings that are essentially social and communal by nature. The focus in virtue theory is on behavior, habitual behavior over time, which becomes character, and character becomes definitive of what kind of person you are, and so what kinds of actions you'll do, and you'll tolerate yourself doing. Character drives actions, and actions reinforce character. This differs greatly from other ethical positions that oftentimes are focused on rule following or obedience to universal laws or divine decrees. Too often rules fail us, as so often when the going gets tough the tough find exceptions. And so we are prone to rationalize after the fact and account for even the gravest of evils as though they were necessitated by whatever guideline or rule we were using at the time. In this regard, David Fisher provides a poignant example. He discusses a case where an officer comes across a young marine in the Vietnam War who, enraged by the death of his comrades, places his rifle to the head of a Vietnamese woman, preparing to kill her in cold blood. The officer, having only a split second to decide how to act, doesn't fall back on the military code of conduct or the Geneva Conventions; he doesn't reiterate to the young soldier that there is a prohibition on intentionally killing noncombatants. He simply says, "Marines don't do that."[38] In this case, it wasn't a rule, a principle, or a command that stayed the marine's hand, it was character, it was honor, integrity, and self-control developed over time into deep character so even when all the rules broke down, when the world seemed to be coming apart at the seams, he could count on himself, he knew who he was, even if he needed a reminder. Johnny Marinville was a Vietnam vet, so this example would surely resonate with him. And Johnny, after being reminded by David that life is about more than avoiding pain, comes around. Johnny remembers who he truly is. Virtue saves Johnny. Virtue will also save Gard and little David Brown: the virtue of philanthropy.

Schopenhauer is a virtue theorist[39] and sees compassion as the road to excellence. He builds his moral philosophy, his response to pessimism, on a simple formula: "Injure no one; on the contrary, help everyone as much as you can."[40] The first demand, to do no harm, is met with the virtue of justice. Justice demands people be treated equally; no one person's good should come at the expense of another—so "good-bye" to egoism. In addition to "do no harm," we ought to help as much as is possible, this is Schopenhauer's virtue of philanthropy, *caritas*.

Philanthropy, for Schopenhauer, is the virtue of loving-kindness, a disposition in us to take the good of others as the motive of our actions. This virtue is exemplified by Gard in *The Tommyknockers*, but it also seems to be the disposition of many of King's protagonists. In *Desperation*, Johnny eventually sacrifices himself in order to imprison Tak. And in his final exchange with David Carver, by means of the blue pass notes, he references 1 John 4:8, "God is love."[41] Most interesting, the strong Christian message in *Desperation*, that God is love, is consistent with Schopenhauer's opinion that "Christianity's greatest merit" is the promotion of compassion as the highest virtue.[42]

In *The Tommyknockers*, Gard faces overwhelming odds as the Tommyknockers take over Bobbi and the people of Haven. He knows he has no escape; in fact, he becomes resigned to the fact that he'll die in the end. But yet he perseveres. In the end, it is David, the young boy stranded on Altair-4, who motivates Gard. He is driven by compassion for a fellow sufferer, by his understanding that our connection to others is what matters. David Brown needs a hand, he needs Gard, and Gard can help.

What gives our actions worth, according to Schopenhauer, is their relation to the good of other human beings. Implicit in his view is a rejection of egoism as an illegitimate, in fact, amoral position. His rejection of egoism seems tied to both the value other human beings hold in themselves, as well as the claim that compassion is a laudable goal human beings should aspire toward. Schopenhauer states, "*Egoism* is . . . the first and principal, although not the only force with which the *moral incentive* has to contend."[43] He adds: self-interest destroys the moral worth of an action, and it is the other's benefit without any reference to one's own good, that gives an action its real moral worth.[44] "The absence of all egoistic motivation is, therefore, the *criterion of an action of moral worth*."[45] In excluding egoistic actions from actions of moral worth, Schopenhauer implies that self-interest is not a moral interest, but perhaps merely a fact, like the self-preservation instinct in animals. An animal saving its own life is not a moral act, but a simple instinct, a fact of animal existence, and egoism in humans stems from the same source, self-preservation, and thus isn't a moral position, it is just a fact of our animal nature. But we are to see to it that we are better.

So it appears an orientation to the Other, an ability to see the Other as oneself, to recognize her as the same as ourselves—empathy—is the beginning of an ethical response to the suffering endemic to the human condition. So the morally praiseworthy route is to begin by recognizing the Other as oneself and then taking her weal, her good, as our object of action. "That other man . . . becom[es] *the ultimate object* of my will in the same way as I myself otherwise am, and hence through my directly desiring *his* weal and not *his* woe just as immediately as I ordinarily do only *my own*."[46] This, according to Schopenhauer, is compassion, "the real basis of all *voluntary* justice and *genuine* loving-kindness."[47]

Compassion, according to Schopenhauer, is the proper moral disposition for humans. Here we see caritas, one of Schopenhauer's cardinal virtues. Caritas is best illustrated, Schopenhauer claims, in the case of the doomed man. This connection to others "appears with special clearness and beauty in those cases where a man, beyond all recovery and doomed, is still anxiously, actively, and zealously concerned over the welfare and rescue of others."[48] It's as if Schopenhauer were thinking of Gard specifically. For with Gard we have the doomed man. He is stuck in Haven. His partner, Bobbi, is no longer human. He is surrounded by those who have been polluted by the ship, slaves to the pull of the Tommyknockers, addicts. He knows he will not get out alive. But in the midst of it all he does not crawl back into a bottle to die. Gard doesn't despair. That's not the kind of person he is. He began this journey out of concern for Bobbi, he has developed himself, as a compassionate person, to be habitually oriented to the welfare of others, and this may be the only habit he's developed that's laudable. So he focuses on one simple thing, saving little David Brown, stranded on Altair-4, lost, alone, cold, and struggling to breathe. Gard even debates with himself, compassion ultimately winning. "The kid would have to come first. *Gard, he's probably dead anyway*. Maybe. But the old man didn't think so; the old man thought there was still a little boy to save. *One kid doesn't matter—not in the face of this. . . .* It was logical, but it was croupier's logic. Ultimately, killer logic . . . *The kid matters or nothing matters."*[49]

This inner debate is telling. In the face of a world collapsing, what does one life mean? A killer can justify killing one among billions, for what matters one insignificant life in the grand, cosmic scheme of it all? Why care about one puny human if in the end we all die anyway? Tens, hundreds of thousands of people die daily and the world moves on without as much as a shiver. How many thousands, tens of thousands die, unnoticed, and we continue on, oblivious and unaffected? One life doesn't matter, so why should it matter to Gard? One life is nothing in the cosmic tally. So why should Gard bother with one measly child as the world crumbles around his ears? But that's killer logic, that's the logic that pulls the trigger and sends the Vietnamese woman into oblivion, and Gard will have no part of it. Calculation in this case seems reasonable. The boy is not worth Gard's sacrifice. Principles fail here; they won't motivate Gard. Abstract language about dignity or duty won't drive him to action in the face of certain doom. He won't redeem his life or find meaning in existence through remembering hollow platitudes learned in Philosophy 101 at Bumblecuss U. But deep character, integrity to who we are, who we've cultivated ourselves to be . . . Well, who can turn their back on themselves? Virtue will save us from nihilism, from the abyss, and the virtue of philanthropy will save David Brown. Even in the face of all this, we have each other.

In the end, either the boy matters or nothing matters. Either there is value in living for others, in living for compassion, or there is mere animality, bestial pleasures in a nihilistic world where only death is certain. We know what Gard chooses. So either we reach out to each other in compassion, or we recognize it's all meaningless, that life has no value other than the little bit of contentment we can eke out for ourselves. If life is to have any value, first we must value it by valuing and caring for each other.

So Gard works zealously to save the boy. He will later sacrifice himself entirely to get the Tommyknocker ship off Earth and into deep space. But it is the boy, a young child suffering, that drives him. Gard will get nothing from the rescue, but he doesn't relent. He focuses on the boy, for the boy matters, compassion matters, caritas matters.

The Tommyknockers and those polluted/addicted to their knowledge and power behave in unthinking and cruel ways toward their fellow humans. Consider Bobbi, who betrays her faithful dog and turns it into a battery, and who does the same to her sister. Bobbi and the others who are "becoming" are blindly driven by ego, by their desire to control the world around them, pursue their own interests, and promote their own good regardless of the impact it has on others. This narrow-minded egoism evinces a self-interest entirely divorced from any consideration of others. The result is cruelty, the view that others are disposable. Those that "become" in *The Tommyknockers* use others to pursue their projects, neglecting their pain and suffering, and so become cruel. Remember, David Brown was sent to Altair-4 by *his own brother* who was blindly driven by his ego, his desire to be the best backyard magician Haven had ever seen.

Yet these evils, this cruelty, isn't foisted on us from outside, it isn't alien. We are always susceptible to it, since we are always at root, egoists. As Schopenhauer notes, egoism is the principal force with which our moral incentive has to contend. Egoism is that primary drive we have to work to overcome. The Tommyknockers are just tinkerers that offer us the "high" of energy, intelligence, and "becoming." They offer to feed our ego, but it is we who give in to their temptations and allow our egos to drive our addictions without reference to the effect it has on others. In so many of King's stories it is egoism, self-interest, that feeds and foments the evil, and it is often compassion that saves the day. Breaking free from his ego, the protagonist fights, often sacrificing himself, for the good of others. Bolstered by virtue, by a character cultivated to caritas, King's protagonists seem inoculated against the evils they face. His characters exemplify philanthropy, in direct opposition to the "monsters"[50] that embody egoism. But this evil often comes from us. Perhaps the supernatural provides a way in, but our all-too-human egos drive it, feed it, and in the end overcoming our egos is what defeats it, at least for a time.

SEE THAT YOU ARE BETTER

Schopenhauer's commitment to compassion and his detestation of egoism are understandable. Add to this the illustrations he provides and the aesthetic presentation of the problem in the works of Stephen King, and one finds it hard to resist the claim that the human condition is, and we as individuals are, defined by our relatedness to others, and so ought to be driven by compassion. This perspective of compassion demands mindfulness of others. And this is another key lesson of *The Tommy-knockers*. The shortsightedness of these tinkerers, who never wonder whether they should do something, but merely whether they can, is the cause of much grief. The shortsighted never see past themselves, past their own interests, and so inflict great harm on those around them (a lesson iterated also in Gard's concerns regarding nuclear power).[51] How often do we act thoughtlessly, or myopically, fully conscious but only of ourselves? Here, Schopenhauer's notion of compassion—injure no one; in fact, help as much as you can—seems to demand that we avoid acting negligently. Avoiding negligence demands that we be mindful of our actions and avoid engaging in those actions that have a reasonable, foreseeable chance of leading to harm in the future.

Stephen King calls horror a dance of dreams, a reaffirmation of life. Perhaps this is the dance of defiance in the face of the dark. Regardless, "if the horror story is our rehearsal for death, then its strict moralities make it also a reaffirmation of life and good will and simple imagina-tion—just one more pipeline to the infinite."[52] In *The Tommyknockers* and through the eyes of Arthur Schopenhauer it appears as just that, a reaffirmation of life through compassion in the face of evil (or the dark, or nihilism), both the natural evil of suffering and the very real human evil of egoism run amok, cruelty. Stephen King shows us the most evil, wicked, and cruelest world we can imagine and in so doing he also shows us the most compassionate, the most heroic style of life.[53] The end of *The Tommyknockers* drives the point home.

Gard saves David Brown. One of his last acts is to bring the boy back from Altair-4, delivered via Tommyknocker technology directly into his brother Hilly's hospital room, where he climbs into bed with his older brother, snuggles in, and goes to sleep. "David's hand groped for the blanket, found it, and pulled it up. Ninety-three million miles from the sun and a hundred parsecs from the axis-pole of the galaxy, Hilly and David Brown slept in each other's arms."[54] Cosmically, David is small, he is tiny. Cosmically he matters not at all to the machinery of the universe. Neither does Hilly. But to each other they are everything; to each other they are the universe. In Gard's final moments he lives heroically; he lives a compassionate life focused on just one small boy, one small boy who matters to just another small boy. But the kid matters, David Brown matters, or none of us matter. Compassion matters, or nothing matters. Gard affirms the value of his own life, the value of the lives of those around him, and affirms that life is about more than just steering a path around pain, or simple contentment. Life is about something greater.

Although the world is sunk in evil, we are to see that we are better; that we are compassionate in the face of grave suffering. The suffering of the world can't be defeated, evil can't be eliminated, but we can make it a little bit better through compassion. Gard doesn't save the planet or the universe from pain and suffering—that will always exist—but he does what he can to alleviate that which it is in his power to, once he reaches beyond himself and takes responsibility for his life and the lives of those nearest to him.

If we are to be more than mere beasts, if we are to set ourselves aside from and above the Tommyknockers who use, abuse, and dispose of others for their own selfish ends, then we must look outward to other people, to our fellow sufferers and lend a hand, even at our own expense. Do no harm; in fact, help as much as possible. There is a fundamental choice between egoism and compassion, between base, animal existence and heroism. We can choose compassion, cultivate our empathy, and so "become" more human, more humane. In the vastness of space, ninety-three million miles from the sun and a hundred parsecs from the axis-pole of the galaxy, we are insignificant except to each other.

NOTES

1. Arthur Schopenhauer, *On the Basis of Morality*, trans. E. F. J. Payne (Providence, R.I.: Berghahn Books, 1995), 129.

2. If this doesn't sound familiar, go back and read chapter 1 in this volume.

3. See note 2.

4. For a good discussion of this topic, see chapter 4 in this volume.

5. Stephen King, *11/22/63: A Novel* (New York: Scribner, 2011), 295.

6. Arthur Schopenhauer, *The World as Will and Representation*, trans. E. F. J. Payne (New York: Dover, 1969), 1:312.

7. Stephen King, *'Salem's Lot* (New York: Pocket Books, 1999), 230.

8. King, *'Salem's Lot*, 68–69.

9. Schopenhauer, *World as Will and Representation*, 1:275.

10. Schopenhauer, *World as Will and Representation* 1:309.

11. Schopenhauer, *World as Will and Representation* 1:312.

12. From Arthur Schopenhauer, cited in Irvin D. Yalom, *The Schopenhauer Cure* (New York: Harper Perennial, 2005), 57.

13. Stephen King, *The Tommyknockers* (New York: Putnam, 1987), 200.

14. Arthur Schopenhauer, "Additional Remarks on the Doctrine of the Suffering of the World," in *Parerga and Paralipomena*, trans. E. F. J. Payne (Oxford: Clarendon, 2010), 2:304.

15. Schopenhauer, "Additional Remarks on the Doctrine of the Suffering of the World," 300.

16. Schopenhauer, "Additional Remarks on the Doctrine of the Suffering of the World," 291.

17. If Stephen King wrote *The Tommyknockers* today, I wonder if Gard might not be more concerned with fracking.

18. This is a reference to *The Killing Joke* by Alan Moore and Brian Bolland. In this comic, the Joker notes to Batman how "all it takes is one bad day to reduce the sanest man alive to lunacy."

19. Arthur Schopenhauer, "Additional Remarks on the Doctrine of the Affirmation and Denial of the Will-to-Live," in *Parerga and Paralipomena*, trans. E. F. J. Payne (Oxford: Clarendon, 2010), 2:322.

20. Schopenhauer doesn't use the term "despair," and it does have a technical philosophical definition that I am alluding to here. Danish philosopher Søren Kierkegaard (1813–1855) is often affiliated with the problematic of despair. See his *The Sickness unto Death*.

21. Nietzsche predicted hipsters!

22. For more on this point, see chapter 10 in this volume.

23. For an interesting analysis of the connection between pain, suffering, hedonism, and sadism, see Colin McGinn, *Ethics, Evil, and Fiction* (Oxford: Oxford University Press, 1997), esp. ch. 4.

24. Schopenhauer, *On the Basis of Morality*, 131.

25. The resolution of *The Regulators* is quite touching—the sacrifice, the bond between Seth and his aunt, and an oddly haunting "happily ever after"— especially as it relates to the notion of compassion. I could easily have used Seth and his aunt Audrey as a case for compassion just as readily as Gard and David Brown. But I chose *The Tommyknockers*.

26. Stephen King, *Desperation* (New York: Viking, 1996), 533.

27. Aristotle famously claimed that a man who can live without society is either a god or a monster. Well, there are no gods among us, but King makes it all too evident there are plenty of monsters.

28. Schopenhauer, *World as Will and Representation*, 1:313.

29. Mary Midgley, *Wickedness: A Philosophical Essay* (London: Routledge & Kegan Paul, 1984), 7.

30. Midgley, *Wickedness*, 117.

31. Arthur Schopenhauer, "On Ethics," in *Parerga and Paralipomena*, trans. E. F. J. Payne (Oxford: Clarendon, 2010), 2:211.

32. Schopenhauer, *On the Basis of Morality*, 169.

33. Schopenhauer, *On the Basis of Morality*, 169.

34. Alasdair MacIntyre, "Philosophical Education against Contemporary Culture," *Proceedings of the American Catholic Philosophical Association* 87 (2013): 45.

35. MacIntyre, "Philosophical Education," 45.

36. Schopenhauer, "Additional Remarks on the Doctrine of the Affirmation and Denial of the Will-to-Live," 322.

37. David Fisher, *Morality and War: Can War Be Just in the Twenty-First Century?* (Oxford: Oxford University Press, 2011), 116.

38. See Fisher, *Morality and War*, 128.

39. For a discussion of Schopenhauer's virtue theory, see David E. Cartwright, "Schopenhauer's Narrower Sense of Morality," in *The Cambridge Companion to Schopenhauer*, ed. Christopher Janaway (Cambridge: Cambridge University Press, 1999)

40. Schopenhauer, *On the Basis of Morality*, n. 92.

41. King, *Desperation*, 690.

42. Schopenhauer, *On the Basis of Morality*, 163.

43. Schopenhauer, *On the Basis of Morality*, 134.

44. Schopenhauer, *On the Basis of Morality*, 139.

45. Schopenhauer, *On the Basis of Morality*, 140.

46. Schopenhauer, *On the Basis of Morality*, 143.

47. Schopenhauer, *On the Basis of Morality*, 144.

48. Schopenhauer, "On Ethics," 219.

49. King, *The Tommyknockers*, 434.

50. In some cases the monsters are clearly defined by egoism; they literally have to survive at the expense of others, like parasites. Consider vampires and werewolves.

51. Again, I think fracking is the more befitting 2016 analogue.

52. Stephen King, *Danse Macabre* (New York: Gallery Books, 2010), 436.

53. NB: Schopenhauer is a pessimist so he ultimately sees no hope of redemption or salvation. However, I'd maintain that the belief is nascent in his thinking, as evidenced by his ethics of compassion. In addition, Nietzsche, who owes a great deal to Schopenhauer, begins from pessimism to ultimately pen a philosophy of affirmation, of "Yes-saying" in the face of nihilism. He also leans

heavily on virtue theory. Nietzsche had to come from somewhere. The seeds of his philosophy were fertilized in Schopenhauer's rich soil.

54. King, *The Tommyknockers*, 558.

INDEX

addiction, 47, 62–63, 203
admiration, 243, 244–245
affective faith, 31–32
afterlife, 176
agency: in *The Dark Tower*, 72–74, 85, 89,
  94; in face of evil and suffering, 279,
  285; in the future, 221–228, 235–236,
  260, 261. *See also* free will
amazement, 243, 245
The Amityville Horror (film), 149, 190
Anselm, Saint, 32
Apt Pupil (King), 131, 134–144
Aquinas, Thomas, 25
Arendt, Hannah, 161, 163–166, 168, 169;
  Eichmann in Jerusalem, 168; *The Life
  of the Mind*, 169
Aristotle: *Eudemian Ethics*, 113, 114, 117,
  125; on knowledge of the future, 221,
  222; *Nicomachean Ethics*, 113, 114,
  117, 124, 127; philosophy of art,
  179–183, 186–187, 257, 273n6;
  Poetics, 179, 183; *Politics*, 114, 182; on
  social nature of humans, 295n27;
  theory of friendship, 113–129
Aronson, Elliot, 132
atheism, 16, 17, 18
Augustine, Saint, 9, 21
avatārs, 88, 93

Bachman, Richard (pseudonym of King),
  161, 170n2, 251n27

The Bachman Books (Bachman/King),
  170n2
Bag of Bones (King), 181
Balzac, Honoré de, 197
Barthes, Roland, 195, 197–198, 201, 202,
  203
Bathrick, Serafina Kent, 40, 41, 42
The Bazaar of Bad Dreams (King), 233,
  236, 249n5
Beardsley, Monroe, 195–196, 204
Beauvoir, Simone de, 36, 37, 38, 39, 41,
  43, 44
Beith, Mary, 70n117
Bentham, Jeremy, 99, 157
Bergmann, Michael, 22
Bernays, Edward, 143
Bhagavad Gītā, 84, 86, 92
bioconservatism, 48, 52, 54, 56–57, 60,
  60–61, 65, 66, 67n18
biotechnology, 50, 51, 67n14, 67n18
the body, 37, 41
The Body (King), 113, 114, 118–119, 121,
  122–124, 127–128, 129
Bostrom, Nick, 49, 50; "Fable of the
  Dragon-Tyrant", 55–56
Bradbury, Ray, 191, 239
Bride of Frankenstein (film), 43
Bruhm, Steven, 160n12
Buddhism, 90
Buffy the Vampire Slayer (television
  show), 41

KA-TET: AUTHOR BIOGRAPHIES

Katherine Allen is a part-time philosopher and full-time horror fangirl. She has written on a variety of topics in the philosophy of literature including the pleasures of disreputable genre fiction, literature's power to enhance empathy, and the philosophical underpinnings of moral panics about violent media. Despite dire bioconservative warnings, Katherine is a tentative transhumanist, and would quite like to become a "New Improved" posthuman (although she would prefer to hang on to her teeth and hair if at all possible).

Randall E. Auxier teaches philosophy at Southern Illinois University, Carbondale. He lives with four very creative but temperamental cats and one similarly talented spouse.

Charles Bane has lived in numerous places all over the country, working variously as a country music disc jockey, an oil refinery demolition specialist, a movie critic, a television producer, an eighth-grade English teacher, and a college professor. Along the way, he managed to earn various degrees including a PhD in literature, film, and theory from Louisiana State University. He is the coauthor of *A Primer of the Novel*, and his articles have appeared in *Hollywood's America: Twentieth-Century America through Film*; *Stanley Kubrick: Essays on His Films and Legacy*; *Papa, PhD: Essays on Fatherhood by Men in the Academy*; and *IRIC: Internationalist Review of Irish Culture*. Currently, he is an assistant professor of film and literature at Harding University in Arkansas, where he lives with his wife, the poet Paulette Guerin, and their three children and three cats.

Matthew A. Butkus is an associate professor at McNeese State University, where he teaches courses in applied ethics. He earned undergraduate degrees from Georgetown University and the University of Pittsburgh, and earned his MA and PhD from Duquesne University. While he has written other work in pop culture and philosophy, most of his publications are in areas at the intersection of psychology, psychiatry, and bioethics. When he is not wearing awesome shoes and dispensing wisdom to the next generation of doctors, nurses, scientists, and engineers, he is teaching Tae Kwon Do, in which he holds a third-degree black belt. He may or may not remind his students of this fact when they come to discuss their grades. He is a lifelong fan of Stephen King, and has been pretty consistent in rereading the Dark Tower series every year or so.

Kellye Byal is a graduate of Kingston University London and Université Paris 8 with an MA in contemporary European philosophy and a BA in philosophy from the University of Oregon. Her specialty is the intersection between philosophy and literature, existentialism, and the philosophy of horror. She has written about Freud, Beauvoir, and Kristeva, most recently on John Waters's *Pink Flamingos*. To date, her telekinetic abilities remain unproven.

Cam Cobb is an associate professor in the faculty of education at the University of Windsor. His research focuses on such topics as social justice in special education, narrative pedagogy, and coteaching in adult learning contexts. Over the past few years his work has been published in a variety of journals including *Per la Filosofia, Cinema: Journal of Philosophy and the Moving Image*, the *F. Scott Fitzgerald Review*, the *British Journal of Special Education*, the *International Journal of Bilingual Education and Bilingualism*, and the *International Journal of Inclusive Education*.

Timothy M. Dale is an assistant professor of political science at the University of Wisconsin, La Crosse. He teaches in the area of political philosophy, and his research interests include democratic theory, political messaging in popular culture, and the scholarship of teaching and learning. He is coeditor of several books on popular culture and politics, including *Jim Henson and Philosophy: Imagination and the Magic of Mayhem* (2015), *Homer Simpson Ponders Politics: Popular Culture as Political Theory* (2013), and *Homer Simpson Marches on Washington: Dissent in American Popular Culture* (2010), and he is coauthor of *Political Thinking, Political Theory, and Civil Society* (2009).

Paul R. Daniels holds a PhD in philosophy from Monash University (Melbourne, Australia). He also completed degrees at the University of Auckland (MLitt), the University of Manitoba (MA), and the University of Lethbridge (BA). He's taught at Monash University, RMIT University, the University of Melbourne, the University of Auckland, and the University of Manitoba. His primary research interests include military ethics and metaphysics. Some of his recent scholarly articles have been published in the *Australasian Journal of Philosophy*, *Philosophia*, and *Metaphysica*.

Joseph J. Foy is an associate vice-chancellor for academic affairs and associate professor of political science at the University of Wisconsin Colleges. Foy is the editor of *Homer Simpson Goes to Washington: American Politics through Popular Culture* and *SpongeBob SquarePants and Philosophy*, and coeditor of *Homer Simpson Marches on Washington: Dissent through American Popular Culture*, *Homer Simpson Ponders Politics: Popular Culture as Political Theory*, and *Jim Henson and Philosophy: Imagination and the Magic of Mayhem*. Foy has contributed over two dozen essays to popular culture anthologies, and serves on the editorial board for the *Journal of Popular Culture*. He really hates clowns. Really.

Jacob M. Held is an associate professor of philosophy and director of the UCA Core at the University of Central Arkansas. He is series editor of the Great Authors and Philosophy series through Rowman & Littlefield and editor of *Dr. Seuss and Philosophy: Oh, the Thinks You Can Think!*, *Roald Dahl and Philosophy: A Little Nonsense Now and Then . . .* , and the book you currently hold. He has also coedited, with James B. South, books on James Bond and Terry Pratchett. His more traditional academic work focuses on legal and political philosophy, and applied ethics. His most recent "academic" publication is *The Philosophy of Pornography: Contemporary Perspectives*, coedited with Lindsay Coleman. And all appearances to the contrary, he is a perfectly normal person who just happens to work on children's literature, pornography, and horror fiction. Nothing at all to be concerned about . . . nothing.

Elizabeth Hornbeck is assistant teaching professor of art history and film studies at the University of Missouri. Her current book project, *Artists' Lives on Film*, unites these two disciplinary interests at the intersection of art and popular culture. Her essay "Who's Afraid of the Big Bad Wolf? Domestic Violence in *The Shining*" is forthcoming in *Feminist Studies*. When she teaches *The Shining* in her course on architecture in film, she often has to explain Jack Torrance's "Heeeere's Johnny!" reference, which she tries to do without destroying any doors in the process.

Greg Littmann is OK. It doesn't matter that sometimes when he opens his front door, there's nothing outside but the mist and the monsters. He just closes it again, and when it reopens, everything is back to normal and he can go to work as an associate professor of philosophy at Southern Illinois University, Edwardsville. No worries! And if softly buzzing things sometimes scratch on his office door and chitter his name, so what? The less he leaves his office, the more work he does. That's how he's published on metaphysics, epistemology, philosophy of logic, and philosophy of professional philosophy, as well as writing numerous chapters for books relating philosophy to popular culture, including volumes on Dracula, Frankenstein, Roald Dahl, Neil Gaiman, and Jonathan Swift. Greg Littmann is just fine.

Bertha Alvarez Manninen is an associate professor of philosophy at Arizona State University in the school of humanities, arts, and cultural studies. She is the author of *Pro-Life, Pro-Choice: Shared Values in the Abortion Debate*, as well as many journal articles. Her primary areas of research and teaching interests are normative ethics, applied ethics, philosophy of religion, social/political philosophy, and public philosophy. She once attended a conference at the famous Stanley Hotel—the inspiration for the Overlook—but stayed away from room 237. When she's not working at ASU, she's at home with her husband, Tuomas, their two daughters, and their wide array of pets—none of whom were found near a pet sematary. She is also deathly afraid of clowns. . . . Thanks, Pennywise.

Tuomas W. Manninen has been an avid reader of Stephen King's works for most of his life, even though he wouldn't consider himself King's "number one" fan. He earned his PhD in philosophy from the University of Iowa, where he studied needful subjects like contemporary analytic metaphysics and history of philosophy. In his youth, he suffered a concussion after being hit by a car on his way to the public library. According to witnesses at the scene, he didn't make much sense when he came to—and according to some other witnesses much later on, he still doesn't. He is working as a lecturer at Arizona State University, where he teaches courses in critical thinking, philosophy of mind, and social/political philosophy. He currently lives in Phoenix, Arizona, with his wife and two daughters. Any similarities between him and the character John Smith from *The Dead Zone* are purely coincidental—but he already knew you would think that.

Garret Merriam is an associate professor of philosophy at the University of Southern Indiana, where he teaches courses in ethics, philosophy of religion, and philosophy of science. He has published on a variety of philosophical subjects including animal ethics, bioethics, the philosophy of disability, and neuroethics. His current work focuses on the relationship between virtue ethics and neuroscience. His lectures can be seen on his YouTube channel, "Sisyphus Redeemed." He has not forgotten the face of his father, but he considers the voice of his mother to be of equal importance.

Michael K. Potter is a teaching and learning specialist in the Centre for Teaching and Learning at the University of Windsor. Previous publications include *Bertrand Russell's Ethics* (2006) and *Leading Effective Discussions* (with Erika Kustra, 2008). He was coeditor of a special issue of the *Canadian Journal for the Scholarship of Teaching and Learning* in 2015, which focused on the neglected role of the arts and humanities in the scholarship of teaching and learning. His research focuses on applications of anarchist, pragmatist, and nihilist philosophy to higher education.

C. Taylor Sutton is a philosophy doctoral student at Purdue University. He has written on the ontological argument for the proof of the existence of God, as well as Kantian deontology, and is working on a dissertation on the foundations of ethics. He currently lives in Indiana with his wife and cat, has never ridden the Bullet, and screams the word "nineteen" into his pillow every night.